CRISIS IN
HIGHER EDUCATION

TRANSFORMATIONS IN HIGHER EDUCATION: THE SCHOLARSHIP OF ENGAGEMENT

CRISIS IN HIGHER EDUCATION

A PLAN TO SAVE SMALL LIBERAL ARTS COLLEGES IN AMERICA

JEFFREY R. DOCKING with CARMAN C. CURTON

Michigan State University Press | East Lansing

Michigan State University Press
East Lansing, Michigan 48823-5245

Printed and bound in the United States of America.

21 20 19 18 17 16 15   1 2 3 4 5 6 7 8 9 10

Library of Congress Control Number: 2014941664
ISBN: 978-1-61186-154-9 (pbk.)
ISBN: 978-1-60917-440-8 (ebook: PDF)
ISBN: 978-1-62895-133-2 (ebook: ePub)
ISBN: 978-1-62896-133-1 (ebook: mobi/prc)

Book design by Charlie Sharp, Sharp Des!gns, Lansing, MI
Cover design by Shaun Allshouse, www.shaunallshouse.com
Cover photo of Adrian College (Lad Strayer/wePhoto)
is used courtesy of Adrian College.

Michigan State University Press is a member of the Green Press Initiative and is committed to
developing and encouraging ecologically responsible publishing practices. For more information
about the Green Press Initiative and the use of recycled paper in book publishing, please visit
www.greenpressinitiative.org.

Visit Michigan State University Press at *www.msupress.org*

Transformations in Higher Education: Scholarship of Engagement

The Transformations in Higher Education: Scholarship of Engagement book series is designed to provide a forum where scholars can address the diverse issues provoked by community-campus partnerships that are directed toward creating innovative solutions to societal problems. Numerous social critics and key national commissions have drawn attention to the pervasive and burgeoning problems of individuals, families, communities, economies, health services, and education in American society. Such issues as child and youth development, economic competitiveness, environmental quality, and health and health care require creative research and the design, deployment, and evaluation of innovative public policies and intervention programs. Similar problems and initiatives have been articulated in many other countries, apart from the devastating consequences of poverty that burdens economic and social change. As a consequence, there has been increasing societal pressure on universities to partner with communities to design and deliver knowledge applications that address these issues, and to co-create novel approaches to effect system changes that can lead to sustainable and evidence-based solutions. Knowledge generation and knowledge application are critical parts of the engagement process, but so too are knowledge dissemination and preservation. The *Transformations in Higher Education: Scholarship of Engagement* series was designed to meet one aspect of the dissemination/preservation dyad.

This series is sponsored by the National Collaborative for the Study of University Engagement (NCSUE) and is published in partnership with the Michigan State University Press. An external board of editors supports the NCSUE editorial staff in order to insure that all volumes in the series are peer reviewed throughout the publication process. Manuscripts embracing campus-community partnerships are invited from authors regardless of discipline, geographic place, or type of transformational change accomplished. Similarly, the series embraces all methodological approaches from rigorous randomized trials to narrative and ethnographic studies. Analyses may span the qualitative to quantitative continuum, with particular emphasis on mixed-model approaches. However, all manuscripts must attend to detailing critical aspects of partnership development, community involvement, and evidence of program changes or impacts. Monographs and books provide ample space for authors to address all facets of engaged scholarship thereby building a compendium of praxis that will facilitate replication and generalization, two of the cornerstones of evidence-based programs, practices, and policies. We invite you to submit your work for publication review and to fully participate in our effort to assist higher education to renew its covenant with society through engaged scholarship.

HIRAM E. FITZGERALD
BURTON BARGERSTOCK
LAURIE VAN EGEREN

This book is dedicated to my family:
my wife Beth
and our four children Jacob, Carter,
Taylor, and Julianna.

•   •   •

Every professional job done well requires two things: hard work and a lot of time at the office. My family gives me the flexibility, support, and encouragement to enjoy both of these privileges at Adrian College. Without them I would have no joy regardless of anything I accomplish professionally.

Contents

Foreword

James E. Bultman, *President Emeritus, Hope College*

There is no dearth of challenges that face American higher education in these early years of the twenty-first century. Ever escalating pricing, competition for students from declining pools, demographic shifts, reductions in state funding, increased governmental regulations, securement of necessary philanthropic dollars, infrastructure upgrades including technology, and the overall relevance of higher education all vie for attention. These challenges are sufficient in scope to keep trustees, administrators, even faculty and staff, awake at night!

We know institutions are resilient, but oftentimes even change to remain viable comes slowly and only with great difficulty. As academics our most natural instincts are to build institutions on the backs of strong and ever-more-reputable academic programs. After all, education in its purest form is about the life of the mind and being comfortable in the world of ideas. Some institutions today have the luxury of an established academic reputation whose worth in the marketplace is well known, accepted, and pursued by prospective students. Other institutions have found their unique niche in the sea of higher education opportunities. This may take the form of unusual fields of study or recognized reputation in a few popular areas. Still others may have strength because of a value-added spiritual dimension that is meaningful for a given constituency, excellence in student development, breadth in co-curricular activities, or even an amenities-laden campus location that makes theirs an attractive choice. Although these less-than-academic reasons may not be the first choice for building reputable academic institutions or saving them, they may be a necessary, likely easier, first step in buying the time to do so.

Earning a recognized academic reputation takes time, resources, and a relentless pursuit of excellence.

In the world of small liberal arts colleges, virtually every president is concerned with enrollment because most are enrollment driven. I've often heard presidents of liberal arts colleges say (tongue-in-cheek) to an admissions director, "You take care of our enrollment, and I'll gladly take care of everything else." Yes, adequate enrollment to operate both effectively and efficiently is that important!

In this book, Dr. Docking makes a compelling case for achieving the necessary and desired student body size by providing enticing co-curricular activities, including especially intercollegiate sports. He does so by implementing his very accountable Admissions Growth model. Lest you gasp at the expedient nature of this model, be assured that it is only step one in the process (described in the book as Renaissance I). Step two (described in the book as Renaissance II) utilizes the revenue produced in step one to enhance academic programs, personnel, and facilities. In fact, the model is so compelling that one has to wonder why it couldn't be extrapolated to include professors, especially in low enrollment disciplines. Shouldn't the physics professor make it his or her business to identify and actively recruit the best area physics students? Or artists? Or German language students? In reality, recruiting the necessary students to correspond with the institutional infrastructure is every employee's business (including the president's) at the small liberal arts college.

Because Hope College, where I was privileged to serve as president for the past fourteen years, is in the same athletic conference as Adrian College, I have seen first-hand the remarkable transformation that has taken place there. Facility improvements are stunningly noticeable, positive morale is palpable, athletic teams are competitive across-the-board, and the results are, well, undeniable. An institution that was in decline only a few short years ago is now vibrantly alive.

To be sure, there was an urgency here that dictated a more revolutionary as opposed to evolutionary change, which might have been allowed had the decline been less precipitous. Dr. Docking freely admits there were the advantages of an institution with a goodly heritage, existing infrastructure capacity, small debt, and available land. Still, I would attribute the saving growth at Adrian College primarily to a very courageous and skillful leader with a willingness to confront the realities of the present with a hope-filled plan for a brighter future. Present with this well-designed plan for enrollment growth and the perseverance to see it through to completion was a trusting constituency willing to give it time to happen.

While this book may be most helpful for those leading institutions where enrollment decline is the root cause of institutional fragility, there is much in this book to commend it for leaders at most every institution. Dr. Docking has shared very transparently a practical model for enrollment growth and how best to implement it. Be assured it will stimulate thoughts about how you can improve the vitality and quality of the institution you serve.

Acknowledgments

While it took the efforts of many people over the past several years to lift Adrian College to higher levels of excellence, two people in particular played a major role in telling the story contained in this book.

The first is Rick Creehan, currently the president of Alderson Broaddus University in Philippi, West Virginia. I met Rick when I hired him as the athletic director of Washington & Jefferson College (W&J) in 2001. I was immediately impressed by his intelligence, work ethic, vision, and ability to craft a plan to grow enrollment at small liberal arts colleges. The smartest move I've made professionally was to hire Rick as my Executive Vice President at Adrian College when I accepted the presidency in 2005.

Together we toiled at Adrian College for six years to raise this college from difficult financial circumstances into the strong and viable institution it is today. Please know that the enrollment growth model that you will read about in this book is *our* model, not my model. Rick introduced me to the basic concepts of this model soon after we began working together at W&J, and we co-created it together once we arrived in Adrian. Rick is indefatigable and focused beyond belief. He is a true believer in how much this model can help small colleges, so much so that he is implementing it as the president of Alderson Broaddus University with great success. When he retires from AB, I have little doubt that the American higher education landscape will have another living example of how this enrollment growth plan can save a struggling small college. To Rick I say thank you for all you have done for Adrian College and me during your years in this town. Those of us who love this college will forever be indebted to you for your efforts to build this institution. I also thank you for your friendship.

The second person who deserves praise far beyond the small number of words I can write in this acknowledgment is Carman Curton, my co-author. Carman is bright, articulate, a beautiful writer, and an even better person. She is a wonderful member of our faculty and a person who has dedicated her life to the most important gift any of us can give to a young adult, the gift of education.

When Carman walked into my office three years ago and expressed a desire to help me write this book, I could not have been more fortunate. Carman is an academic who can organize thoughts and write prose as well as anyone with whom I've worked, and I was overjoyed that she wanted to help me. More important than her intellect was her personal experience on campus with how this model can help small liberal arts colleges. Carman lived the experience at Adrian College both before and after the model was implemented. Like many faculty members, she worried about Adrian College's future when it dipped below 1,000 students, and she celebrated our success when we grew to over 1,700 students in less than eight years. She combined a clear understanding of the model, having seen it in action, with visceral and emotional relief at how it helped the college she loves. These two aspects of Carman's experience with the model—the cerebral and the visceral—combined with her reputation as a seasoned and respected member of our faculty make her the perfect person to help me pen this book. For this I say thank you and express my sincere appreciation for her work. I feel confident that my gratitude will be felt by many others who will use this book to strengthen enrollment on their respective campuses even as high school graduation rates fall and budgets are squeezed even tighter.

In addition to these two outstanding individuals, I want to thank two important groups of people. First, the trustees of Adrian College took a big risk—albeit a calculated one—when they decided to go "all in" on the enrollment growth model nine years ago. If the model had failed, Adrian College would have quickly gone out of business and defaulted on several million dollars in loans. But the trustees were smart in realizing that Adrian College would benefit from cutting its own path in admissions. Their great risk reaped great rewards, and I am as happy for them as I am for the institution that their faith and trust in this model benefitted the college so much.

And finally I want to thank the students of Adrian College who have endured mud on their shoes, pounding hammers in their ears, and the continuous sounds of construction vehicles these past several years as we have rebuilt the campus around them. It is not lost on me that today's students have 2,500 institutions from which to choose and over 600 private liberal arts colleges to send their enrollment deposit. But our students chose this college, and we are honored by their choice. We sincerely hope that the education you received in the classroom is worthy of the decision you made.

CHAPTER 1

Why Higher Education Needs This Book

I am writing this book because I am worried. I am worried about the plight of small liberal arts colleges in America. I am afraid many are going to run out of money, reach insolvency, fail the federal financial responsibility audit (as 150 small privates did in 2011), close their doors, or be swallowed up by large state universities as satellite campuses over the next several years (Field & Richards, 2011). If this happens, if small liberal arts colleges continue to struggle to the point of insolvency, we will lose one of the greatest educational assets this country has. Small privates offer students a different type of education, an education where students can get tremendous amounts of personal attention and where faculty are committed to "teaching first." Many students who would fall through the cracks of large lecture halls at huge public institutions will lose the option to enroll in places where professors actually take attendance in class and will pull students aside for a talk after class if they are falling behind in their work. Many students need this type of environment in order to graduate. Without this option they simply will not earn a college degree.

Additionally, small communities in which these colleges are located will lose the largest economic engine they have to supply prosperity, jobs, and cultural activities to the businesses surrounding the college. Many restaurants, bookstores, markets, and small retailers rely on college students and their guests to spend money in their establishments to stay afloat. The loss of a college not only hurts educational options for students, it severely impacts the surrounding community. The loss of students and their disposable incomes is compounded when the highly educated workforce that is required to teach and administer an institution is gone. These individuals and their families fill the K–12 buildings in a town as well as buy homes and attend cultural events. When a community loses such people, the effects that ripple throughout it are hard to calculate.

Finally, small private colleges traditionally offer a religious and values-based education that is hard to replicate at state-funded institutions. The separation of church and state, of course, does not apply to private institutions. Those students who want to participate in campus-sponsored worship services, meet regularly with a campus pastor, blend their educational experience with their spiritual life, and join openly with others (including professors) who share their religious viewpoints may be lost if religiously centered colleges can't remain prosperous.

My anxiety is not without merit. A recent survey by Moody's Investors Service (2013) noted that 19 percent of private nonprofit institutions self-reported that they expected net tuition revenue to decline, and 23 percent of these institutions project that net tuition revenue will grow slower than the current inflation rate of 2 percent. During the past ten years more than thirty institutions shut their doors for the final time, terminated their faculty, and told their students to transfer to other schools. This list includes the following colleges (Brown, n.d.):

- Barat College (Lake Forest, IL)
- Beacon University (Columbus, GA)
- Bethany University (Scotts Valley, CA)
- Bradford College (Haverhill, MA)
- Cascade College (Portland, OR)
- Chester College (Chester, NH)
- College of Santa Fe (Santa Fe, NM)
- D-Q University (Davis, CA)
- Dana College (Blair, NE)
- Eastern Christian College (Bel Air, MD)
- Far North Bible College (Anchorage, AK)
- Kelsey-Jenney College (San Diego, CA)
- Lambuth University (Jackson, TN)
- Lon Morris College (Jacksonville, TX)
- Marycrest College (Davenport, IA)
- Marymount College (Tarrytown, NY)
- Mary Holmes College (West Point, MS)
- Mount Senario College (Ladysmith, WI)
- New College of California (San Francisco, CA)

- Notre Dame College (Manchester, NH)
- Pillsbury Baptist Bible College (Owatonna, MN)
- St. John's Seminary College (Camarillo, CA)
- Sheldon Jackson College (Sitka, AK)
- Southeastern University (Washington, DC)
- Summit Christian College (Fort Wayne, IN)
- Trinity College (Burlington, VT)
- Vennard College (University Park, IA)
- Wesley College (Florence, MS)
- William Tyndale College (Farmington Hills, MI)

These colleges had an average life span of 87 years. Some had been in operation over 150 years. Many seemed resilient and impenetrable. Several were established soon after our country was founded, and they survived wars, the Great Depression, epidemics, and natural disasters. It seemed highly unlikely—if not impossible—that these wonderful schools would ever go out of business, but they did.

And I believe that many others will do the same over the next several years unless we adopt a new paradigm for attracting students. Clearly, I am not alone in this worry. On September 18, 2013, I spoke at a hearing before the Subcommittee on Higher Education and Workforce Training in the U.S. House of Representatives on this very topic (see appendix 1 for the full transcript). Michigan representative Tim Walberg introduced me to the committee by saying that our unique business model utilizing strategic investments, quantifiable results, and recruiting accountability at Adrian College is one of the most positive success stories he has ever seen in his district. My testimony highlighted our enrollment growth and all that it produces: annual budget increases, high retention rates, new facilities and ongoing renovations, and most important of all, more qualified students and better resources with which to provide a higher quality education. At the conclusion of the panel testimony, the committee vice chair said our session was the most enlightening and helpful hearing he had attended on the topic thus far. This is why I am writing this book.

To the casual observer, small liberal arts colleges in America are just fine. One could even argue that they are robust. Many have multimillion-dollar endowments and an alumni base that appears willing to send additional millions quickly every time they launch another capital campaign. Their buildings look strong and hearty, their ivy is green and neatly trimmed, they have at their disposal outstanding investment firms to manage their cash and equity portfolios, and they have dedicated board members to support the president and administrators. Most importantly, they have students, bright, eager, energetic, passionate students who represent the future of America and all that is good in today's youth. Certainly nothing can be wrong within this Norman Rockwell–like picture.

But if we look beneath the ivy, something is wrong, terribly wrong. Fewer and fewer students perceive they can afford to select these types of schools every year (GDA Integrated Services, 2010). As costs escalate within each institution, tuition soars for students, and a major storm is brewing in the distance that could lead to the end for many historic and wonderful colleges (Fairbanks, 2011; College Board Advocacy & Policy Center, 2011; College Board Advocacy & Policy Center, 2012).

There are several factors that led to this facade of health and prosperity at many colleges. Part of the problem is a function of the towns in which these colleges are located. Many schools were founded at the same time that their villages were incorporated. Often the town and the college grew up together as America was becoming a nation. They welcomed each other as academic, community, and business leaders all appreciated what the others had to offer. Timeless traditions grew up: Homecoming parades wove through towns, and community bookstores catered to "book rush" each semester. At the same time, city councils passed zoning ordinances permitting colleges to expand their borders and build impressive buildings. Lectureships, athletic events, and student philanthropy projects created an illusion that the colleges were healthy, but, without fresh eyes and constant oversight and vigilance, no one noticed that these schools have begun floundering.

For administrators and trustees who are forced to make the decision to close a college, the disappointment lasts a lifetime. They not only feel that they have let down their current employees and students, they feel the weight of history in knowing that they were the captains of the ship when the ship went down, and they are disappointing everyone who has ever been affiliated with the college, including alumni, friends, and families. The loss of a college is a death in the academic family and is a true loss to the community in which the college is located.

While it is true that many factors precipitate taking a college off life support, the final decision is always a function of one thing: *money*. When the money runs out, an institution ceases to exist. It is that simple. Money is the life-giving nourishment that every college needs, and when there is no money, there is no college. You can write long and detailed books on why the money runs out. Presidents can be second-guessed, poor decisions can be regretted, inexpensive online competition and a host of other reasons can be offered as excuses for insolvency, but none of these excuses matter when the money runs out. The only thing that matters is that the institution can't meet payroll or pay back the banks or meet the financial obligations of student aid. And the casket closes.

Now it is certainly true that some schools have tremendous financial assets. For the elite institutions in America, an abundance of money is available. These schools have no fear of closing because enrollment is temporarily down or because of a few wild Wall Street fluctuations in the equities market. Seventeen private colleges in this country have between $1 billion and $2 billion in their endowments. Seven have between $2 billion and $3 billion, and twenty-one colleges have over $3 billion. (Presidents and chief enrollment officers at these institutions can stop reading this book now. It is not for you.) Another nineteen colleges have over $500 million in their endowment. (This book is probably not for you either.) But the vast majority of the five hundred small private liberal arts colleges in America have far less financial strength than the few colleges mentioned above. Over 70 percent of private colleges have less than $100 million in their endowment, and nearly 20 percent have less than $20 million (National Association of College and University Business Officers, 2011). Many of these schools live on the edge, an edge that is becoming increasingly precarious as the financial landscape changes for families trying to afford college.

These problems are compounded—and the perfect storm continues to gain strength—when college administrators engage in denial. Many believe that the longevity of their institutional history ensures the security of their future. "We've made it almost a hundred years," they say, "what are the odds that we'll run out of money any time soon?" But this point of view is blind to the changing demographics that are converging to make it extremely difficult for private colleges to survive. Although a record number of students have graduated from American high schools in recent years, the number of graduates is projected to grow by only 1 to 2 percent in total through the next decade. Even so, the number of high school graduates will fall in at least twenty-seven states, especially states in the Midwest and Northeast, but this trend does stretch all the way south to Louisiana and as far west as Washington State (National Center for Education Statistics, 2011, 2012). In addition, online education is growing at a seemingly exponential rate, and these potential students will find it increasingly convenient and financially attractive to forgo traditional education in order to grab an online degree. Most importantly, small private colleges are now charging such an extraordinarily high price that, at first glance, the general public is unwilling to even consider attending these colleges (GDA Integrated Services, 2010). Sticker shock is real. Students won't look at a college if they believe that the price tag is completely outside their reach. Why get your hopes up when you know that your parents will ultimately say no?

Financial concern within families is compounded by current economic realities in America that lead many people to believe that our most prosperous days are behind us. Although average family incomes for the top 40 percent of earners are up over the last thirty years, family incomes for all earners in our country have fallen recently. And these recent drops in income have nearly all come since 2007 (College Board Advocacy & Policy Center, 2011), so families with high-school-age and college-age students are understandably skeptical about their ability to pay for their kids' education. Further, competition overseas continues to erode the labor market; America lost more than two million manufacturing jobs between 2007 and 2009 to inexpensive labor markets in Mexico, China, and beyond (Barker, 2011). These factors lead many families to think twice about paying for private education when the entire house of cards could come tumbling down on the financial markets in America again as it did in 2008.

Does the future look bright for American consumers? A huge percentage of people say no, as reported in a recent poll that showed 71 percent of Americans do not believe that the future will be as good as the past (Gallup, 2013). This feeling is exacerbated in families of college-age students as fears grow that the higher education "bubble" may burst (Gillen, 2008; Kawamoto, 2011; Lacy, 2011). With entry-level wages for college grads falling, debt rising, and stagnant unemployment rates expected to continue for the next few years, these fears are absolutely understandable as well as realistic. This insecurity does not bode well for expensive private higher institutions that fail to help families to understand that they *can* afford to pay for a higher quality college education. Too often, private colleges don't do enough to inform families about the number and amount of scholarships available to students. Many parents don't realize that private and federal grants greatly reduce the "real price" of an education at many excellent small private institutions.

Why Share the Secret to the Sauce?

In 2005 Adrian College faced all of these realities, and we developed a revenue-building enrollment model that saved our institution. I am writing this book because I think that this model can work for other colleges as well. But you are probably asking why I would do this. Why am I sharing the strategy to our success at Adrian College when many people reading this book may be competing with us for students? I believe the answer is that small private institutions are not in competition with each other. We are competing with the large public universities. Most small liberal arts colleges only need about four hundred incoming freshman every year to stay viable. That's really a very achievable number. But it is vital to remember that small institutions should not see these students as a closed pool of freshman they are taking from each other. For the most part, institutions like Adrian College can focus on recruiting students who are thinking about enrolling at the large public state colleges and universities, but who would be better served at a smaller private college, where they will be coached, mentored, taught, and otherwise guided individually, in a closer and more intimate setting. Implementing the enrollment strategy outlined in the following pages is, in the end, focused on finding the students your institution will serve *better* than a large university can and showing them why they should apply and enroll and participate and graduate at *your* institution.

Even more importantly, I am sharing the secrets to the sauce and giving other college leaders the recipe that we at Adrian College used to pull ourselves back from the edge of financial ruin because I love our type of college, and, as I said earlier, I worry for our collective future. While small privates may not be the right educational experience for every student, they certainly are the right choice for many young adults, especially those who need small classes, personal attention, a "teaching first" faculty, and an institution that wraps its arms around each student and says, "You can do this, you can earn a college degree, and we will help you through to graduation." And this is not a fictional romantic scenario. The Michigan Colleges Foundation, an organization of fourteen of the most selective small liberal arts colleges in Michigan, recently hired the research firm SimpsonScarborough (2013) to explore and clarify attributes of these small private institutions. The presidents of these fourteen colleges were not surprised to learn that, taken as a whole, our mean four-year graduation rate is double that of Michigan's public institutions. Although this is not a statistic most of our target audience is well aware of at present, it is a significant one, one that reminds us how important institutions like ours are. Our schools are excellent investments for our students and their parents. We provide positive outcomes, and students know they stand a good chance of improving their career options when they enroll at a small private.

Students need to graduate, parents deserve to get the best bang for their buck, and employers want to find qualified, skilled professionals. Our economy *needs* our type of college. Parents and students alike are worried about achieving the income required to pay for a college education, and students articulate that their primary motivation to attend college is to acquire a better job. But many people do not see the real value of a liberal arts education to their future professional success. Students perceive that the employers in the "real world" want hard skills and preprofessional training, but they and their parents believe that a liberal arts degree is filled with esoteric classes that teach no hard skills, such as those in the philosophy, ethics, or literature. However, employers themselves know better. The Association of American Colleges and Universities (Hart Research Associates, 2013) reports that a recent survey of 318 employers showed an explicit understanding that a liberal arts education provides students with the broad knowledge base and demonstrated ability to think critically as well as to solve complex problems that they so desperately need in the workplace. Eighty percent of the business owners, CEOs, presidents, and high-level executives queried recognized their businesses' need for professionals with a "broad knowledge in the liberal arts and sciences" (22). Over 90 percent of these difference-makers in our economy recognize that critical thinking and complex-problem-solving skills are more important in their hiring decisions than a student's undergraduate major. Employers in this survey also approved of the kind of teaching we offer across the liberal arts curriculum, courses that utilize creative problem solving, group activities, community service, and senior capstone projects. They understand that activities like these in a stimulating and academically rigorous setting will prepare students for the economy of the future, one that will reward the innovation and originality every business needs to continue and thrive in a global economy.

Add to the value that students gain from a liberal arts education the undeniable importance of assistance in the form of career development and job placement assistance, references from faculty who actually *know* their students, small classes and individualized assistance, opportunities for collaborative research with faculty, and the plethora of future leadership positions available on a small, but active campus, and it is obvious that small colleges like ours give students what they need most to prepare for their futures in the new economy.

Our students and our country need the leaders that our small private colleges and universities are preparing today. Institutions like Adrian College give students the assistance they need to successfully complete their degrees and the skills they require for success in their professions. We support our communities socially, culturally, and financially. If you, the institution's leader, don't keep your college alive and thriving by bringing in the enrollment it needs to keep its budget in the black, then the damage will ripple across the local community and the students you serve. If you are interested in this prescriptive formula to add students and revenue to your college, read on. I am confident that this book will be helpful to you.

Key Takeaways

1. There are good reasons to worry about the financial future of small liberal arts colleges in this country.
2. During the past ten years, at least thirty institutions have closed their doors. Before closing, these colleges had an average life span of eighty-seven years.
3. While it is true that many factors contribute to the death of a college, one factor overrides all others: money. When a college does not have money, it does not survive.
4. The economic engine for nearly all of these colleges is the students who pay tuition, room, and board.
5. Economic insecurity throughout the country compounds enrollment problems at many small private colleges because parents and students believe students won't find jobs that will enable them to pay off college debt.
6. Small private baccalaureate institutions are *not* in competition with each other
7. Students at small private institutions graduate at twice the rate of those at public institutions in Michigan.
8. Our type of college offers real advantages to students and employers: the critical-thinking and problem-solving skills needed in our new economy
9. The sole purpose of this book is to propose a unique enrollment growth model that can be replicated at every small liberal arts college in the country to build student capacity and to grow revenue.

CHAPTER 2

A Typical Small Private Baccalaureate Institution

Perhaps you can find yourself and your institution in the following description: In 2005, Adrian College was about as typical of a small private baccalaureate institution as it gets. It had roughly nine hundred students, about three-fourths of whom lived on campus but who went home most weekends to see their families and friends from high school. Like many four-year baccalaureate colleges in this country, Adrian College was a small, friendly place that had a certain kind of look that appeals to young adults and their parents when they visit. It's on a fairly small campus in a fairly small town. It's the kind of place where everyone's friendly. You can walk from one side of the campus to the other and it doesn't take you very long. You look at it and you can see instantly how different it is from large state schools with tens of thousands of students, where you literally have to drive or take a bus from the classrooms to the library. You can look at the classrooms and the other facilities at Adrian College and know that your son or daughter is going to have a safe place to take classes, and they're not going to be sitting in a giant lecture hall with six hundred students where the professors rarely know their names or even whether they're regularly attending class.

But in 2005 Adrian College, like so many other small schools, had deep problems just beneath the surface. A close look revealed that the most essential maintenance and repair issues had been ignored for many years. The same basements flooded, the same lights did not work, and money never seemed to be available to fix these problems. The campus was run down. Deferred maintenance seemed like the easiest way to save money because people learned to adapt to these inconveniences, and after a while they stopped complaining or, worse yet, they simply didn't notice anymore.

As the curb appeal declined, the patience of the faculty, students, and staff ceased to matter. Even if they didn't want to be patient, even if it pained them greatly to see the school they loved fall apart around them, what option did they have? They could leave, which many did, but leaving always presents another set of problems (relocating family, finding a new job, taking care of elderly parents, moving the kids to a new school), so most faculty and staff stuck it out. Patience was not only a virtue, it was a required adaptive strategy.

Another problem Adrian College shared with many small schools was constant belt-tightening. Although it was promoted as a small school with small class sizes, implying that smaller classes automatically meant higher quality, the college increasingly relied on underpaid adjuncts, instructors who spent the minimum amount of time on campus and who could not provide much of the time and information that students need.

When you combined these internal problems with the external reality that Adrian is a small rural town, perceived by soon-to-be-college-educated young adults as dull and lacking the exciting amenities of "the big city," it became increasingly difficult to attract quality students to attend the college. "There's nothing to do in Adrian," students would say. "If I'm going to attend a college that's smaller than my high school, I at least want to be in a big city like New York or San Francisco or Chicago so I can have fun on the weekends."

What is vital to understand about these problems, though, is that they are all connected, and they are all linked to the biggest problem of all: low enrollment! Enrollment accounts for 90 percent of our income; we are dependent on tuition, room, board, and fees. When enrollment declines, budgets suffer, and when budgets suffer at small privates, the cascading effect is lethal. If money is the ultimate cause of death at small privates, as I am suggesting here, then poor enrollment is the disease. If you can cure the disease, you can save the patient.

If you ask small private college presidents what they fear most, it is not under-prepared students, an insufficient endowment, or even tensions with the faculty. It is low enrollment, because everything begins with strong first-year classes and the ability to retain these classes through to graduation. Once you establish a model that guarantees perpetually strong admissions numbers, presidents can solve most of the other problems that confront them.

Enrollment is the answer.

In 2005 Adrian College implemented an enrollment plan that works. In five years, Adrian College watched its first-year class nearly double and saw total enrollment grow by 100 percent. The Admissions Growth plan that we instituted, with the support of the Board of Trustees and administrators and faculty members across the campus, has saved Adrian College. It can save your college, too. All you need is the courage to launch it and the fortitude to see it through. Let me tell you about where this plan came from and where it can take your institution.

The Standard "Fixes"

I'm going to go back a little bit from here and start at the beginning. The story of this situation unfolds like this: In 1997, I accepted the dean of students position at Washington & Jefferson College (W&J), in Washington, Pennsylvania. One year after I arrived, W&J hired Dr. Brian Mitchell as its eleventh president. Dr. Mitchell was a young president, forty-five years old, progressive, and willing to take risks to grow enrollment. Shortly after he arrived he announced that his highest priority was to move the needle from twelve hundred students to fourteen hundred in five years. For many years W&J had been stuck at twelve hundred students, and they could not figure out how to grow quickly without lowering their admissions standards and compromising their academic quality. Dr. Mitchell made several adjustments that other schools often make. He lightened up on an oppressive set of rules that were created over many years to control student behavior, rules that in my opinion were unnecessary and, frankly, did not work, in addition to driving students off campus and into other schools. He cultivated strong relationships with students and became known as an accessible president who listened well and cared about student input. He terminated the contracts of several employees whom he believed could not build the type of school that he wanted to create, a school with momentum and excitement. He invested heavily in information technology and website development that clearly was becoming increasingly important to students in the late 1990s. He expanded the student center and he ended an antiquated dining service, contracting for better meals and creating a new, attractive dining room. He worked well with the faculty, conducted a curriculum review, started new majors, and increased academic budgets. He improved the look of the place by installing beautiful patio areas with umbrellas, small coffee shops, and new landscaping.

Dr. Mitchell's most urgent and expensive project was the completion of a stately academic building in the middle of campus. This building was partially completed during his predecessor's administration, and he had no choice but to finish the fund-raising and invest millions in this facility. Then, shortly after he arrived, he met a donor who gave him $5 million for an information technology facility with state-of-the-art "smart" classrooms and two hundred computer work stations (Carbasho, 2005). The Technology Center is gorgeous. Its architecture is award-winning—it has a stone exterior and a very classic look that blends beautifully into the campus. Despite all of these changes, W&J did not grow its enrollment by a person. Not a soul. We just flatlined the whole way. Nearly three years later W&J was still stuck at twelve hundred students.

Admissions Growth Is Born

At this point, W&J just continued to tread water until 2002, when the athletic director retired. After two failed national searches, someone recommended I meet Rick Creehan, a successful athletic director at Allegheny College in northwest Pennsylvania. So we sat down and we talked in late 2001, and Creehan introduced me to an enrollment model that had worked very well for him at Allegheny. He told me that this model would be expensive, it would be met with skepticism by the faculty, and the trustees would need to agree to borrow money, something that many small colleges do not like to do. However, borrowing funds is necessary because to implement this plan, he said, a college will need to add personnel quickly and to invest in people who will need at least one year to produce results. Many of these new hires would be full-time coaches to replace part-timers who did not have the time or talent to recruit. Part-timers, he explained, are people with day jobs: they have families to provide for, and they can't travel to high schools to recruit. Schools hire these part-time coaches because they are cheap, sometimes working for nothing, but colleges lose on the other end because these coaches don't recruit and bring in new students or provide a quality athletic experience for their student-athletes.

In addition to investing in full-time coaches, Creehan suggested that our athletic facilities at W&J were poor, often below the standards set by the high schools from which we wanted to attract students. We played football on a flood plain, baseball on an undersized field, and basketball in a gym that had not been updated since it was built in 1970. We needed to make a major investment in athletic facilities that would "wow" potential students.

When it became clear that Creehan would oversee major investments to drive enrollment growth, it also seemed logical that he should sit on the senior staff. We gave him a seat at the table and told him to report directly to the president. Any person who oversees this much capital investment, staff, and enrollment growth should have a direct line to the president.

Creehan joined W&J in March 2002, and work began shortly thereafter. We

W&J Total Enrollment

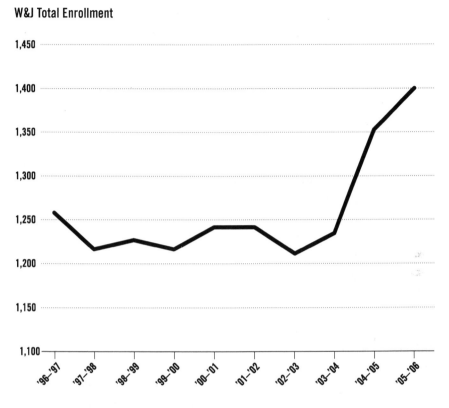

FIGURE 1. We accomplished about 70 percent of our enrollment goals at Washington & Jefferson College. (Source: National Center for Education Statistics, 2013b.)

immediately started lacrosse teams for men and women, and club hockey soon followed. We added field hockey and hired full-time coaches for all of our sports. We built a new softball field, soccer field, and baseball field, and we refurbished our football stadium so it could accommodate field hockey.

As the plan was moving forward and enrollment was growing at W&J, Dr. Mitchell accepted the presidency at Bucknell University in 2004, and it became unclear to Creehan and me whether we could implement our entire set of objectives. As you can see in figure 1, we estimated that we were 75 percent complete at that point with 1,355 students (National Center for Education Statistics, 2013b).

Creehan and I continued to talk. He knew that I believed in this method of enrollment expansion. I told him that if I were ever to achieve a presidency I would encourage him to join me as an executive vice president, and I would give him tremendous freedom to implement the entire Admissions Growth plan. Two years later I began my work as president of Adrian College, and, as we had agreed, Creehan became my executive vice president.

At my interview, the Adrian College trustees spoke about the enrollment problems. I told them I understood that enrollment was at the heart of all of the problems at Adrian College, but also that I had a plan with which enrollment could also be the key to all of the solutions.

I told the trustees that a viable enrollment growth plan is a panacea at most small colleges because it can provide the money to fix the little things like dandelions, dirty windows, cracked sidewalks, and leaky roofs, as well as provide for the big things like fully staffed academic departments, a well-paid faculty, new computer labs, and upgraded classrooms. The entire campus can improve with an infusion of significant dollars, and for a new president, enrollment is your best hope—perhaps your only hope.

I learned during my interviews at Adrian College that the next president would be a very lucky person, because the trustees showed me an adjacent piece of land on which we could build the needed facilities, facilities that would host new and expanded athletic teams and cocurricular activities. Admittedly, most colleges do not have thirty-five unused, wide-open acres for expansion and growth. This certainly was a bonus I inherited from the former president at Adrian College. But the enrollment plan that I will articulate in the following chapters does not require this much expansion space. There are ways to implement the plan without the benefit of unused space. For us, that empty, thirty-five-acre field is now the site of the Multi-Sport Performance Stadium, as well as of Arrington Ice Arena and Nicolay Field—one of the premier Division III baseball facilities in the country. It also houses indoor batting cages, our track & field complex, twelve new tennis courts, and three practice fields.

On the other side of the coin, I discovered through the interview process that, if I should be hired, I would inherit a $1.2 million annual deficit and an incoming class of roughly 250 students. I also learned that morale was low and that many students were not capable of doing college-level work, that faculty were passing students with questionable skills because they knew the institution couldn't afford to have all of these kids fail and drop out.

One especially insightful professor at Adrian College, a biology professor, described to me a sense that had overtaken the faculty in particular, but the community in general as well, something that was described by a metaphor she had read in a book called *Good Natured,* by Frans de Waal. The feeling in the community was that the faculty were all like cave men and cave women, with limited resources, who knew that there wasn't enough food to go around, so they would try to hold what they could gather as tightly as they possibly could, and if they could forage a little over here, they would get it and hide it, and they would try to keep whatever resources they could to themselves because they were so afraid that if they let go or loosened up, others would get their resources because their colleagues were doing the same thing. The result was a culture of forced selfishness. And that attitude was just lying heavily on everybody's shoulders.

Low enrollment and limited resources created additional cultural problems as well. Upon arriving at Adrian College, I quickly learned that at various points in the college's recent history the faculty had passed curriculum changes that were not necessarily in the best interests of the institution. Instead, they had been implemented to provide job security. Our foreign language department was a good example. Regardless of whether a two-semester language requirement for all majors is a good idea, our foreign language professors knew it would further shield them from layoffs during lean years. The thinking was that you can't eliminate language professors if the two-semester requirement was part of the core curriculum. This kind of resources insecurity leads people to think only about their own positions, or more broadly, their own departments, but not about what's in the best interests of the institution or of the students.

A second example of curriculum changes driven by job security and not student need was apparent in the Art Department. The art faculty loaded students with distribution requirements in art to the point that art became a requirement for every major, not just art majors. These unnecessary requirements left no flexibility in the curriculum, so we were losing students for that reason as well. Driving students out of Adrian College in this manner was not helping the problem at all, of course. What tied these situations together was layer on top of layer on top of layer of morale and organizational behavior issues that, in my opinion, were built on a base of a lack of resources. Every decision by administration and faculty was not driven by a growth strategy: How can we invest in the institution to bring in more students and improve their experiences here? Instead the thinking was always: What can we cut next so we can still keep our own program/department/office going?

The last part of the Adrian College story to note with respect to the Admissions Growth plan is that it became clear to me early on that those who were in charge of enrollment and retention under the old system needed to move on to other opportunities outside of Adrian College. I accepted the resignations of the director of admissions and the dean of student affairs. I reassigned the athletic director to another department, and the vice president for academic affairs retired, as he had planned before my arrival. Before too long the vice president of development resigned, and the chief financial officer moved to a new job in Virginia.

The trustees were very supportive of these moves, not because they did not appreciate the contributions these individuals had made to the college, but because they recognized that the Admissions Growth model was a unique and untried plan that required fresh eyes, fresh hands, and a new openness to doing business differently at Adrian College.

The beauty of small liberal arts colleges is that, unlike their large public counterparts, the community feels more like a family than a group of professional colleagues. The downside of this pleasant environment is that presidents are often reluctant to terminate individuals who no longer serve the institution. While this is heartfelt and compassionate, it often neglects to recognize that our first duty is to the health and well-being of the institution. Money needs to be spent on the right people in order for the Admissions Growth plan to work. This may require colleges to reallocate money from existing personnel or programs. We certainly had to do that at Adrian College. During the first years of the Admissions Growth plan we chose not to fill positions in undersubscribed majors. We carefully ana-lyzed all academic programs, and those that carried too many faculty members vis-à-vis enrollment were left unfilled after retirements and departures. We have continually and gradually asked employees to increase their healthcare copays. We cut several part-time staff members in a variety of departments and delayed filling some vacancies in plant maintenance up to one year in addition to cutting a full-time building manager position in athletics because it was not a position that helped us increase enrollment. We redirected all of the money saved from these salaries and benefits cuts into the model, so that it could fund new coaches who would recruit. It was not only employees who took on the burden of helping to fund Admissions Growth. We also ended a First-Year Experience program that was yielding poor results, partly due to a lack of common readings and common core learning objectives, and we discontinued our field hockey program as soon as we realized it was just not going to be successful at our school, which I will address in later chapters.

By the fall of 2005, we were taking the first steps to put the Admissions Growth program fully in place at Adrian College. In the chapters to come, this book will show you exactly how the plan was implemented at this small four-year institution.

My goal in telling this story is to make the steps we've taken at Adrian College transparent. You will see on these pages the steps we took to launch the Admissions Growth plan and then the work we did to follow through with that plan. The proof that this strategy works is in the numbers—not just the numbers of students admitted to Adrian College, but the number of applicants, the four-year retention rate, the team GPAs, and of course, the tuition dollars all of these students bring in and the budget they provide for the expansion and upgrades that happened and continue to happen across campus. When you see these numbers on the following pages, you will see that this approach to enrollment has saved Adrian College. The Admissions Growth plan can help—even save—*your* institution as well.

Key Takeaways

1. Many small colleges face the same financial worries.
2. The response is often constant belt tightening, increasing reliance on underpaid adjuncts, and flat budgets and salaries.
3. The top concern among small college presidents is not underprepared students, a small endowment, or tensions with the faculty. It is low enrollment.
4. At small liberal arts colleges with small endowments and donor bases, strong enrollment is the solution.
5. Without strong enrollment numbers, money is scarce, resources are difficult to acquire, and a culture of forced selfishness often pervades a campus.
6. Resource insecurity can also lead to unwise curricular changes as departments attempt to pass mandatory requirements in order to make it difficult to lay off professors.
7. Implementing this enrollment growth plan usually requires a president to take a fresh look at his or her personnel and terminate those individuals who can't get the job done.

CHAPTER 3

Growing Enrollment

Why Choose Admissions Growth over Other Plans?

Before I outline in precise detail how the enrollment growth model works, I need to show you why presidents and senior-level administrators must do two things: First, they must reject nearly every piece of conventional wisdom that has traditionally guided admissions offices on how to grow enrollment. This "wisdom" includes fads, gimmicks, quick fixes, hip trends, and most of the suggestions provided by consultants. Most of these strategies don't work (that is why small private colleges are in trouble), and they are nearly impossible to measure. They are not effective, they are expensive (some are complete budget busters), and they rarely, if ever, live up to their promises. It is easy to spend tens of thousands of dollars quickly on admissions-growth ideas and not know for sure whether they lead to any enrollment growth whatsoever.

How Many Students Select a College

The root of the problem with most of these ideas is that they are completely disconnected from the mind of a high school senior. They are ideas of people my age (the fifties) or thereabouts who have forgotten what motivates a student to select a college, or they are plans of individuals who are out of touch with the millennial generation. Their ideas lack relevance and show the difficulty of getting into the mind of a seventeen-year-old. When we broached the initial Admissions Growth presentation to our Board of Trustees, I really drove this point home. I tried to help them understand this generation by asking the trustees to imagine a hypothetical high school student named John Smith. In selecting his college, John probably woke up one morning his senior year and said, "Well, Mom, it's time I start looking at colleges. I'd like to look at five colleges: Kalamazoo College, Michigan State University, the University of Michigan, Hillsdale College, and Adrian College." And so, as many families do, John took a day or two off from school, and Mom or Dad, or maybe both, took time off from work. Then they drove the circuit together, and they visited each one of those schools. As they took the tours and visited with admissions counselors, it was immediately clear to John and his parents that the colleges had many similarities. They all have big green lawns and huge buildings and cheerful students who act as tour guides. They have a buffet of majors and fun activities. They promote diversity and give you convincing statistics about graduation rates and successful graduates. They require work in the classrooms, but overall they are a veritable carnival of fun for any student desiring to enroll. Now, soon after the family arrives home, they have a decision to make. Mom will ask, "Well, which college do you like best?" And, of course, if John wants 110,000 people at his football games on the weekend, then Adrian College is not going to win that battle. The University of Michigan is going to win that battle. If John says, "I want to go to a school that has 250 majors," we aren't going to win that battle either, Michigan State is going to win. And if John says to his mom and dad, "I want a small liberal arts experience where I can get to know my professors and receive an excellent education," then we are still only one of three schools on that list—Hillsdale and Kalamazoo also offer small classes, personal attention, and a strong liberal arts emphasis. And so Adrian College has only a one out of three chance of getting John to enroll. But if we have something to separate ourselves from those other two schools, like a team or a cocurricular activity such as hockey or marching band, then we have John, because neither of the other two liberal arts schools on that list have these activities that John wants to participate in in college. So this student might say, "Well, all of those schools had something that I liked, but I want to keep playing hockey, and only Adrian has that." And so John now wants to come study at Adrian College and play on our hockey team.

Eight Enrollment Strategies That *Don't* Work

The second thing presidents must do is create clear and concise goals regarding the number of freshmen they want to enroll each fall, the total number of students they need in their student body to run the college effectively (to keep the lights on, so to speak), offer annual raises, and offer an exciting, creative, innovative educational experience. Later in this chapter you will be asked to answer some questions that will help you establish these goals. Once you answer these questions, you will have the data and goals you need to effectively implement an Admissions Growth model specifically tailored to your campus. These are the details you need to know before you launch the Admissions Growth plan. But first, a few things that don't work and why. Essentially, below you will find eight ideas, suggestions, and pieces of advice you should forget, ideas that are very popular right now, but ideas that, unfortunately, do not work.

So let's begin by looking at eight things that don't work to grow your enrollment. If your college is spending money on these efforts right now, my advice is to cease and desist, move in a new direction, save your money, and invest instead in the strategies outlined in the following chapters, strategies that have worked so well on our campus.

1. Rebranding

Rebranding your institution is a very popular fad right now. Marketing firms and consulting agencies suggest that every college has a unique story, a warm and welcoming history that when "packaged" correctly can be articulated in such a way that it will move the hearts and minds of young people to flock to your campus (Sevier, 2010).

Branding has been a major fad in higher education for the past ten years and, quite honestly, I do not see the results. The concept of "branding a college" or "rebranding a college" has several clear problems. First, it is incredibly expensive to create a marketing campaign with the power, reach, and redundancy that is truly required to create a new image in the mind of the consumer (i.e., a potential student). When we think of great brands in this country we immediately think of great products like Coca-Cola, McDonalds, and Ralph Lauren. Or we think of stores like Tiffany, The Gap, Apple, or even JCPenney. Each of these products and institutions has a brand, an identity, an image that immediately tells us what to expect when we walk into their stores and purchase their products. These brands—and the perceptions they conjure up in each of us—were created over decades and were supported with millions of dollars in advertising and marketing campaigns. They were created by the greatest minds in marketing in New York, Los Angeles, and Chicago. They were reinforced in billboards, television ads, radio spots, and endless other marketing campaigns. Most importantly, the marketing efforts were supported by the products themselves, through which customers *experienced* the truth of the appeal when they purchased the food, apparel, computer, or jewelry. Tiffany's jewelry *is* elegant, McDonald's food *is* inexpensive, JCPenney clothes *are* durable and moderately priced.

The problems for colleges that try to rebrand are numerous. First, few small colleges have the financial resources to truly rebrand themselves in the marketplace. We simply don't have millions of dollars to create a new image for students. Second, many panels, articles, and academic conferences promote the success of rebranding campaigns, but these publications and presentations are woefully short of actual facts and evidence. The questions these administrators cannot answer is this: Can you really say your new branding efforts have brought any tuition-paying students to campus? How many? Which students? It is not possible to measure the efficacy of branding.

In addition, as much as we might hate to admit it, a college experience does not differ wildly from one campus to another. In fact, the experience is quite similar at most small liberal arts colleges. We may think they are different and even want them to be different, but they are not. Classes, cocurricular activities, dorm life, and cafeteria food are similar, by and large, at most colleges. Beyond that, we do not need to be rebranded. Our brand is solid. Private higher education is perceived as extraordinarily strong. When students think of a small private school, what comes to mind is a safe and beautiful educational environment with small classes and knowledgeable faculty mentors. Students envision warm and inviting Homecoming parades and quiet walks between classes with new friends and classmates. They see chapel services on Sunday mornings and graduation ceremonies on the college green. All of these images are positive, and all are inviting to many prospective college students. We don't need to change our brand, our brand is just fine.

So, you are probably asking, if our brand is this strong, why don't more students select small private colleges? In other words, why are enrollments falling and why are so many colleges in financial distress? The answer is that students rarely pick a college based on its brand. When presidents and trustees think about what makes their school stand out to high school seniors trying to make a very big decision about where to spend the next four years of their lives, they need to remember that they're trying to get into the mind of a young adult here. This young person probably has as idea about a career path or at least a major, but he or she is not responding to a slogan, that is, a brand. It doesn't happen. Moreover, many of our colleges have been in business for nearly one hundred years. Our brands are well established. Students and their parents see us in a particular light. This brand is not going to change with a few years and a few million dollars' investment in advertising. Regardless of how much I spend to rebrand Adrian College, it is never going to be seen as another Grinnell College in my lifetime.

2. Adding Satellite Campuses

Satellite campuses are also a recent "fad" for growing enrollment and increasing revenue. Some small private colleges have relied on these campuses to attract students, often using the revenue to sustain their traditional main campus. While this strategy may work in the short term, it is risky because satellite campuses are antithetical to the *type* of education we believe in philosophically and have successfully offered to our students for over a hundred years. (Put differently: satellite campuses are antithetical to our well-established brand, as discussed above.) Satellite campuses are commuter campuses for nontraditional students. They are usually located in rented buildings hundreds of miles from the main campus and offering no housing or out-of-class experiences and few opportunities for meaningful relationships with professors. True liberal arts education is an experience, a four-year journey of the mind that transforms individuals into critically thinking, lifelong learners capable of citizenship and social engagement to an extent beyond that available to those who are not fortunate enough to have this educational experience. The philosophy that supports liberal arts learning simply can't be captured on most satellite campuses. Of course, there are exceptions. Your institution may have access to a well-defined population of students that you can serve with targeted programs for nursing, teaching, or other professions that would utilize a part-time or commuter curricula. However, let me state unequivocally, here, that these programs must be very targeted, with a clear and defined strategy outlining how and why these students would enroll in your institution. They must also be fully funded from the beginning, as I will discuss in future chapters, and each program must be led by someone who is accountable for recruitment and retention. Further, it is risky to rely on revenues from satellite campuses to support the traditional main campus because most of us don't know how to operate these distance learning institutions. We are wading into unfamiliar waters, here. We are trying to start a new type of business—one about which we know very little. We know small privates, we like small privates, we believe in the value of small privates, many of us graduated from small privates. That is why we entered the field. We should use the knowledge and passion to serve our college instead of searching for a gimmick that will supplement a struggling main campus.

3. Investing in Online Education

Growing enrollment through online education is even less attractive than adding satellite campuses if we want to remain true to our original mission. Few educators try to argue that online education promotes class discussions, meaningful faculty-student dialogue, and the rich exchange of ideas that transforms individuals into deep thinking, progressive, highly engaged learners. Online education is disengaged education; it is education that places students in front of a computer screen instead of in front of a professor and mentor. It is education directed at the head at the expense of the heart, at the mind at the expense of the soul, at the individual at the expense of the community. I have taken online classes, and I encourage presidents and admissions administrators to try to find an online course that can replicate the experience our students receive in small, on-campus classes. You will discover that these classes and experiences do not exist. While they are convenient and often less expensive, convenience does not translate into knowledge production. Great thinking requires hard work, work that is rarely accomplished in online learning. The bubble has already started to burst with respect to the efficiency of online learning. Congress, the Department of Education, and many professional educations are increasingly asking for proof that deep learning is taking place in these programs.

4. Adding Preprofessional Programs and "Trade School" Certification Programs

Small liberal arts institutions need to avoid what I call the DeVry trend: part-time classes focusing on skilled trades and instant income. Trade school education does not appeal to the students we are aiming to enroll. Remember, most of us need about four hundred new students a year to maintain a thriving institution. The types of students who select our colleges are not looking for the jobs these programs prepare them for, jobs like emergency medical technician, HVAC mechanic, or veterinarian's assistant. Our potential students are looking for experiences that will guide them toward leadership positions. They want to be successful professionals and major change agents in society.

When you offer part-time, evening, and commuter classes that provide graduates with credentials such as emergency medical technician certifications and associate degrees in computer networking, you are not bringing in ambitious young leaders who want to pursue a liberal arts education. Just like adding satellite campuses, creating these career tracks is incompatible with our brand of baccalaureate instruction.

5. Building New Academic Facilities

At the risk of sounding iconoclastic, my experience suggests that new academic buildings and technology centers in and of themselves do not significantly grow enrollment. We may *wish* that these academic investments would persuade high school students to attend a college, but, except for a few students at the margins, new buildings don't fundamentally improve enrollment numbers in large and transformative ways. While both are essential to the academic process and are necessary for student learning, admissions counselors and college administrators must confront the hard facts of the college selection process: seventeen-year-olds do not choose where to spend the next four years of their academic life based on the size of an institution's academic buildings or the dimensions of their technology center. Yes, it is true that a high level of quality in these facilities must be met—I am not suggesting that presidents should ignore their academic spaces—but, once an acceptable threshold is achieved, most colleges will not see a noticeable difference in the size of their student population by investing heavily in academic infrastructure.

I have personal experience in this area. At Washington & Jefferson College (W&J) we built a $12 million business building, named after Howard Burnett, who had been president of W&J for twenty-seven years. We spent an additional $20 million on the Technology Center. Neither of these buildings grew the enrollment by any substantial margin. Perhaps they didn't grow the campus by any students at all. It is impossible to know because it is impossible to measure whether a student selects a campus because of a new academic building. You can invest millions of dollars in new academic buildings and have no way of knowing for sure whether these investments have worked.

Moreover, there is no way to require accountability when you attempt to build your enrollment through investments in new academic buildings. Admissions counselors and coaches can't hand out brochures encouraging students to study at an institution because of a new building. When you don't have accountability you don't have responsibility, and when you don't have responsibility you have no way of going back to individual employees who are not recruiting new students. The impossibility of judging how many students a building brings to campus ignores the fact that enrollment at small privates needs to be built on accountability. Each program must have an individual who is responsible for attracting a certain number of students through the offerings that the college has. And unless you have somebody who's dedicated to going out and getting students who are excited about a new music building or a business building or a science lab, you are never going to know if that expense is being leveraged to build enrollment.

One of the reasons new academic buildings, libraries, and technology centers don't work in and of themselves to increase enrollment is because public universities, which of course receive state money and significant federal money, will always have bigger and more elaborate buildings. Small private institutions don't want to get into an arms race where they're trying to out-public the publics by enhancing the academic buildings so much that the students are more impressed by your buildings than they are by those at the larger public schools. In addition, if you look at the physics building, for example, at a small institution like Adrian College, versus a place like Michigan State University, which recently received $220 million from the federal government to build a state-of-the art research facility for the study of rare nuclear isotopes (Schultz, 2008), or if you try to compare business buildings or science laboratories or foreign language buildings or even communication arts buildings at small privates to those at The Ohio State University or the University of Michigan, then you will see the smaller institutions simply can't put up buildings on that scale. You can try to approximate these huge buildings or build a charming small building, instead, that will be more attractive to a small segment of people, but if you really want to get into building larger academic buildings at small privates, it's very, very difficult to overtake the publics.

Larger and more beautiful academic buildings and technology centers also don't work to grow enrollment because students simply assume that you have academic buildings that will be sufficient for teaching and learning. Potential students take for granted that administrators and professors at colleges that have been around for 100 or 150 years have had plenty of time and brain power and sufficient money to put together adequate buildings. It's difficult to sell students on the idea that a new building is really that much different at a small private or a large public institution. Another way to say this is that buildings are not "difference makers" in a high school student's mind.

6. Increasing Library Holdings

An additional strategy often employed by presidents to grow enrollment is to significantly increase the number of books and periodicals in their library. Unfortunately this also does not work to tip the scale in a young person's mind enough to make him or her say, "I want to go to Adrian College because they have a bigger library." We must remember that, in the minds of young millennials, nearly everything they want is available online. Students assume that they can find all the research materials they want either on the Web or through co-op agreements and interlibrary loan programs that small private schools have with other private and public colleges. For example, at Adrian College, if a student needs a book that we don't have, then we have a shuttle that runs among a consortium of many libraries throughout our area so students can get the books they need. Most students are already familiar with these kinds of systems through their high schools. So finding research materials, articles, and the like is not something that is a difference maker in the student's mind.

7. Publicizing Faculty Research

In a 2009 survey performed by GDA Integrated Services, only 6 percent of students indicated that a record of strong faculty research was "essential" to their college choice. So research and writing and publications are not things that generally attract students at the undergraduate level. While it is true that students like to see their professors quoted in articles and books, there is no research or data to suggest that it plays a role in their college selection process. At the graduate level, this is not true, of course. Strong graduate program enrollment is often a function of the professors serving individual disciplines and the research accomplishments of those professors. But at the undergraduate level, all research suggests that research and publishing is far down on student's priority list.

8. Manufacturing Fun outside the Classroom

An eighth approach that doesn't work very well is to "manufacture fun" for students through off-campus trips, club activities, visits to sporting and cultural events, and highly active student unions. Weekend bus trips are one example of this effort. While all of these ideas are important, especially in rural areas like Adrian, which is perceived by students as a slow social environment, there is no data to show that students will select a college because student affairs professionals make extra efforts to create fun experiences. College students know how to have fun. They prefer to create their own activities instead of following chaperones to college-organized events. These students are looking for independence, a break from the constant oversight they had in high school, and freedom to spread their wings and be impulsive outside the classroom. We did try to stage some activities at Adrian College, but they did not grow enrollment. A smattering of new activities is appreciated by students and certainly creates momentum and needed social opportunities, but it does not grow enrollment. Students don't make their college selection based on these kinds of fun trips, even though they help entertain students outside the classroom. And a seventeen-year-old doesn't decide to go to a college because it has more ski trips or more trips to amusement parks.

What You Need to Know to Launch the Plan That *Does* Work

So now we have sifted through all of these ideas that many institutions have tried, and we have plenty of evidence that they haven't worked. You will see in subsequent chapters that the Admissions Growth plan does not use any of these strategies. Before we outline a plan that does work, you still have some homework to do, homework that will give you the data you need to move forward with clear goals in mind and to create a plan to fit the needs and culture of your campus. Please get a pen or pencil (go ahead!) and answer these questions for your institution.

1. What size is your college now? __2500__
2. What is your ideal college size? __2800 - 2900__
3. What is your discount rate? _____
4. What is your ideal net tuition revenue? _____
5. How much revenue do you need to make from each student to realize your revenue goals? _____
6. What is your ideal freshman class size? _____
7. What is your ideal in-state/out-of-state ratio? _____
8. What is your campus capacity? _____

Then, review your historical institutional data:

1. How many new students can you count on every year with your current recruitment efforts? _____
2. What is your annual retention rate? _____
3. Why do students leave your college early?

_____   _____
_____   _____
_____   _____

In 2005, at Adrian College, the answers to some of these questions were the following:

1. What is your ideal college size? __1,400__
2. What is your ideal net tuition revenue? __1,400 × 20,000 = $28,000,000__
3. What is your ideal freshman class size? __400__
4. What is your ideal in-state/out-of-state ratio? __60/40__
5. What is your campus capacity? __1,400__

Adrian College's historical institutional data were the following:

1. How many new students can you count on every year with your current recruitment efforts? __120__
2. What is your annual retention rate? __59 percent (2005)__
3. Why do students leave your college early?

   Academically unprepared   _Inadequate IT resources_
   Too few majors   _Rural campus_

When you formulate the answers to these three questions,

- What is your ideal college size?
- What is your ideal net tuition revenue?
- What is your ideal freshman class size?

then you have a goal, the number of students you need to bring to campus each year to keep your institution fully funded.

Keep in mind, too, that growth during this period must be controlled as well as planned. Admissions Growth is a monetarily frontloaded program. However, adding students above your campus's capacity will require adding buildings and facilities you do not yet have the income to fund. This will reduce your revenues and diminish the amount of money that can ultimately be directed to funding academic improvements.

The next step is to look at the programs your school offers and ask these questions:

1. How many students is each athletic team and each cocurricular activity bringing in now?
2. How many students should each activity be attracting?
3. Who is accountable for recruiting these students for this activity?

After you have a firm grasp of the enrollment potential of current activities, then you begin to add programs. And I am going to emphasize one more time here that each program must have a recruiting goal associated with it, as well as a coach or staff member responsible for achieving that goal.

The next chapter will get you started answering these questions by showing you exactly how Adrian College sets recruitment goals and then tracks the progress for each of those goals, student by student, week by week, activity by activity. You will, of course, need to tweak the Admissions Growth program to fit your institution's resources and needs, but what you will find on the following pages is the secret to the sauce. What follows are the steps that will avert the coming crisis in higher education. This strategy is how the Admissions Growth plan saved one small liberal arts college in Adrian, Michigan.

Key Takeaways

1. Reject all tricks, gimmicks, fads, and most advice from consultants on how to grow enrollment. Their strategies nearly always fall short of expectations because they fail the ultimate litmus test: understanding the mind of a seventeen-year-old high school student.

2. Rebranding doesn't work. Neither do satellite campuses, online education, increasing library holdings, reducing room and board fees, or attempting to "manufacture fun" outside the classroom. While all of these are important, none are essential to grow enrollment.

3. Attempting to grow enrollment with new academic buildings and computer labs does not work. You will never be able to out-build large public universities with their heavily subsidized tax base. (Adrian College will never be able to compete with the University of Michigan on facilities alone. We need to beat them in other ways.)

4. Students assume their professors are knowledgeable, skilled teachers who will help them to succeed. As long as you offer their preferred major, they will make their college decisions based on other factors. Only 6 percent of students indicate that a record of strong faculty research is essential to their college choice. Be careful about placing too much emphasis on credentials.

5. Students know how to have fun. Don't spend too much time or money on organized activities outside the classroom (ice cream socials, pizza parties, etc.) since these do not strongly influence college selection.

6. Do your homework. Write down your enrollment goals including the financial requirements to run the college.

7. Consider your current student capacity when setting your ideal enrollment numbers. If a college grows too quickly and needs to build several new buildings, this will divert funding that should go first to academic enhancements.

8. After you have set firm enrollment goals and financial objectives, assess the recruiting potential for each of your current extracurricular and cocurricular activities. Once each of these steps is in place, then plan which activities you will add to your campus, and include quantifiable recruiting goals for each activity.

CHAPTER 4

Getting Started

To get started with Admissions Growth you need a plan, the plan must have a (goal,) and the goal must have a clear deadline and benchmarks. WIG Establishing your overall goal and getting everyone on campus working to support it is a critical part of creating an Admissions Growth strategy that will work for your institution. We have discussed breaking down the goals in chapter 3 and will discuss how to achieve those goals in chapter 5. In this chapter we will address setting goals and getting your house in order so that you can take the specific, concrete steps necessary to reach your goals. These steps are vital, because if you don't know where you are going, you have no way of measuring your progress. Quantifiable goals are extremely important to the entire process; they give you your endpoint, both in terms of an ideal and in terms of the hard data to allow everyone in your community to work toward a common aim. Most importantly, goals clearly enumerate the benchmarks you must attain in order to know whether your financial investments are paying a return to your institution.

Six Simple Steps

The short version of the strategy I'm going to roll out for you in this chapter and the following one is actually a very simple, straightforward formula. But to achieve your goals with Admissions Growth, it is necessary to prioritize the steps you will take, so that each effort builds on the step that came before it in a way that will create a stable base for growth. As figure 2 shows, you need to follow these steps:

1. Do your homework and set goals.
2. Build and upgrade required facilities.
3. Fund teams and activities fully and set recruiting goals.
4. Focus on return on investment by holding recruiters accountable.
5. Redirect new income to academic facilities and programs.
6. Continue to build and utilize momentum for further growth.

Step 1: Do Your Homework and Set Goals

Now it is time to take a look at the homework you began in chapter 3. At Adrian College we looked at our campus capacity, including our dorm space, classroom space, dining hall space, and ideal professor/student ratio. We also looked at the amount of money we needed to support our educational mission, and, of course, we looked at the average amount of money we earned on each student. For us, that number was $20,000 a year. From this we determined that we needed fourteen hundred students. This was our goal. We published it widely. We told the Board of Trustees we could accept nothing less than this number if we hoped to build a quality institution. Everyone on campus—from the faculty to the secretaries to the administrators—knew the number we needed to reach.

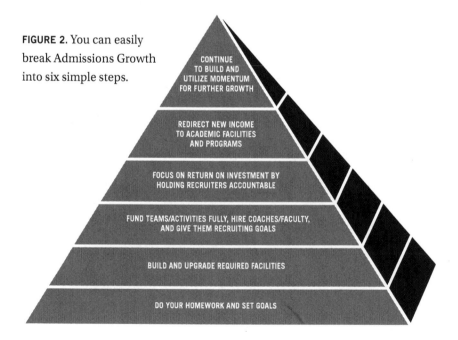

FIGURE 2. You can easily break Admissions Growth into six simple steps.

We even had a name for this effort; we called it Renaissance I. Everything that we did to reach this goal fell under the umbrella of Renaissance I. Everyone knew what "Renaissance I" meant: it referred to our ultimate enrollment goal. We used this term so often and so widely that not only did the people on campus understand its meaning, the town also embraced the concept and the name. I would bump into people in the grocery store or the barber shop or city hall, and they would say, "Hey, Prez, how is Ren I coming along?" Alums would arrive for Homecoming and inquire about Renaissance I. And of course our donor base knew that we needed money to support Renaissance I, and their gifts were acknowledged as critical to our Renaissance I goals. Even the *Chronicle of Higher Education* got on board by running a front-page article on the amazing enrollment results from our Renaissance I efforts (Sander, 2008). This common vernacular created understanding and momentum, and it allowed all of us to work toward a common goal. It was a simple idea that everyone could understand and play a role in.

IMPLEMENTING STEP 1: GET ALL CONSTITUENCIES
ON BOARD AT AN ALL-CAMPUS RETREAT

In order to get everyone on campus involved and to emphasize the critical importance of their efforts, we took a number of strategic steps that both refined the plan and gave all constituencies ownership for its implementation and success. We not only needed the entire campus community to know the goal and understand the plan, we needed them to *believe* in the plan, to affirm in their own minds that it could work.

The first thing we did was to schedule a campus-wide retreat shortly after I was hired, in order to broach the broad outline of the enrollment growth plan. The purpose of the retreat was to provide as much transparency as possible. We stayed at a large hotel in Ypsilanti, which is about forty miles from Adrian. Nearly everyone on campus was invited: faculty, administration, secretarial staff, the trustees, our physical plant leadership team, cafeteria leadership group, and a few student representatives. (You can only do this on a small campus, but it is extremely effective.) We hired a moderator for the two-day workshop, Dr. Richard Kneedler, retired president of Franklin & Marshall College. Dr. Kneedler is a person of great integrity. He has a commanding presence and people trust him. He knew about the Admissions Growth plan that I intended to introduce to the community, and he believed in its efficacy. He helped me use the forum as a kickoff, explaining what we needed to do and why we needed to do it. While we were in Ypsilanti, we talked about our budget problems openly, and we discussed problems on our campus that dissuaded potential students from choosing Adrian College. We squashed rumors and we exposed secrets. We did not shy away from conflict, and we confronted every brutal fact that had driven our enrollment to potentially catastrophic lows.

This catharsis produced real and positive results. Most importantly, it showed everyone in the room that at small liberal arts institutions like Adrian College enrollment is the answer. Only when enrollment is strong can we produce the revenues necessary to meet the myriad needs on our campuses.

Including faculty and staff and administrators in this planning process at every level of the college, I believed, would create a sense that everybody matters and that everybody's opinion was important. As a result of these efforts, if people didn't feel that they had special expertise or interest in the Admissions Growth model when we rolled out the plan in November, then they could get involved in enhancing the school in other ways. The result was that by the end of the retreat in August 2005, committees were planned, faculty members were engaged, people were committed. Academic Dean James Borland put together a series of work groups that would continue the process begun in Ypsilanti through the school year, work groups that allowed all members of campus a say in the Renaissance I revitalizing process.

All of these plans and working groups and committees notwithstanding, I asserted during the retreat that we could *not* use the next two years to plan and plan and plan some more, as is often the case on many campuses who hire new leadership and hope for a turnaround. It was clear to me, and I made it clear to everyone present, that changes needed to be made quickly. We needed growth quickly, and like so many small privates, we didn't have two years to wait. I emphasized that major changes needed to be in place and working by Thanksgiving of that year. At that time, I would gather the reports, and I would stand before the community, and I would announce those areas that would receive immediate investments and improvements to the extent that we could with the budget we had.

I recall that there was an audible gasp in that meeting room in the Marriott when I said "by Thanksgiving." I don't think anyone believed it. And it took enormous discipline on the part of the college community to keep every working group and committee motivated, focused, and on schedule over the next few months. In the beginning, if there could be said to be any resistance to the Admissions Growth plan at Adrian College, I think the speed of planning and implementation were where we were most likely to find it.

Even so, by November 2005, we had that plan. In less than five months we identified our largest problems and put a plan in place to fix them. Each constituency contributed, and administration codified the plan in a strategic five-year document. In fact, by June 2010 that plan had pretty much been accomplished. Essentially, well over 85 percent of that plan is now in place, and maybe 5 or 10 percent of the plan is still in process. I would say about 5 to 8 percent of plan has been revised or removed and probably is not going to happen.

UNDERSTANDING STEP 1: SPECIFY QUANTIFIABLE GOALS
TO AID FOCUS AND PREVENT RESISTANCE

All of these efforts—the retreat, involving people who help the campus function at every level, making the Admissions Growth plan as transparent as possible when we began implementing it—played a major role in making the idea of Admissions Growth more palatable to all the constituencies at Adrian College. We in the administration did this on purpose. We did it for strategic reasons, although I'm not sure that everyone understood that. So part of the point of the August 2005 retreat was to get input and feedback on curriculum, enrollment, staffing needs, and the like, but I felt it was also a vital part of getting future buy-in on the plan from all parties involved. The institution needed to get everybody involved and focused. With a very small set of specific and measurable goals in mind, senior administrators could keep various working groups and individuals from working at odds with each other, and reduce the chances that some faculty or staff members would actively sabotage the plan or speak out against it. That kind of divisiveness would lower morale and defeat all of the work we were doing toward improving the atmosphere and creating a new vitality on campus.

I certainly don't want to suggest that the retreat and the subsequent work groups miraculously created acceptance of our plan for enrollment growth wholeheartedly across campus. I did get a modicum of pushback from some faculty, and some administrators were less than enthusiastic about the model. A few of these people left the college of their own volition. They saw where the institution was going and they didn't want to be a part of it. I respected their candor and their decision to leave. Others were given incentive and retirement packages, and still others were terminated.

Step 2: Build and Upgrade Required Facilities

The next major step was taken at the October Board of Trustees meeting. Here I presented the Admissions Growth plan in its entirety to the trustees. The Board had heard only a little bit about the plan during my interviews and early days on the job. I believed I needed to roll the whole thing out to them all at once so that they could see how everything fit together. Showing them the Admissions Growth plan that way helped them understand how my request for a large investment in facilities, and probably more important, a major, major leveraging of money from local banks, would ultimately pay large dividends. I was very concerned that if I piecemealed it out, this would give some of the members of the Board the opportunity to get nervous, to say, "I don't know . . . That's a lot of money. Can we really trust this guy?" I thought they should see it all at once, in color, on a screen in front of them.

BUILDING A STRONG BASE FOR STEP 2: BROACH THE PLAN TO THE BOARD OF TRUSTEES

At that trustees meeting I laid out the Admissions Growth plan in a PowerPoint presentation. At the end of the presentation, I told them that the plan would cost $30 million to implement; I agreed to raise $15 million if they would borrow $15 million. This may seem like an insurmountable amount of money to many college presidents and their boards, but when you consider that the loan will be paid back over twenty-five years—and the return this investment will immediately bring to campus—it really is not that much money. On top of that, many small colleges are already hemorrhaging cash. At that time in our history Adrian College was gushing $1.3 million in red ink annually, so borrowing $15 million to halt that outflow truly was not the drastic measure it appeared to be to those who did not know the severity of the crisis at Adrian College.

UNDERSTANDING STEP 2: KNOW THAT YOU CANNOT CUT YOUR WAY TO PROSPERITY

Making this large investment is consistent with another mantra that guides my philosophy of managing small liberal arts colleges: You cannot cut your way to prosperity. Here is why: Small private institutions need to understand that we are not in competition with each other; we compete with the big state universities. These large institutions, because of their size and their access to tax dollars, are constantly reinvesting in themselves. Once we start cutting, we lose ground to these schools. Just as importantly, cutting diminishes everything from curb appeal to staffing to faculty support. This diminution in quality and services is obvious to prospective students. They see weeds all over campus and treadmills that don't work in the fitness room. They see classrooms that are not clean and professors harried from departmental cutbacks. They feel the strain of the cuts when they visit campus and the poor morale that inevitably takes over when people are not getting raises and when money is not available to fund creative ideas.

The only thing that keeps our colleges on the front line of progress is constant improvement and the momentum that inevitably surfaces when people know that they are part of a prosperous and thriving institution. Attempting to create this momentum through cuts is antithetical to real and perceived progress. As the leader of your institution you need to start the momentum by getting the ball rolling with your own initiative. Remind your staff and faculty what your trustees probably already understand: You have to *look* successful to *be* successful.

Once the trustees saw the plan and understood how these investments would lead to big returns, they fully supported borrowing and raising the money. The vote was unanimous. I really have to give credit to the Board of Trustees. I gave them these numbers, they understood the plan, and they agreed to go for it.

IMPLEMENTING STEP 2: BEGIN FACILITIES UPGRADES IMMEDIATELY

We immediately got in touch with the best architectural firm in the country for the construction of sports facilities, Hastings & Chevitta, out of St. Louis, and we said we need you to design a multipurpose performance stadium, and we want to break ground January 2 of 2006. That means you need to work quickly, and you need to put together a stadium that costs no more than $6 or $6.5 million. And of course, that's what they did. They put the plan on paper. We followed up by quickly getting contractors—everyone from bricklayers to cement contractors to steelworkers to turf installation professionals—and broke ground on the new performance stadium on January 2, 2006, just as we planned.

A lot of people will want to ask why we began with the stadium. We had a couple of strong reasons, and these reasons are at the heart of Admissions Growth. We thought we would get the largest enrollment boost out of the stadium. Why? Because not only would the football coaches be able to recruit more readily, but we could also move our men's and women's soccer teams on campus. At the time, the soccer teams were playing over at a local elementary school field. The football team wasn't playing on campus then, either. In 2005, the football team practiced on campus but played its games at the local high school field. College athletes do *not* want to play sports at a high school. In their minds, they are done with high school. "High school fields are for kids," they're thinking, and *they're* young adults. So, if you can get into the minds of seventeen- or eighteen-year-olds, you know that they want to play in a stadium. When Adrian College recruited students prior to 2006, the coaching staff was so nervous about showing potential students the stadium we were using that they literally would not even tell recruits the games were not on campus because they were afraid that the students wouldn't even consider enrolling. The coaches would show recruits our practice field, and they would say that they practiced on campus, and then they would hope that players would assume, "Well, the games must be somewhere around here, too." That strategy did not work beyond the initial recruitment, and our retention showed it. We had fifty-one players leave the football team *and the college* midyear in 2004. Among other reasons, they did not want to play at a local high school. So the stadium was the base of the Admissions Growth plan because we knew it would help us reach our enrollment goals and would boost retention as well.

With a performance stadium in place, we could also start men's and women's lacrosse in this new and beautiful facility. Lacrosse is the fastest-growing sport in America according to some estimates, and it is inexpensive to start (NCAA, 2011). In addition, the stadium could serve dozens of intramural programs that nonvarsity athletes participate in as well. Retention would be served as these students got to use the great facilities that our best athletes utilized for major contests. Even the community began to sponsor events—and help our bottom line—by renting the stadium for many local teams. So we built the stadium. And the enrollment growth followed.

Following the success of the stadium as part of our recruiting strategy, we quickly built a track & field complex. Shortly thereafter we built an ice arena, a baseball stadium, and tennis courts, as well as refurbishing the women's softball field. We started teams and built healthy rosters in women's synchronized skating, hockey, tennis, and many other sports.

Step 3: Fund Teams and Activities Fully and Set Recruiting Goals

The most efficient and most effective way to grow enrollment is to leverage extracurricular and cocurricular activities designed to attract interested and academically capable students to campus. You must not simply implement teams and randomly add other activities. The viable extracurricular and cocurricular activities you recruit for depend for success on your geographic area, your campus culture, the attitudes of your surrounding community, your personnel and facilities, and the types of students you hope to bring, or to bring more of, to campus. Implement and emphasize the activities that have the most traction at your particular institution.

For some of these activities, your college will already have the facilities and personnel needed to support a particular team or cocurricular. For example, at

Adrian College, we had a women's volleyball team and volleyball facilities that were very adequate for recruiting students. We also had basketball courts for our men's and women's teams, and we had a softball field. We did not need to build new facilities for these sports; we used the existing facilities on campus. At the same time, as I mentioned previously, we needed many new facilities for our existing and expanding sports program, including a multisport stadium for football, soccer, and lacrosse; a baseball field; a track & field complex; tennis courts; an ice arena; and several practice fields.

And here we come to a difficult part of the plan: in addition to building these expensive facilities, we also needed to hire coaches and recruiters at least one year prior to fielding these teams. This means we were paying salaries and benefits one year before we enrolled new students. We did not see a return on investment until we built the facilities, hired the coaches, and gave them a year to recruit high school students for the following fall. This model is front loaded. This plan is expensive, and it is very expensive for at least a year before the institution sees significant returns. At Adrian College we spent a lot of money twelve months before we knew we would see any results because we believed that students would flock to our college with these new facilities, coaches, and cocurricular activities in place. They did.

IMPLEMENTING STEP 3: FUND EXTRACURRICULARS AND COCURRICULARS FULLY

Costs to build, improve, renovate, and upgrade facilities are enormous, of course, but your coaches and cocurricular advisors will need ample funds up front, as well. At Adrian College, we gave our coaches and our marching band director generous recruiting and travel budgets as well as sufficient funds to buy attractive uniforms and equipment that would draw students to Adrian College. We also needed to replace facilities and equipment that were actually driving students away. Earlier I mentioned that our football team played on a local high school field and the retention problem that created. As a matter of fact, our athletes actually traveled to those games in the yellow public school buses that we rented, too. Executive Vice President Rick Creehan made changing that a priority. Almost immediately after arriving on campus, he invested in one new bus for the teams to travel in, and trustee Dick Sweebe donated another. Both are very spacious, with cloth seats, air conditioning, stereo radios, and CD players so our athletes can travel in a relaxed and comfortable manner. That this improved morale 100 percent should go without saying, but it also aided our retention numbers. And keeping students and their tuition dollars at Adrian College was the point. In addition to simply enabling your coaches and advisors to do the actual work of recruiting, the equipment and supplies you fund show potential students that your institution is serious about supporting their activities, activities that are going to bring students into your college and keep them sufficiently involved and engaged in campus life that they will stay for four years and complete their degrees successfully.

MAKING STEP 3 QUANTIFIABLE: SET RECRUITING GOALS

We gave coaches generous travel budgets and encouraged them to purchase new uniforms that would be attractive to aspiring young athletes. These funds came with an obligation, though. We made it clear to our coaches that they should use these resources to bring qualified students to campus, students who would play *and* stay *and* be very successful in the classroom. We demanded accountability from our coaches, and if these coaches did not recruit full teams, then we terminated their contracts.

While it is true that large investments always involve an element of risk, this risk comes with verifiable rewards for your college. It is not easy, but leaders can no longer leave enrollment to chance and luck. If you want your institution's enrollment to grow, you need to create a plan. And that plan must be strategic, which means it must be deliberately designed to grow enrollment, it must be measurable, and it absolutely must be executed in a way that holds those who carry it out accountable. It is not enough to say that we want our freshman class "to grow" and that our results in recruiting this year were "good" or "better than last year." College presidents need to implement a plan designed to bring students to campus, and each person working with that plan needs to have a recruiting goal, and those coaches and other recruiting personnel who don't meet their goals must be terminated. It sounds harsh, but small private institutions run on tuition income, and this is the best model I am aware of that ensures the strong financial future of small colleges in our country.

ENACTING STEP 3 WISELY: FOCUS ON ACTIVITIES THAT
"FIT" WITH YOUR CAMPUS CULTURE

Some may misinterpret Admissions Growth as a program that is all about athletics, but it is not. This plan is first about numbers, about bringing students—academically qualified students—to campus, but it also has the added advantage of bringing in students who can add more than just a body to your college. Our student population here at Adrian College is made up of about 900 athletes, but building on athletics is only one way to grow enrollment, and if all we had done when we started this plan was to start marching bands and hockey teams without asking if these are the right activities and sports to fit in with our existing culture, activities, and sports that could be successful and add vibrancy to our campus, we could have failed miserably. *You need to identify activities that will work on your campus.* What the president and senior staff of a small institution need to ask is: what can work in our area of the country, what fits our mission and culture, and therefore, what can be immediately successful with our student population? You want to add programs that will draw students who would not otherwise attend your college.

One of our earliest recruitment initiatives at Adrian College was to identify cocurricular opportunities for students that were consistent with our academic mission, that were suited to our area, and that would create unique and exciting activities outside the classroom. For example, here at Adrian College, we have enjoyed a long and storied history of excellence in music. In that first trustee meeting in October 2005 when I presented the Admissions Growth plan to the Board, I pointed out to them that, at that time, our music program offered several music degrees. Students could earn a bachelor of music in performance or a bachelor of music in education. They could also graduate with a B.A. in music, musical theatre, or arts administration, and the program offered a music minor, as well. What Adrian College had at that time was all sorts of ways to get a music degree, but we did not have a marching band. As I explained to the Board of Trustees, we needed to leverage this opportunity to build our enrollment. I argued that many high school seniors love playing in the marching band—it's their peer group, it's a big part of their social lives, and it's an important part of their identities. If we offered a quality marching band opportunity, we would quickly get one hundred or more students on campus who would not be there otherwise.

One recruiting advantage Adrian College uses is a result of our size. Most kids active in high school bands are never going to play in the marching band at large state universities. Bands at those schools are too competitive. But the Adrian Marching Band has a "no cut" policy, so every student who wants to play is guaranteed a spot on the "team." A student who wants a good education and that experience of playing in the band on the field every home game is going to choose Adrian College.

However, enrollment is not the only advantage when you bring these student musicians to campus. A marching band is big, it's loud—often it has more than a hundred members. A band is a highly visible group on campus, and it enhances school spirit. It raises the morale not just of the team, but of everyone in the stands during home games as well. Our marching band, therefore, is highly successful for many reasons. First, it resonates with our academic programs in music. We

Table 1. Marching Band Return on Investment

Start-Up Costs (Director's Salary and First-Year Budget) $145,000

Ideal Roster Size 80

Number of Students Recruited Per Year... 25

Annual Return on Investment* (Four-Year Total)................................$359,600 ($1,438,400)

* In this and subsequent tables, the ROI is calculated as $24,800 (tuition/room/board × number of students) × 0.58 (effective rate after discount) (2006 costs and discount rate). Discount rates change, sometimes dramatically, with each entering class. For our purposes, I have used a 42 percent discount rate, which is roughly the ten-year average at Adrian College.

have many students on campus who simply love to play and be a part of musical performances. Second, folks on our campus like sporting events, noisy crowds, school spirit, and "cutting loose" at the gym, rink, or field. A band adds to this atmosphere and fits hand in glove with our activities and culture.

One huge advantage that most four-year colleges have if they want to launch a marching band, of course, is that they've already got the facilities up and running. We did not have that at Adrian College in 2005. At that time, the football team, as I mentioned earlier, was playing on the local high school field. That year, though, we were already getting financial backing in place, and we knew that by fall 2006 we were going to have a beautiful new Performance Stadium where the football team would play on Saturdays. So facilities costs for a marching band are essentially nothing, and uniform costs are small overall. You get all of these just wonderful benefits to the college, and then you also realize that it really takes a minimal staff and faculty to build and maintain a marching band. You can see the economic advantages of starting a band illustrated in table 1.

One of our faculty members, Dr. Marty Marks, was enthusiastic about the idea of creating a band, so I gave him time off from teaching some of his classes to recruit, and I gave him a goal of twenty-five students per year. He has met and exceeded that goal ever since he began recruiting in 2006. Our goal, as you can see in table 1, was to have an 80-member marching band after four years. By 2007, the first fall that the band was actually active, Dr. Marks had 72 students participating. It was up to 84 in 2008, 94 in 2009, and by the fourth year, that band had 109 students. Most of those students would not have selected Adrian College without a marching band and without Dr. Marks approaching them at a high school band festival or concert with a warm smile and the words, "I want to recruit you to play in my marching band at Adrian College."

Every institution has a different discount rate. Adrian College has a rate that fluctuates between 40 percent and 50 percent. Even so, as the information in

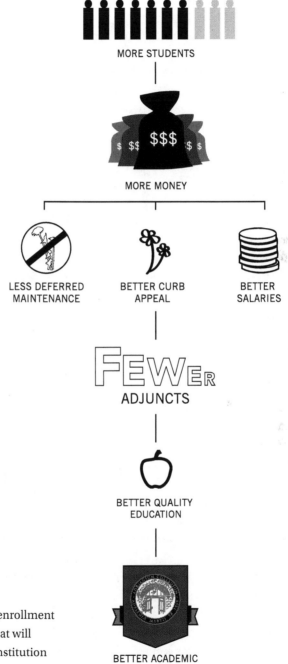

MORE STUDENTS

MORE MONEY

LESS DEFERRED
MAINTENANCE

BETTER CURB
APPEAL

BETTER
SALARIES

FEWER
ADJUNCTS

BETTER QUALITY
EDUCATION

BETTER ACADEMIC
REPUTATION

FIGURE 3. Focusing on enrollment produces the results that will help strengthen your institution academically.

table 1 shows, because this one part of the Admissions Growth plan is bringing twenty-five or more students to campus every year, the economic return is now easily surpassing the original planned return on investment every academic year.

All of the money spent for these improvements was closely scrutinized by our business office to ensure that the dollars we received in enrollment growth far exceeded the costs of starting each new program. As a nonscholarship school, our assets must far outweigh our liabilities. By 2008 we were making far more money than we were spending. Our recruiting efforts were bringing more, and more active, students to campus, we were building facilities that would entice even more students to enroll, but for the first time in years, we could also afford to treat those students who were enrolling to first-rate accommodations, amenities, athletic equipment, and food service facilities, in addition to highly qualified coaches and respected professors. Among all of these other benefits, our increased budgets allowed us to begin academic programs, institutes, and outreach efforts that connected Adrian College to its local community in lasting and productive ways. We were cash rich for one of the few times in our institutional history, and everything changed on our campus.

The Admissions Growth plan answers the questions that many administrators ask when they see enrollment declining, budgets getting pinched, and costs exceeding revenues: Where do we begin? What should be prioritized? The answer is always enrollment. Focusing on enrollment first solves the greatest number of problems quickly. It really builds momentum for all of the other solutions an institution's leaders need, as shown in figure 3. The equation is really very simple: More students equals more money equals less deferred maintenance equals better curb appeal equals better salaries equals fewer adjuncts equals a higher quality education equals a better academic reputation. And now you have reversed the downward spiral because the fun, the excitement, the momentum created by the new students and the new activities on campus and the new reputation for excellent academic programs means more students will *want* to come to your campus.

What you see here in the story and the statistics on Adrian College's marching band is the heart of what I will cover in chapter 5. Step 4 of Admissions Growth is "Focus on Return on Investment by Holding Recruiters Accountable." The next chapter presents the evidence that Adrian College is not a success story based on luck.

Adrian College implemented the Admissions Growth plan in the manner outlined in these six steps, making it strategic, measurable, and accountable. Of course, every institution's leader will have to make some strategic decisions of his or her own. Not every single aspect of the plan as rolled out at Adrian College will work at every small baccalaureate institution in the country. You may want to change the plan to emphasize whatever parts of it have the most traction at your institution and tailor it to meet the political and cultural realities of your school. Suffice it to say that this plan can work for you, and I encourage you to read further to see how it can be a major impetus to improving other institutions.

Key Takeaways

1. Much like a fund-raising campaign, a campaign to grow enrollment should have clear goals as well as a catchy name and be easily understood by all.
2. When you create your plan and kick off your enrollment campaign, organize an all-college retreat so everyone—faculty, staff, trustees, custodial services—understands the strategy and the goals.
3. Do not bog down the plan in a two- or three-year planning process. This plan is simple enough to strategize quickly (in two to three months). Then get to work on funding and implementation.
4. While you plan to work toward broad acceptance of the plan on campus, it is time to broach the subject with your Board of Trustees. Be prepared to show them exactly how much the plan will cost and what they should expect to see in return for their investment.
5. You can't cut your way to prosperity.
6. Once you decide to adopt the Admissions Growth plan, move quickly to raise money, borrow funds, and build facilities. This will give you the quickest results and create believers out of skeptics.
7. Fund extracurricular and cocurricular activities fully and in advance, before you begin to look for recruitment results.
8. Create clear, quantifiable goals so people can see progress and be accountable for reaching benchmarks.
9. This plan can be tailored and modified to fit the needs and the culture of any liberal arts campus.
10. I do not encourage you to copy the Adrian plan in precise detail. Instead, I encourage you to copy the philosophy that undergirds the plan: make investments that will lead to measurable results and hold people accountable for reaching those results.

CHAPTER 5

Implementing the Admissions Growth Plan

In this chapter I'm going to continue to show you clearly and persuasively how the Admissions Growth plan worked at Adrian College so that you can adapt it to your campus. The next step, if you are one of the seven hundred other small four-year institutions in this country (Carnegie Foundation, 2013), is to ask how you can apply this plan to help your own college grow. But first, remember that small privates are *not* in competition with each other. Many small liberal arts colleges only need about four hundred new students each year to maintain the enrollment income they require to keep their campuses fully funded. However, they do not need to recruit these students from each other. Instead, they should appeal to students who intend to study at a large public university without thought for how or whether they will find success at such an institution. Moreover, only 10 percent of college students choose small privates. This means that you have very large pool of students, nearly seven million currently, from which to pull those four hundred students who will be better served by attending your institution (National Center for Education Statistics, 2013a)

This chapter spends significant time discussing step 4: "Focus on return on investment by holding recruiters accountable." I am going to spend a whole chapter on this because built into step 4 is accountability. And accountability is what distinguishes the Admissions Growth plan from every other enrollment fix being bandied around in books and magazines and on websites addressing the current crisis in higher education. The Admissions Growth plan, as enacted by Adrian College, was successful, I believe, extraordinarily successful, because the plan pays particular attention to the costs associated with each initiative and to the financial return gained from each strategic investment as well as to how much profit will be returned to the college through tuition and room and board. In other words, we know how much we will spend on each sport and activity. And because we hold our coaches accountable for the recruiting goals set for them, we know how much income we can expect from each team every year.

Step 4: Focus on Return on Investment by Holding Recruiters Accountable

Let's go back for a second to the six steps outlined in chapter 4 and illustrated in figure 2:

1. Do your homework and set goals.
2. Build and upgrade required facilities.
3. Fund teams fully, hire coaches, and give them recruiting goals.
4. Focus on return on investment by holding recruiters accountable.
5. Redirect new income to academic facilities and programs
6. Continue to build and utilize momentum for further growth.

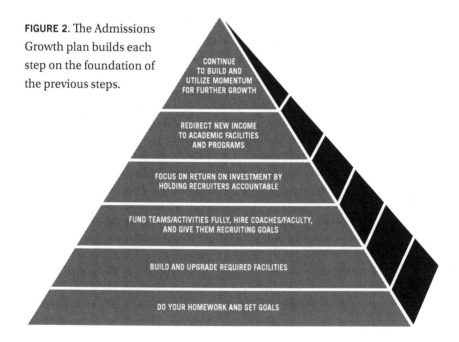

FIGURE 2. The Admissions Growth plan builds each step on the foundation of the previous steps.

CONTINUE TO BUILD AND UTILIZE MOMENTUM FOR FURTHER GROWTH

REDIRECT NEW INCOME TO ACADEMIC FACILITIES AND PROGRAMS

FOCUS ON RETURN ON INVESTMENT BY HOLDING RECRUITERS ACCOUNTABLE

FUND TEAMS/ACTIVITIES FULLY, HIRE COACHES/FACULTY, AND GIVE THEM RECRUITING GOALS

BUILD AND UPGRADE REQUIRED FACILITIES

DO YOUR HOMEWORK AND SET GOALS

Following the Admissions Growth program means that you develop a plan to implement activities that will bring students to campus, and you fully fund those activities. But a vital part of the strategic focus at your institution is accountability. You will need to hire good people and give them attractive facilities they can use to bring students to your college. Each person working with this plan needs to have a recruiting goal. Those coaches and other personnel responsible for recruiting who don't meet these goals must be terminated. Saying to your coaches and advisors, "You are accountable and you need to reach these goals or move on to another position at another college where you can serve better" is harsh, but as the leader of your institution, you are implementing a plan designed to grow enrollment. Accountability for recruiting is absolutely key to this growth.

UNDERSTANDING STEP 4: WHY RETURN ON INVESTMENT MATTERS

Creating new programs to grow enrollment is only part of the formula when you're trying to turn around a campus with very little curb appeal, poor academic standards, and a moribund social atmosphere. Part of curb appeal, of course, is what the buildings look like: Are they in good shape? Is the landscaping attractive, or is everything dead? Are the entry areas appealing, or are they just plain bleak? Taking a close look at curb appeal also means asking: Is there anything happening when you're walking through campus between classes or at the end of the day? Do the students actually have anything going on? As I explained in chapter 4, a marching band and all of the big and small activities that come with it are part of what makes the campus attractive to both visitors and the students who live there every day. When Adrian College began recruiting for a marching band, we began building up our curb appeal. When we've got a band on campus at Adrian College, we have students, in addition to the athletes, who participate in every home football game. And it's not just football. These students have a pep band that plays at home hockey and basketball games. They also march in the Homecoming Parade, and they play in the Music Department's Fall Showcase every November. They participate in Marching Band Exhibitions for local high schools, and they perform annually at the United Way Rally downtown, too. So these students are now involved and are involving others in the performing arts, in community service, in cocurricular activities, and of course, in building social and working relationships. All of these activities are part of how we measure student engagement on campus. And study after study confirms that student engagement in cocurricular and extracurricular activities is one of the primary factors in improving and maintaining retention, not

Table 2. Cheer and Dance Teams Return on Investment

Start-Up Costs (Coach's Salary and First-Year Budget) $48,000

Number of Freshman Expected Each Year 6

Annual Return on Investment (Four-Year Total). $86,304 ($345,216)

THEY DON'T NEED TO BE LARGE #s

to mention promoting deep, integrative learning and higher order thinking skills (Gayles & Hu, 2009; NSSE, 2012).

Another opportunity for recruiting that Adrian College was really missing out on, an activity that adds life and spirit to your campus, was a cheerleading and dance team. This extracurricular activity delivers a group of students whose goal is to raise the spirits of other students and to create excitement on campus and at special events. Our Athletic Department was tasked with hiring a coach to recruit for and guide dance and cheerleading teams. Our goal was to bring to campus a full-time professional who would be available to travel to recruit as well as to coach and who would be assigned *clear recruiting goals.*

Again, one of the keys to the Admissions Growth plan is that it pays particular attention to the costs associated with each initiative as well as to the financial return gained from each strategic investment. So I asked Angie Lewis to build the team. She's a talented coach and an athlete who was on the World Champion High School Cheer Team and is probably best known for being the Purdue Marching Band twirler called The Girl in Black. Lewis worked to recruit a specific number of students each year. But her passion for recruiting and building capable dance and cheer squads also led her to set additional goals for herself and her teams. She set out in 2008 to triple the size of each team in three years, which she absolutely has done. Lewis also has built teams that travel and compete nationally, and she achieved another goal—that of bringing men into the sport and making the Cheer Team a coed squad—in 2009.

So the cheer and dance programs were set up with an eye on return on investment as illustrated in table 2. By 2010 Lewis had brought to campus twenty-two new students, after having surpassed her own goal by recruiting nine new team members the year before. Again, the students she recruits and what they contribute to the campus community are about more than just bringing a specified number of warm bodies to Adrian College, although this certainly is the most important benefit of her work. Recently, our Dance and Cheer Teams were the 2010 U.S. Finals

Champions, and the Dance Team won Grand National Champions at the 2010 Great Lakes Championship competition. Also, these student athletes have participated in Math Nights at the local school and in the Rake 'N Run fund-raisers. In addition they take seriously their charge to raise school spirit at athletic events as well as at homecoming and other campus activities.

THE KEY TO ADMISSIONS GROWTH: STEP 4 HOLDS COACHES ACCOUNTABLE

Cocurricular activities like the marching band and extracurricular activities such as cheer and dance teams are only one part of the Admissions Growth plan, though. During the fall of 2005, when I asked the Board to support the plan, we had some coaches at Adrian College who were successful recruiters, while others did not recruit at all. Remember, the real key to the success of this strategy is that we were absolutely committed to *not* making any investments in particular parts of the plan if we did not see a clear return on investment. Understanding this commitment meant that all coaches would, from that point forward, have specific goals for recruiting and maintaining their teams. Coaches would now be accountable for recruiting a set number of students who would not otherwise attend Adrian College. If they did not recruit and meet their goals, we would have no choice but to relieve them of their duties.

So, finally, we get to the key to the Admissions Growth plan. The core of Admissions Growth is an Athletics Department that will commit to building and maintaining quality teams grounded in the Division III athletics philosophy. That is to say, it is committed to creating an environment where athletic participation is integral to the students' academic experiences. And every member of the Athletics Department is going to have to provide a solid block of the foundation of this program. That block is aggressive recruiting. Remember that recruiting is vital because cocurricular activities and athletics work in support of the campus by contributing to the Admissions Growth program. As we have demonstrated here at Adrian College, the keys to this plan are the changes we have to make to steadily grow the enrollment that pays for the education that we provide our students.

Before I presented this plan, I constructed a data table for the teams that were active at the time at Adrian College. This graphic served two purposes. First, and most important, it was a way to show coaches specifically what they were accountable for. We wanted them not to just recruit new students but to also retain those students. It was their responsibility to maintain a full roster for their sport after a specified start-up period. And this goal was for the good of the students as well as the college. This meant that coaches had to recruit students who were academically prepared to complete four years of study.

Adrian College fielded sixteen athletic teams in 2005: football, baseball, softball, women's volleyball, men's and women's basketball, men's and women's track, men's and women's cross country, men's and women's soccer, men's and women's tennis, and men's and women's golf. If you look at the Admissions Growth plan superficially, then these sixteen teams should have been bringing in enough students to grow enrollment and maintain the retention needed to keep Adrian College financially healthy. The reasons this sixteen-team model broke down and produced very poor results were these:

- Part-time coaches
- Poor facilities
- No accountability in holding coaches to recruiting goals
- Not enough teams

What you see in table 3 is a listing of the athletic teams that existed at the college in 2005 and the enrollment goals we established for each coach soon after I arrived.

As I detailed above, this sixteen-team model broke down and failed to produce the needed return on investment because it used part-time coaches, and it did not hold coaches to recruiting goals. In addition, with the recruitment efforts in place at the time, sixteen teams were not enough to sustain enrollment growth. And finally, this model utilized Adrian College's current facilities, which were unattractive, substandard, or nonexistent. Before adding new teams we first had to get our own house in order in terms of managing the teams we had.

IMPLEMENTING STEP 4: ELIMINATE PART-TIME COACHES

Right now, all over the country, there are small institutions trying to save money on coaching in two ways: First, they are hiring part-time coaches for many of their teams. Most of these teams are not the showcase teams for the college like football or basketball. Instead they are lower-visibility teams such as golf, tennis, and cross country. When a college makes its first mistake, trying to cut corners on its intercollegiate teams, administrators often hire part-time employee-coaches. Sometimes they hire faculty to coach, and usually the plan is that the professor is still teaching full-time and getting an additional stipend to coach. Often, though, they'll also hire people from the community, someone who lives nearby and has

Table 3. Snapshot of Potential Annual Return on Investment by Sport in 2005

SPORT	IDEAL ROSTER SIZE	NUMBER OF FRESHMEN EXPECTED EACH YEAR	ANNUAL RETURN ON INVESTMENT (FOUR-YEAR TOTAL)	
Baseball	30	10	$143,840	($575,360)
Men's Basketball	18	6	$86,304	($345,216)
Women's Basketball	18	6	$86,304	($345,216)
Men's Cross Country and Track	27	9	$129,456	($517,824)
Women's Cross Country and Track	27	9	$129,456	($517,824)
Football	150	50	$719,200	($2,876,800)
Men's Golf	12	4	$57,536	($230,144)
Women's Golf	12	4	$57,536	($230,144)
Men's Soccer	27	9	$129,456	($517,824)
Women's Soccer	24	8	$115,072	($460,288)
Softball	18	6	$86,304	($345,216)
Men's Tennis	10	4	$57,536	($230,144)
Women's Tennis	10	4	$57,536	($230,144)
Women's Volleyball	24	8	$115,072	($460,288)

a real passion for lacrosse, for instance, but can only do it on the weekends. For instance, when I arrived at Adrian College in 2005, one of our secretaries in the Administration Building was coaching the women's golf team. As you can see in table 4, this institution had eleven teams being coached by part-time coaches at that time. Part-time coaches just don't have time to recruit. These men and women are too busy trying to juggle their coaching duties and traveling to games with a job and family obligations to do any recruiting at all.

The second shortsighted cost-cutting measure that an institution will try is forcing the few coaches they do hire to coach two teams in two different sports. Before we instituted Admissions Growth in 2005, our head men's basketball coach also coached the men's golf team, Obligating coaches to follow this practice creates three problems. The first is that such coaches can be truly proficient in only one sport. The second problem follows from the first: no matter how much a coach is committed to helping all of his or her students, this person is often genuinely passionate about only one sport. And finally, when you think of the time and travel and effort involved, a coach can only recruit in one sport. Often a coach will put all of his or her time into one sport, traveling and recruiting and advising players, and the second sport will just take walk-ons or maybe some student who came because

Table 4. Sports Formerly Coached by Part-Time Coaches

TEAM	START-UP COSTS	IDEAL ROSTER SIZE	NUMBER OF FRESHMEN EXPECTED EACH YEAR	ANNUAL RETURN ON INVESTMENT (FOUR-YEAR TOTAL)	
Women's Basketball	$53,000	18	6	$86,304	($345,216)
Men's Cross Country and Track	$28,000	27	9	$129,456	($517,824)
Women's Cross Country and Track	$28,000	27	9	$129,456	($517,824)
Men's Golf	$19,000	12	4	$57,536	($230,144)
Women's Golf	$19,000	12	4	$57,536	($230,144)
Women's Soccer	$40,000	24	8	$115,072	($460,288)
Men's Tennis	$19,000	10	4	$57,536	($230,144)
Women's Tennis	$19,000	10	4	$57,536	($230,144)
Women's Volleyball	$40,000	24	8	$115,072	($460,288)
Total	$265,000	164	56	$805,504*	($3,222,016)*

*Does not include $76,000 yearly savings on salaries currently paid to part-time coaches.

he or she knew this sport was available at Adrian College. But that student will see that this coach knows very little about the sport and really isn't giving the team the care it deserves, and he or she will quit the team and quit the school. When you realize that's happening, you need to ask yourself: Why are you even funding that team? Commit or quit.

When small colleges cut corners this way, they erode their coaches' abilities to leverage their athletic teams to grow enrollment. When colleges do this, they demonstrate that administrators have lost their focus on return on investment. When I arrived at Adrian College in July 2005, the school employed twenty-four part-time coaches to serve sixteen intercollegiate athletic teams. So the next step in implementing the Admissions Growth program was to eliminate part-time coaches at Adrian College. Of those sixteen teams that I inherited in 2005, only five had full-time coaches. I immediately hired full-time coaches for every program and gave them clear recruiting goals. Then we committed to funding all sixteen teams fully, which, of course, meant front-loading the expenses for these teams and giving them adequate budgets to purchase equipment, travel, and recruit.

IMPLEMENTING STEP 4: KEEP YOUR FOCUS ON THE PLAN

Another purpose the information in table 3 served was not aimed at the coaches. It and all of the other tables you see in this chapter were a way to make sure the senior administrators all stayed focused on the plan. This table would remind us every time we looked at it that the point of all of this investment at Adrian College was enrollment growth. When we look at that Return on Investment column in the table, first of all, the vocabulary there reminds us what our work is: an *investment*. Adrian College absolutely was not going to grow unless we brought academically capable students to campus, students who would enroll and pay tuition and stay through graduation. Recruiting in athletics and a few other important cocurricular activities was going to be the mechanism that would do that for us. If Adrian College did not achieve the recruitment goals on this table, then we didn't have the return on investment that we needed to keep this institution going. And return on investment is why the coaches were going to be held accountable. We had some coaches who just could not bring in the students they were required to bring in, and so they had to go. We brought in new coaches, and when they saw the numbers and the return we were expecting from Adrian College's investment in the teams and in them as coaches, then they knew exactly what they had to do to be a successful part of this program.

In addition to the original sixteen teams at Adrian College, we've added fourteen extracurricular or cocurricular activities since 2005, and you can see their current recruitment goals in table 5, as well.

Every year, the coaches and our athletic director, Mike Duffy, work with recruitment goals, as you can see in table 6. The coaches know, in writing, year by year, what their recruiting goals are for each team. But giving them numbers and sending them out on the road is just the beginning. The job of the vice president for enrollment is knowing what is happening, both in terms of contacting students and then getting them interested in the program and having them matriculate at Adrian College. Table 6 shows that we don't just send the coaches out with a goal in mind and wait for them to bring students in. We track inquiries, applications, and acceptances, and we compare them year-to-year as well. This chart is a year-end report for the 2010–2011 academic year. But we also follow these numbers, by team, on a weekly basis. Every Monday throughout the year, I receive an updated report that I scrutinize closely. This gives me a lot early warning if a coach is falling behind.

The results of holding coaches accountable for recruiting are plain to see. In 2011–2012, via athletic recruitment alone, we had over 7,000 inquiries and 1,985 applicants. Remember, in 2004, the year before this model was implemented, we had only 1,204 applications to Adrian College *in total*.

You can see from the evidence on these pages that these teams did exactly what we wanted them to do—they brought more, and more enthusiastic, capable

Table 5. Snapshot of Activities Added since 2005

TEAM	IDEAL ROSTER/ACTIVITY SIZE	NUMBER OF FRESHMEN EXPECTED EACH YEAR
Women's Bowling	14	6
Cheer	20	6
Dance	30	10
Women's Equestrian	25	8
Men's Hockey	26	8
Women's Hockey	26	8
Men's ACHA Div-I Hockey	26	8
Women's ACHA Hockey	26	8
Men's ACHA Div-III (Gold) Hockey	24	8
Men's ACHA Div-III (Black) Hockey	24	8
Men's Lacrosse	32	8
Women's Lacrosse	32	8
Marching Band	80	25
Orchestra	62	20
Synchronized Skating	24	8
Men's Volleyball	24	8
Total	*495*	*155*

young people to campus. It *seemed* like the next step was to create even more teams and keep growing the Admissions Growth plan. Once we made the financial and organizational commitment to get our current teams in order, then the time came to continue expanding the Admissions Growth method. But one thing I want to emphasize here is that it is absolutely *vital* that administrators at this time not get carried away and just start adding athletic and cocurricular activities randomly. When you have this plan, stick with the plan. And part of the plan was looking at activities that our campus would support, activities that could be successful in our school as well as in our area of the country. At the same time, these activities must add something important to the quality of the campus.

HELPING YOUR COACHES GET THE MOST OUT OF STEP 4: ADMISSIONS
GROWTH UTILIZES FACILITIES TO MAXIMIZE RECRUITING

By fall 2005 our campus was preparing to add a new Multi-Sport Performance Stadium, a genuinely premier facility with a FieldTurf surface, twenty-five hundred

Table 6. 2010–2011 Athletic Recruitment Goals

SPORT	GOAL*	INQUIRIES	APPLICANTS	ACCEPTANCES	DEPOSITS
Baseball	10	270	81	61	11
Men's Basketball	7	197	59	44	8
Women's Basketball	6	197	59	44	8
Women's Bowling	6	223	67	50	9
Men's CC & Track	9	346	104	78	14
Women's CC & Track	9	346	104	78	14
Cheer	6	167	50	38	7
Dance	10	270	81	61	11
Women's Equestrian	8	124	37	28	6
Football	50	1,353	406	305	55
Men's Golf	4	124	37	28	5
Women's Golf	4	124	37	28	5
ACHA (Club Hockey) 4 teams	32	617	185	139	25
Men's NCAA Hockey	8	223	67	50	9
Women's NCAA Hockey	8	366	110	83	15
Men's Lacrosse	8	270	81	61	11
Women's Lacrosse	8	270	81	61	11
Men's Soccer	8	223	67	50	9
Women's Soccer	8	223	67	50	9
Softball	7	197	59	44	8
Synchronized Skating	8	167	50	38	7
Men's Tennis	4	124	37	28	5
Women's Tennis	4	124	37	28	5
Men's Volleyball	8	197	59	44	8
Women's Volleyball	8	265	43	34	9

*These are all *minimum* recruiting goals.

chairback seats, and a pavilion for pre- and postgame events. That stadium was on target to be open by fall of 2006, and we had four groups of students who were going to be using it in the fall: the football team, two soccer teams, and the marching band. So, if we are always thinking about how to maximize our current assets, how to improve the return on our facilities investments, what Adrian College needed was more ways to utilize that performance stadium. The next step, then, was to

Table 7. New Teams Utilizing the Multi-Sport Performance Stadium

SPORT	START-UP COSTS (COACH'S SALARY & FIRST-YEAR BUDGET)	NUMBER OF FRESHMEN EXPECTED EACH YEAR	ANNUAL RETURN ON INVESTMENT (FOUR-YEAR TOTAL)	
Women's Field Hockey*	$55,000	5	$71,920	($287,680)
Men's Lacrosse	$60,000	8	$115,072	($460,288)
Women's Lacrosse	$60,000	8	$115,072	($460,288)
Total	*$175,000*	*21*	*$302,064*	*($1,208,256)*

*Women's field hockey was the only activity we implemented during these years that wasn't successful. I discuss why this extracurricular program did not have any traction in our institution in chapter 9.

add teams that would be able to make good use of the field when it wasn't being occupied by the current teams. So the senior staff put together a plan to expand Admissions Growth recruitment by frontloading the funding on three new teams: men's and women's lacrosse and women's field hockey. You can see our expected return outlined in table 7. We added these teams not only to maximize the use of the stadium, but to grow enrollment with sports that we thought would surely succeed at the college. We thought we could persuade John—that hypothetical seventeen-year-old we met in chapter 3—to select Adrian College over others on his list, with these unique offerings. At that time, in 2005, not one other college in Michigan offered NCAA varsity lacrosse. If John wanted to play lacrosse in college in Michigan, he had only *one* choice: Adrian College.

I want to emphasize that the key here is that we had a plan and we stuck to it. First we envisioned cocurricular activities that would bring accomplished and passionate students to campus. Then we got our own house in order by funding athletics appropriately—we ended the practice of part-time coaches and coaches who were doing double duty on two teams. Next we began to add and build teams that would continue to enhance the new, lively atmosphere of the campus. And as part of that step, these teams produced the return on our investment in new facilities.

The first of these facilities was, of course, the Performance Stadium, which gave teams like football and lacrosse a place to play where they could be proud of their home field. We knew our next move was to continue bringing to campus students and activities and facilities that would raise the level of excitement at Adrian College. But we continued to follow the original plan, and to do that we had to keep in mind that the key to Admissions Growth is always return on investment. One of our state-of-the-art athletic showpieces on campus now is the Arrington Ice Arena, and this facility is an excellent example of a good return on investment. It was clear to me as I spoke to trustees and to alumni and to people

Table 8. Men's and Women's Hockey/Skating Return on Investment

SPORT	START-UP COSTS (COACH'S SALARY & 1ST-YEAR BUDGET)	NUMBER OF FRESHMEN EXPECTED EACH YEAR	ANNUAL RETURN ON INVESTMENT (FOUR-YEAR TOTAL)	
Men's NCAA Hockey	$90,000	8	$115,072	($460,288)
Women's NCAA Hockey	$90,000	8	$115,072	($460,288)
Men's ACHA Hockey Div. I	$40,000	8	$115,072	($460,288)
Women's ACHA Club Hockey	$40,000	8	$115,072	($460,288)
Men's ACHA Hockey, Div. III, Gold	$40,000	8	$115,072	($460,288)
Men's ACHA Hockey, Div. III, Black	$40,000	8	$115,072	($460,288)
Synchronized Skating	$40,000	8	$115,072	($460,288)
Total	*$380,000*	*56*	*$805,504*	*($3,222,016)*

in the area that we already had so much pent-up enthusiasm in this community that we did not need to borrow *any* money to build the ice arena. Recognizing and working *with* the culture and geography of Adrian was key to identifying a campus activity that would generate enthusiasm and excitement among future athletes, coaches, professors, members of the community, and the student body at large. This is an area with a popular professional hockey team nearby, the Detroit Red Wings, and several well-supported college and minor league teams fairly close by. Parents in this area were already driving their kids sixty to seventy miles to youth games and hockey clinics. Adrian was a community just waiting for the chance to have an active hockey organization. This enthusiasm became evident when I began to solicit funds to build an ice arena. Two brothers, Dr. Robyn Arrington Jr. and Colonel Harold Arrington, gave the college $3.2 million to pay for much of the construction of the arena. In addition, some trustees and local business benefactors wanted to be part of the new expansion and success at Adrian College, and they pledged their support to the new facility. The result was that the Arrington Ice Arena was a $6.5 million project that was paid for the day that we opened it. Because all of the facility costs were covered through donors, all of the tuition income from all of the hockey teams and synchronized skaters on campus went right to the bottom line. Even if Adrian College hadn't received these generous gifts, even if we'd had to borrow every last penny, the arena would have still been a good investment. Table 8 shows why.

The return on investment with the Arrington Arena is even bigger than we first anticipated. First of all, the hockey program is so popular that we actually field six teams every season. Adrian College now offers NCAA men's and women's intercollegiate teams as well as four American Collegiate Hockey Association (ACHA) teams, three for men and one for women. And, on average each year, we expect eight recruits per team. Then, in 2007, we were able to get a coach and put a women's synchronized skating team on the ice, as well.

ONE LAST TIME: ADMISSIONS GROWTH FOCUSES ON RETURNS

So the short version of all of this is: If you want to vastly improve and grow, look at what this platform for enrollment growth has done for Adrian College. When you look at all of the books and presentations out there on how to revitalize higher education, you'll see that many will tell you to "improve your infrastructure" or "reposition your brand" or "revitalize your unique culture." These strategies do *not* do what Admissions Growth does for your institution. Admissions Growth keeps the focus on measurable goals by tracking your *return* on investment. When you apply this model to your institution, whether you are investing in cocurricular activities or athletics or new facilities, you always set a goal for what the return on that investment will be, and you judge your success based on that return. To do this, senior staff, your board of trustees, everyone involved in recruiting, all have to understand the Admissions Growth initiative, they have to believe in it, they have to trust in it, and they have to stick to it. The returns are obvious when you begin to see that your investment doesn't simply bring more students to campus, it brings more engaged and better prepared students. These students will bring momentum to your campus. And you will be able build on early successes to grow until you have achieved your needed returns on your investments, just as we have here, at Adrian College.

Key Takeaways

1. Small baccalaureate institutions are not in competition with one another.
2. This plan is successful because it pays close attention to the costs associated with each activity and to the financial return gained from each investment.
3. Accountability is the key to the enrollment growth your institution needs.
4. Admissions Growth is more than just numbers. It also improves curb appeal, school spirit, campus vitality, and a host of other aspects of campus life.
5. Hire coaches and leaders of cocurricular activities (i.e., marching band, etc.) who are so deeply passionate about their sport/activity that they will bring in far more students than you require.

6. Eliminate part-time coaches. Most do not have time to recruit, and because they are part-time, they can't be held accountable for recruiting goals.

7. Each person responsible for recruiting must have a quantifiable goal, in writing, and the administration should track progress toward that goal on a regular basis.

8. This model is 100 percent data driven because it focuses on return on investment, which makes it easy to monitor the process for success.

CHAPTER 6

Using Admissions Growth Income to Support Your Institution's Mission

Step 5: Redirect New Income to Academic Facilities and Programs

As figure 2 reminds us, Admissions Growth supports academic investment as step 5 of the plan redirects new income leveraged from your extracurricular and cocurricular recruitment successes into new academic facilities and programs. When I launched Renaissance I in 2005, remember, I made clear to the faculty that it was part 1 of a two-part plan. Renaissance II focused on academic needs of the college. If, after revitalizing athletic and cocurricular activities on your campus you don't follow through with improvements to academic plans and buildings, then you will lose the momentum you've been building on campus during the previous few years. Remember, Admissions Growth improves recruiting to increase enrollment to raise tuition income to improve academic offerings. This goal is how you promoted your plan to donors, trustees, recruiters, and faculty. This is how you follow through on that plan. At Adrian College we have poured our new funds into renovations that directly impact the students and their educational and preprofessional experiences. We have made additions and renovations to the buildings housing our English, business, science, and visual and performing arts departments, as well as to our divisions of communication arts and modern languages. We have added faculty and majors, we have funded academic and field learning experiences, and we have founded institutes to improve the academic experience as well as to prepare students for their careers or for professional and graduate school.

FIGURE 2. Each step of Admissions Growth provides a strong base for the next step.

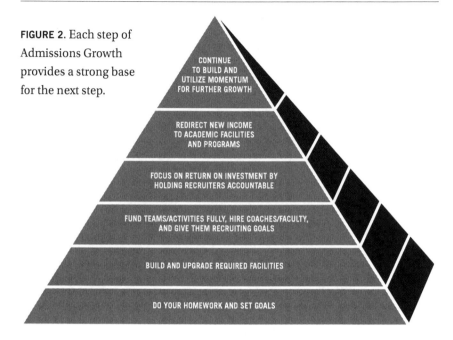

CONTINUE TO BUILD AND UTILIZE MOMENTUM FOR FURTHER GROWTH

REDIRECT NEW INCOME TO ACADEMIC FACILITIES AND PROGRAMS

FOCUS ON RETURN ON INVESTMENT BY HOLDING RECRUITERS ACCOUNTABLE

FUND TEAMS/ACTIVITIES FULLY, HIRE COACHES/FACULTY, AND GIVE THEM RECRUITING GOALS

BUILD AND UPGRADE REQUIRED FACILITIES

DO YOUR HOMEWORK AND SET GOALS

ADMISSIONS GROWTH REDIRECTS INCOME TO FACULTY INVESTMENT

More important than the buildings and programs that we built, improved, and renovated are the professors. Begin the next step of the Admissions Growth plan, "Redirect new income to academic facilities and programs," with the professors, because they make it happen. Students want to come to a campus with activities they are interested in, but they know they are here for an education, too. We've increased the number of full-time, tenured, or tenure-track faculty by 35 percent since 2005. Adrian College has strengthened its academic offerings by creating tenure-track lines in nearly every department. In the past five years we've hired geologists, physicists, chemists, mathematicians, rhetoricians, musicians, clinical therapists, and entrepreneurs—professionals and specialists who work in their professions and teach in their fields. These professors have plenty of expertise and offer students an intensive academic experience as well as key information and practice using their knowledge in "real world" applications.

ADMISSIONS GROWTH REDIRECTS INCOME TO ACADEMIC FACILITIES AND INFRASTRUCTURE

I've emphasized earlier that new and big buildings don't bring students to campus, but students certainly will notice if your facilities are crowded, dingy, run down, and plagued by flickering lights, leaky ceilings, and cracked windows. Students envision themselves surrounded by historic, ivy-covered buildings (and their parents want to send them to such an institution), but they are not interested in a campus that is crumbling around them. This is why we have spent so much of our new tuition income on the Adrian campus in the past few years to repair, renovate, and construct new academic buildings. In December 2011, we received a generous donation of $1 million to build the Spencer Center for Music. Adding to that momentum, the college put over $700,000 into the building, and the resulting facilities improve the student experience every day. Spencer Hall is a busy place. The practice rooms are now well equipped to meet the needs of our music majors, but non-majors who love music are frequent visitors, as well. The sound and audiovisual equipment in the classrooms has greatly facilitated our professors' ability to teach classes, and the rehearsal hall is large enough to accommodate every ensemble on campus. While the music faculty has been key to bringing about a high level of student participation and enthusiasm, this building allows our students to play, work, and learn in comfortable and professional performance facilities. When students see the quality of the space provided for them to study, practice, and perform, they know that our institution values their effort and participation, and more important, values their presence on campus by giving them the space and supplies they need to prepare for their careers, whether in teaching or performance.

During the same period Adrian College has made significant and extensive improvement to Downs Hall Theatre as well as to lecture halls and classrooms across campus. Knight Auditorium, Peelle Lecture Hall, and the Jones 110 classroom now offer free Wi-Fi and multiple recharging and electrical outlets at each desk. They also feature top-of-the-line seating, desk, and lectern facilities, in addition to high-resolution projectors, with video playback and sound, in a comfortable and acoustically absorbent environment. These showcase classrooms and lecture halls are also available to the community and offer an attractive locale for hosting speakers, seminars, and other public events.

The building housing the Department of Modern Languages & Culture on the Adrian College campus also had a complete interior renovation in 2010. Improvements to the physical environment of our institution, like those we made in the lecture halls and language lab on our campus, are important and impressive. They are very visible and demonstrate that Adrian College values academic endeavors. However, just as important to the learning experience are the improvements we make to campus that are not necessarily visible. In addition to state-of-the-art headphone sets and microphones, the language lab in Goldsmith Center supporting student learning offers three Linux desktops, two PCs, and two iMacs. These powerful computers run an impressive range of software applications that allow students access to language lectures, multimedia exercises, workshops, demonstrations, videos, and games. The computing facilities in the Modern Languages building also allow students access to multimedia editing software, applications that allow a user to access a keyboard in languages in addition to English, as well as powerful programs offering phonetic analysis. The students do not necessarily see or think about this expensive software when they are visiting or using the language lab, but these programs improve the quality of their learning experiences every day.

The improvements to the language lab in Goldsmith Center demonstrate that as important as the physical environment offered for students to study and work in are the upgraded computing power and Internet access offered on campus. Adrian College implemented Admissions Growth in 2005, and by 2007 our institution was able to spend $40,000 of its new tuition income on an impressive Mac Lab in the Mahan Center for Art & Interior Design. These twenty-one iMacs each offer the full Adobe Creative Suite, as well as professional photography and video editing programs like Photoshop Lightroom and Final Cut Pro. All of these applications are the industry standards for professionals. This lab is instrumental in keeping our students current and marketable in their future careers, and also prepares those who choose to apply to graduate school. Again, these improvements are not immediately visible to students and visitors, but they are the types of investments that Admissions Growth is specifically designed to fund. Another almost "invisible" improvement that today's students expect and need for their personal use as well as for their academic work is free and convenient access to wireless Internet. In the summer of 2012, our institution added over $200,000 in infrastructure upgrades to our core system. During that time, we installed 148 wireless access points in the academic buildings and many of our residence halls. As part of the same investment, upgraded laptops were installed in many classrooms, and all but a very few of our academic classrooms are now completely technology enabled, allowing professors to utilize laptops, the Web, projectors, speakers, and DVD players whenever they choose. Our faculty members are now able to offer students an incredible array of learning and participatory experiences in a variety of media, which are literally limited only by their imaginations.

ADMISSIONS GROWTH ALLOWS FUNDING FOR INNOVATIVE
PROGRAMS AND SCHOOL-COMMUNITY PARTNERSHIPS

To guide our students through the complexities of acquiring academic excellence as well as a wide range of experiential learning opportunities required to successfully apply to graduate programs, Adrian College has founded eight institutes:

- George Romney Institute for Law and Public Policy
- Institute for Career Planning
- Institute for Creativity
- Institute for Education
- Institute for Entrepreneurial Studies
- Institute for Ethics
- Institute for Health Studies
- Institute for Study Abroad

Each year, 40 to 50 percent of our entering freshmen express an academic or career interest in life science and health-related fields. Yet they have enrolled at a liberal arts college. Simply stated, our students understand that a preprofessional degree would provide only one skill set. Given the pace of technological and social change in their lives, they know intuitively that a liberal arts education is a valuable commodity. Some of our current students will work in roles we cannot imagine today, and they will need every skill we can teach them to build a sustainable and creative future. The Adrian College Institute for Health Studies anticipates this future. Delivery of health care, research in the life sciences, and development of innovative biomedical technologies are broadly understood as complex tasks requiring concrete skills. The technical skills on which these services depend are, however, only one component of quality care. These skills are best applied by an individual who habitually connects ideas across disciplines, who extends critical analysis to each task, who communicates effectively within and across cultures, and who is skilled in written communication—in short, the precise capacities one acquires in a quality liberal arts education.

At Adrian College, our institutes perform another important function. They fulfill our campus mission of providing service to our local and global community. Our Institute for Education is an outstanding example of how Adrian College serves its students and its community in a vital capacity. The Institute for Education offers models for and trains students in the most current research-based best practices in teaching and learning. Simultaneously, as part of the students' experiences and education, this institute broadens Adrian College's outreach to the community through strengthened ties with education professionals throughout our area. This institute functions to offer relevant experiential opportunities through student teaching as well as to allow our education students to put current research and theory into immediate practice in the field.

For instance, in 2012, the Adrian College Teacher Education Department, in partnership with YMCA and Lincoln Elementary, opened a laboratory classroom site that offers preschool and childcare services to Adrian College faculty and members of the local community. But what is key to understanding how Adrian College works to serve the community is to note that the superintendent of the Adrian Public Schools system approached us for help in expanding and strengthening the local schools' offerings by integrating the International Baccalaureate World school curriculum into their preprimary program offerings. During 2011 the director of the Institute for Education, Dr. Andrea Milner, began a yearlong discussion with public school administrators about ways Adrian College could strengthen its relationship with nearby Lincoln Elementary School while building a new master of education degree program at the same time. It was Professor Milner who saw that Adrian College could utilize the resources of the Institute to serve all three needs. In the fall of 2012, Adrian College, working in a three-way partnership with Adrian Public Schools and our local YMCA, opened a preschool at Lincoln Elementary. This three-way partnership serves the college community and its neighbors in a number of ways. This program means we can now offer affordable, nearby childcare to our faculty and staff as well as to our local community. The Lincoln preschool offers quality early childhood education through college students who engage in fun learning activities with young children, under the supervision of highly qualified professors and public schoolteachers. While serving their community, our students are gaining indispensable experience needed to pursue a teaching career in this economy.

When the planning for this new preschool offering was ongoing, our institution was also pursuing its own International Baccalaureate certification as well as accreditation for a master's program, and both were approved by their respective organizing bodies in the 2012–2013 school year. During the same time period, the Adrian Public Schools system received permission to begin the process of joining the International Baccalaureate Primary Years Programme. Each of these accomplishments, a new preschool, an energized, state-of-the-art classroom laboratory for teacher education students, a new master's degree in teacher education at Adrian College, and the upcoming International Baccalaureate World School certification in the Primary Years Programme, was made possible when the director of the Institute for Education had the vision and the motivation to work in partnership with the Adrian Public Schools superintendent. Adrian College supported this partnership by providing the time, the resources, and the administrative support necessary to achieve these accomplishments, accomplishments that are so important to Adrian College and its neighborhood community.

This YMCA Preschool at Lincoln partnership, facilitated by the Institute for Education, is just another example of how increased recruitment and enrollment have funded academic programs and facilities vital to the growth of our college as well as to the people in our community. So what I would like to emphasize, here, is that our local community wanted to engage with the college to improve early childhood and primary education, but we did not have the means to support such a partnership less than a decade ago, no matter how much we may have wanted to. The six hundred to seven hundred more students who enroll at Adrian College every fall as a direct result of our Admissions Growth initiative, who enroll because they want to be involved in our exciting extracurriculars and cocurriculars like women's hockey or men's volleyball or the Drum-Line, help fund the Institute for Education, and so underwrite all of the activities our professors and students engage in every day that fulfill our mission of service.

ADMISSIONS GROWTH SUPPORTS COMMUNITY ENGAGEMENT ABOVE AND BEYOND SIMPLE PARTNERSHIPS

Of course, any college's primary mission is to provide a high-quality education. Enrollment supports that education and all of the structure it requires. Adrian College founded and supports the institutes I discuss throughout this chapter to give our students the very best opportunities to achieve academic excellence, at Adrian College and beyond. But the institutes have also become a pipeline that feeds community engagement. Historically, business education has focused on the corporate model, and relatively little time and attention have been spent educating students about entrepreneurial and start-up ventures. Our economy relies on the income and innovation resulting from small, entrepreneurial businesses. So to give our students the knowledge and skills they need to undertake such important tasks, a few years ago I recruited Dr. Oded Gur-Arie, a professional who has published core articles in the history of business research, a former member of the University of Michigan Business School who served on its faculty for ten years, and a very successful consultant and businessman in his own right. I asked him to join us at Adrian College to teach in our Business Department and to become the founding director of a new institute that would add to our students' skills and opportunities as well as offer a much-needed boost to start-ups in our area. The Institute for Entrepreneurial Studies, launched in 2009, helps our students develop the skills and tools necessary for success in such pursuits. In the fall of 2012, the institute opened a Business Incubator to support students and local community members who have an idea for a small business, by offering guidance and physical resources to get start-up companies off the ground. The incubator offers people trying to launch an entrepreneurial enterprise a physical space to get started: desks, computers, phones, conference rooms, all on campus and close to the Jones Business Building, with a separate entrance and plenty of parking, as well. It's not a place to set up a permanent office, but it is a place to begin your work, to meet with potential clients and investors while you're getting started. Several Adrian College students have already launched small businesses with the help they received from the Institute. The Business Incubator also matches up students with local businesspeople in order to share experience and expertise. For instance, Dr. Gur-Arie might work to pair up a small business owner who needs a marketing plan with a student who has a business major and plenty of ideas and information about marketing and who wants to put all of his knowledge to use and gain some experience writing a marketing plan for a currently operating business. Or a student might have ideas of his own about how to start a new business, but he's never written a business plan. So the Institute director, Dr. Gur-Arie, will pair him up with a business owner who wants to expand and needs help writing just such a plan. The owner gets the writing expertise of someone with plenty of knowledge about the format and specialized vocabulary of an expansion plan, and the student gains valuable, real-world experience that he just cannot get in a classroom.

The Institute for Entrepreneurial Studies and its affiliated Business Incubator also hosted an Entrepreneurial Boot Camp, made up of three days of minicourses such as Federal and State Income Tax Implications for Entrepreneurs, Writing a Viable Business Plan, New Product and Service Innovation, Financial Statements and Selective Ratio Analysis, and A Lender's Perspective on Managing Working Capital. Adrian College carried most of the cost of this boot camp, with some aid from the Lenawee Economic Development Corporation and the Michigan Small Business Technology and Development Center. About this time, the institute also hosted a daylong Social Media Workshop, aimed at local small businesses, and open to the public. A few weeks after this workshop, someone from the General Federation of Women's Clubs called the Institute and asked if Federation members could be invited to the next such workshop we had planned. Well, we were about to wrap up for the summer and didn't have any other events planned, but Dr. Gur-Arie offered to host a workshop just for the Federation members. At Dr. Gur-Arie's request, the session facilitator solicited questions and problems from the attendees before the event and then presented a list of topics to him before the seminar. So he tailored his presentation to answer their questions and solve their problems. And the result was everyone attending heard research or an anecdote on a topic of interest to her. Every single person attending got exactly what she asked for. Topics included the pitfalls of social media, the dangers of using social media and appropriate solutions, how to use social media effectively without exposing yourself to predators, and plenty of additional practical advice. For instance, Dr. Gur-Arie reminded participants that when you choose a "secret question" to authenticate your identity when changing an online password, be sure it is not a question anyone who looks at your Facebook page can find the answer to. A good example of a poor authentication question is: "What high school did you attend?" The professionals who attended this seminar loved it. They were glad to know that Adrian College cares about them, and they have already asked us to present another seminar again, soon.

When you grow enrollment via Admissions Growth strategy, remember, you grow not only the number of students at your college, but also the amount of tuition income that you bring in. And this income is precisely what funds our Institute for Entrepreneurial Studies and all of our other college-community initiatives, strengthening our ties to the local community. This tradition of service, and especially of service at the request of community members like the Federation of Women's Clubs mentioned above, is part of the mission of engagement at liberal arts colleges. In 1995 the National Association of State Universities and Land-Grant Colleges, with the support of the W.K. Kellogg Foundation, established a national commission to examine and offer guidelines to revitalize the role of higher education in our country. During the following years, the Kellogg Commission met repeatedly and issued a series of reports on its findings and recommendations, and report number 3 was entitled *Returning to Our Roots: The Engaged Institution* (1999). The executive summaries of these reports, published in 2001, emphasize several guidelines for measuring an institution's engagement with its community. Among those guidelines are sharing the college's expertise and intellectual capital, responding to community requests for assistance and knowledge, and, very importantly, committing sufficient financial resources to the tasks of community activities and service. The Kellogg Commission (2001) was tasked with specifically researching and offering advice to public universities and state and land-grant colleges, but I would like to argue, here, that small private colleges also have much to gain by strengthening their engagement with their communities. Such endeavors work to build trust and mutual respect, in addition to reminding such colleges and the small towns and villages that surround them of the mutual benefits of sharing goals, resources, and activities. When we aid each other, we all learn from the experience—local residents and businesses gain new respect for the knowledge, research, and expertise people who have dedicated their lives to learning can bring to a new preschool program, for instance, and members of the academic community are reminded of the value of experience dealing with multiple constituencies in a public school district. Most importantly, students at all levels benefit when students in primary and secondary classrooms get opportunities to interact with teachers and assistants and student teachers who bring a variety of methods and styles to the classroom, while student teachers gain vital experience working with students before graduating and gaining sole responsibility for classroom planning, preparation, and management. Private colleges have a long and proud record of service to their communities, and that does not arise from an elitist sense of noblesse oblige. Rather, its source is our understanding, often built right into our mission statements and engraved into the cornerstones and lintels of our oldest buildings, of the rewards of service, of the importance of community, our obligation to return effort to those who have supported us so substantially.

By the time you have reached step 5 of Admissions Growth, "Redirect new income to academic facilities and programs," it will become apparent that this program has acquired its own momentum. This momentum is what transforms an active and vital campus from simply a place of students and teachers and classrooms into a community filled with knowledgeable professors, lecture halls filled with students engaged in hands-on learning in multimedia environments, and institutes that link professionals, students, and public institutions to serve a wider constituency. It is this momentum, and the long-term benefits it brings to your small college, that I will address in chapter 7.

Key Takeaways

1. Use the added income from increased enrollment to serve your college mission. Redirect revenue to academic facilities to improve students' educational experiences.

2. When reinvesting increased tuition income in your institution, start with your faculty members. Students will choose your institution for the extracurriculars and cocurriculars that interest them, but ultimately, they want an education whose quality will serve them after graduation.

3. Reinvest in your campus by building and renovating facilities that will improve students' academic experiences. Comfortable and professional-quality academic spaces show students that your institution values their presence and their work.

4. Newly renovated classrooms, language labs, and computer facilities will also become showcase spaces for your campus. They show students, parents, and visitors that your campus is thriving and offers state-of-the art facilities where students can acquire marketable skills.

5. Reinvesting added tuition revenue from the Admissions Growth plan allows your campus to thrive by funding programs and personnel who will offer innovative teaching, programming, and community partnerships.

6. Reenergized and well-supported faculty and departments will become more involved and responsive to community needs. Active community engagement will create new learning and internship opportunities for your students and fulfill your mission of service to the community.

CHAPTER 7

Admissions Growth Generates Its Own Momentum

Step 6: Continue to Build and Utilize Momentum for Further Growth

When you implement the Admissions Growth model at your institution, your primary goal is to leverage investments in facilities and programs to bring more students to your campus. Small private colleges can only run on tuition, and tuition comes from students, plain and simple. But more students and improved facilities bring so much more to campus than just tuition dollars. They work together to create a plethora of additional benefits that will make your campus vital and will ensure that your institution thrives. As you can see in figure 2, we come here to the capstone of the Admissions Growth plan, step 6: "Continue to build and utilize momentum for further growth."

SELF-RECRUITING

The first visible momentum emerging from Admissions Growth model is that teens tell other teens about your college when they have a positive experience there. The best recruiters we have at Adrian College are our current students. So having more students, of course, simply means that more people are telling your story to other, future students. Teenagers are incredibly social beings. They talk, they ask questions, they want to know, and they want to share what they know. When you implement this plan you have more eyes and ears passing the word about your college. Having a student go home and tell her siblings and her friends in high school that Adrian College is an awesome place to attend is worth more than any pamphlet or call from an admissions counselor can ever be.

FIGURE 2. The capstone of the Admissions Growth plan is the point at which your institution has built enough momentum to sustain growth.

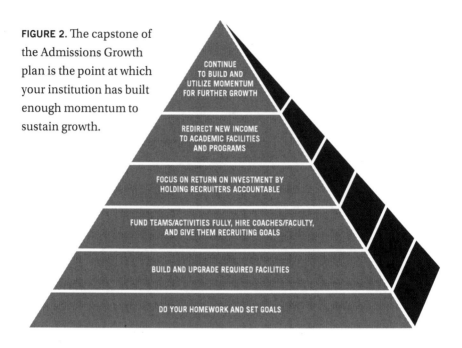

CONTINUE TO BUILD AND UTILIZE MOMENTUM FOR FURTHER GROWTH

REDIRECT NEW INCOME TO ACADEMIC FACILITIES AND PROGRAMS

FOCUS ON RETURN ON INVESTMENT BY HOLDING RECRUITERS ACCOUNTABLE

FUND TEAMS/ACTIVITIES FULLY, HIRE COACHES/FACULTY, AND GIVE THEM RECRUITING GOALS

BUILD AND UPGRADE REQUIRED FACILITIES

DO YOUR HOMEWORK AND SET GOALS

SOCIAL MEDIA ONLY INCREASE THESE EFFECTS

More than any other word, "connectivity" is the key to describing this generation of young people. If a student plays a great lacrosse game or enjoys an exciting hockey game, then he immediately texts or tweets it to his friends or posts it on Facebook. This is instant advertising, and it goes on all the time after you put Admissions Growth in place because students are constantly engaged in activities they enjoy. At Adrian College, even the president tweets, uses Facebook, and texts birthday wishes to students. We even have our own YouTube Channel where students can post their videos. This medium presents a constant inflow of fun activities that students capture and post for others to see what they're doing and experiencing. After seeing a video posted by students taking a break by singing karaoke-style in our MAC lab, one viewer commented, "AMAZING!!!!!!! couldnt stop watching it! i only wish we had that spirit/equipment at my school:P." That kind of student-to-student interaction is advertising no institution can buy or manufacture. When students genuinely enjoy what they are doing on your campus, the authenticity of their experiences will show in all of their communications, and social media will amplify that to your institution's benefit.

MOMENTUM

This model creates tremendous momentum for the college that decides to implement it. Your teams *will* win. Adrian College just won its first national championship: ACHA Division III Hockey. But in recent years we've also won league titles in football, men's lacrosse, women's lacrosse, baseball, men's hockey, women's hockey, and women's soccer. We've also experienced great success in many other sports, including softball, bowling, men's volleyball, men's basketball, and track & field. Your teams will win because they now have great coaching, excellent facilities, good equipment, and the financial resources to help them strive to the limits of their potential. Hiring quality coaches means student athletes have clear expectations and defined roles. When teams are started up "on the cheap" and continuously underfunded, they do not thrive, regardless of talent level. When you fund your extracurricular activities appropriately, they win because they wake up each morning wanting to get better, so they practice, they prepare. Winning is a function of momentum and sustained energy. You start that ball rolling by demonstrating to your students that you believe in their team enough to provide what they need to be successful. Winning certainly requires talent, but it also needs skilled people who expect total devotion from themselves and from others around them. Winning teams have a synergism that is created when the whole is bigger than the sum of its parts. Sufficient funding is the first part; it supports the rest of the program and allows your teams to grow, to thrive, to succeed.

These successes garner media interest that, of course, increases the momentum you've begun through enrollment growth. The local sports pages are now filled with stories about successful Adrian College teams, and one of those teams will make the front page of our local newspaper several times a month. In addition, national publications like *Athletic Business* and the *Chronicle of Higher Education* have featured our institution on their covers. The momentum you've begun keeps building after this coverage. Campus spirit grows, enthusiasm builds about activities in and out of the classroom. You now have a vital and active campus, which will produce happy students and upbeat alumni. You will attract better students, which will please your faculty members, creating an even more positive attitude on campus as well as a greater depth of purpose.

But the real momentum produced by all of these changes to your campus is in future recruitment growth. Athletes want to join teams that are successful. Students want to come to a campus that is lively and fun. Your coaches and recruiters believe in your institution and they will work enthusiastically and cheerfully to meet their recruiting goals. And that brings you back to the only solution: enrollment.

The momentum provided to your school by the Admissions Growth plan will build additional creativity in your faculty, staff, administrators, and coaches. The improved morale and campus spirit spurred by your new momentum are positive energies. They are motivating and captivating. They make people want to reach higher, do more, have fun, and find ways to be better and to distinguish themselves. All of these positive side effects are happening now on our campus because we have more students, more faculty members, more events, more creative energy, and more visible signs that people with great ideas and the ability to implement them are welcome here. In 2012 we made sure that welcome message was explicit by founding an Institute for Creativity, an office whose mission is to provide workshops, activities, and events that promote a culture of creativity campus-wide. The Institute also hosts an Annual Creativity Award competition, challenging faculty and staff to submit ideas to improve campus life. The first award was handed out in 2012 to Dr. Scott Elliot, a professor who suggested further "greening" our campus by instituting a bike-sharing program—a program that is now fully in place on our campus. This award provides a $1,000 prize to the winner and funds the idea with a $10,000 budget. These cheerful bikes, painted in Adrian College's school colors with bulldog logos on them, are now available for students and other members of our campus to check out from the student union, the Caine Center. They use them to travel across campus, downtown, to the local video store, and just for rides in the pleasant neighborhoods around our campus. Dr. Elliot's creative idea not only benefits our campus, it also supports the economy surrounding our small institution. Students have an environmentally friendly option for quick trips to local businesses, and the initial funding purchased bikes from a local shop, Adrian Locksmith and Cyclery, as well as paying for fleet maintenance from another local business, Re-cycle Lenawee.

Of course, we find creativity among our students and faculty members when they are working at their best, and this happens all the time, all over our campus, not just through institute-sponsored contests. I discussed in chapter 6 how our Institute for Education's innovations were key to creating a community-partnered preschool program to serve the needs of our faculty, community members, and the local public school system. Even more recently, the institute director, Dr. Andrea Milner, has been working, at the request of principals and teachers at Adrian Public Schools, to improve the preparation of student teachers before they reach the classroom. She is in constant communication with both student teachers and their cooperating teachers in the classroom, helping to make clear what we expect from students during their student teaching and making sure everyone is aware of deadline requirements for various forms and evaluations. In the course of making communications clearer and more frequent between Adrian College students and the teachers they assist, Dr. Milner learned that the mentoring teachers felt they really needed more information about their potential student teachers. The supporting teachers wanted more information, before being matched to student teachers, about their majors, their prior experiences in the classroom, the quality of their academic work, their graduation dates, and the like. Dr. Milner's excellent and creative insight came when she realized that Adrian College already collected much of this information in an electronic archive that we maintain for our regular communications with the Teacher Education Accreditation Council. It was really just a short, but very imaginative, step to repurpose all of that information by building electronic "profiles" of our students. These profiles are then maintained in an online portfolio available to the Adrian Public Schools teachers as they are being matched to student teachers each year.

Low campus morale from underfunded departments, overworked staff and professors, and shoddy work spaces can kill the kind of innovative thinking Dr. Milner shows every day. This genuinely innovative leap that she made as director of the Institute for Education, the ability to see how information that was already organized and stored can be reused to solve problems of communications and expectations between community teachers and their Adrian College student teachers, is clearly the result of a campus-wide attitude that encourages, recognizes, and rewards creative thinking. And such an attitude is a direct result of the momentum built by a successful Admissions Growth program.

Developing creative ways to continue to support and broaden our growing partnership with area public schools, the Institute for Education also teamed up with a professor from our Modern Languages and Cultures department in response to requests from the superintendent of Adrian Public Schools to enhance their language instruction. Working with four area public schools, Dr. Milner and Dr. Bryan Bott developed a collaborative Japanese language and culture class for select gifted fifth graders from four area school districts. The class met on Saturdays during the spring of 2012 and introduced students to Japanese language and culture. Four undergraduates in the Teacher Education program were recruited to teach this class to these eager fifth graders. This collaborative learning partnership between our institution and the public schools reinforced our commitment to strengthen teacher preparation while offering a unique learning opportunity to local elementary students. At the end of each class, the students demonstrated the concepts and vocabulary they had acquired that day, and during the final class, each learner had the opportunity to perform a short speech in Japanese for an audience of their parents and other family members. Our undergraduate students were guided throughout this learning and teaching experience by Dr. Bott, who coached them in language acquisition methodology, as well as by Dr. Milner, who met with them after each class to review best practices in pedagogy. Such opportunities for students and professors to continue pursuing creative collaborative projects with members of the Adrian community at large are a result of the creative attitudes fostered on our campus. In addition, classes such as this Japanese outreach experience model for our students how professors use creative problem solving to improve the educational process for a variety of constituencies simultaneously. This unique, collaborative class improved and broadened language offerings to public school students in our area, helped local school districts serve their gifted and often overlooked students better, and created valuable classroom experiences for our future teachers. And I might add here, that Dr. Milner receives the support she needs to design and develop these innovative programs because making her the director of the Institute for Education gave her the ability to devote the time required for everything from conception through implementation. When I arrived at Adrian College in 2005, the Teacher Education department had only four full-time positions. The increased tuition revenue brought about by Admissions Growth allowed us to add two full-time positions, including that of director. And being able to fund this institute, this director, has made all the difference in this department's ability to serve these students, the campus, and our community. This is the kind of momentum you unleash when you are able to fund new programs with income realized by the Admissions Growth strategy.

The momentum your leadership creates when you utilize Admissions Growth to bring high-achieving, active, involved students to your school moves beyond professors and classes to every activity on campus. Creativity and excellence flow when professors, students, and campus organizations are well supplied and well funded. In October 2013, student members of our campus organization Not For Sale made a presentation to the national Historians Against Slavery conference in Cincinnati, and in the words of our campus chaplain and group advisor, "They brought the house down." These students conceived and executed a program that began with a minimalist five-minute segment of audio and voice recordings detailing how and why they became involved in the movement to end human trafficking. They then shared an engaging interpretation of their work and their plans for the future. The students closed with a very moving and informative video

What Kids Want

they produced and took questions from the audience. Adrian College's students were the only undergraduates present at the conference, and other attendees have shared with me that they were impressive, professional, and excellent ambassadors for our college. Chaplain Chris Momany told me that the conference was filled with the most respected professionals from a variety of disciplines, and he believes that every single one "was deeply moved." The creativity of the program these students produced is astounding. Their self-motivation, their ability to conceptualize the program far in advance of its presentation, and their willingness to learn and perfect the video-editing skills necessary for production demonstrate not just creativity but their ability to imagine and then produce a presentation for such a purpose as improving awareness of human trafficking, which is still ongoing, even now, even in the United States, and especially in Michigan, because of the border we share with Canada. The founder of Historians Against Slavery, Dr. James Brewer Stewart, was impressed enough to write to me praising our students and the organization advisors:

> It quickly became clear to everyone that Adrian's representatives exemplify a rare and compelling synthesis of teaching learning and social engagement. Following their presentation admiring comments about the value of replicating the "Adrian Model" became ubiquitous. Participants in significant numbers followed up with numerous questions of Chris, Deborah and your students. All of us saw clearly that Adrian's antislavery group truly does "make a difference" and that the students involved are finding fruitful answers to important moral/vocational questions. . . . In closing I must attempt to convey some sense of the deep admiration your students developed in the estimate of so many of our conference's participants. Such smart, deeply informed, justifiably confident and ethically informed people—a wonderful example what an authentic "learning community" is all about. (Personal communication, October 28, 2013)

This praise is all the more significant since it was completely unsolicited. Dr. Stewart recognized the level of concern and the amount of time, care, and effort these students have invested. So much of that is enabled by Adrian College professors who are provided the time and funding to support such student programs. History professor Deborah Field and Chaplain Momany were able to use a new Adrian College van to take students to the conference at the National Underground Freedom Center in Cincinnati. Additional funds to support the students' activities and presentation were available through Chaplain Momany's office and from an umbrella student organization. All of this financial support comes from the student fees and tuition that undergird so many of our campus successes in the past few years. Our students' overwhelming show of creativity demonstrates that what Admissions Growth has done for our campus is to recruit and then empower future leaders, those difference makers who are going to change the course of our culture and our economy in the coming decades. This is the kind of learning, critical thinking, innovation, and creative problem solving skills that you enable with the tuition income the Admissions Growth plan will bring to your school.

ADDITIONAL REVENUE CENTERS

Adrian College is bringing in much more nontuition income than we did a few years ago, as a direct result of improved facilities that our campus now has. The activities hosted in these facilities are just another product of the momentum created through Admissions Growth. Youth camps and conferences brought in over $530,000 during the summer of 2011, alone. When we host K–12 kids on our campus, we encourage our coaching staff to offer these families camps and individual lessons for their children. Many young athletes, especially the highly skilled players, want this expert-level coaching. To have an opportunity to be taught by a college coach is an opportunity that is too good to pass by. Parents love to give their children these opportunities to learn from full-time coaches at the college level. These camps and lessons create relationships that not only lead to stronger connections with potential students, they give our coaches an opportunity to earn a little extra money. We at Adrian College like our coaches to supplement their income using our facilities because this keeps them motivated and serves the community at the same time.

Part of the reason we can afford to maintain our improved grounds, buildings, and athletic fields is that they do not sit empty and unused when school is not in session. We don't have enough weekends to fulfill the number of requests from brides who want to be married on our campus. We don't have enough room on our football field for all of the football camps and band camps who want to use our facilities for preseason practices. What we do have are opportunities to host Detroit Red Wings old-timers' games in our ice arena as well as Detroit Lions' charity basketball games in our gym. Our own events are continuing to grow in popularity, also. Ticket sales to campus sporting events have nearly tripled in the last five years. Excitement is gravitational—it pulls people in. The same is true for concert performers, convocation guests, commencement speakers, and various musicians, artists and performers. They *want* to come to campus because of the momentum here and the positive energy it has created for our institution. Recent guest speakers on our campus include Michigan State University basketball coach Tom Izzo, Governor Rick Snyder, educator Alfie Kohn, Senator Carl Levin, author Temple Grandin, astrophysicist Janna Levin, and Olympic athlete Sheila Taormina. Student Affairs has brought to campus big-name performers such as Jake Owen, Neon Trees, Sean Kingston, and Switchfoot. Students and faculty alike appreciate and enjoy opportunities to hear speakers and see performers they might never have the chance to see otherwise.

The momentum of increased attendance builds on itself, too, as many local and national advertisers now want to buy space on our hockey rink boards, our baseball outfield fence, and around our track & field complex. In 2012, our institution pulled in over $100,000 in advertising revenue alone.

Our hockey arena's success and popularity has also attracted a new national restaurant, the WOW Café American Grill & Wingery, and our lease with it pays the college a significant percentage of its profits. Our food service provider was so anxious to capture this business opportunity that it gave the college $1 million to construct the restaurant that serves students and faculty daily. So we continue to provide a fun and exciting destination spot for our students, faculty, and members of the community, and part of what all of these people spend when they're having a fun lunch or a great night out also supports the college. This is how the campus momentum continues to grow and to build on itself.

Additionally, businesses use our campus lecture spaces to hold off-site meetings for their employees. These groups pay rent to use our space at Adrian College. All of this revenue is a direct result of the facilities investments we made as step 1 of the Admissions Growth plan. But, more important, all of these people come to Adrian College and they have a good time and they go away with happy feelings about their time at Adrian College and they become good ambassadors for our campus. While Adrian College is growing the number of people who may become future students and future alums, our campus also simultaneously serves our local community by offering top-flight locations for conferences (we can host from five to two thousand people), corporate training, sports camps, junior hockey games, summer art experiences, wedding receptions, family reunions, and a variety of community and public school events, not to mention a really excellent restaurant, overlooking Arrington Ice Arena and open to the public, not just to ticket holders, even on game nights. Adrian College serves the community in myriad ways, and it is not a small or inconsequential thing to serve our tiny city in a fairly rural area by improving the quality of life of all of the residents in our area by sharing our attractive and distinctive facilities.

Building the number of visitors who will become future students or goodwill ambassadors for your institution, of course, is not the reason you embark on a plan such as Admissions Growth. Your first and primary responsibility to your institution when you make such a move is increased enrollment. But every investment you make in improving facilities that will attract more and more involved students will also bring additional, if unintended, benefits to your institution in the form of an inviting and exciting campus that will continue to draw students, produce satisfied alumni, and provide additional income sources over the short and long term.

Adrian College continues to attract more academically qualified students, students who want to continue their education at the graduate level, and so another positive, if unintended, consequence of Admissions Growth is that we have recently initiated four new graduate programs in athletic training, criminal justice, accounting, and industrial chemistry. Next year we will add a masters of education. During our first two years, Adrian College enrolled nine graduate students, we brought in more than twenty the next year, and we anticipate nothing but further growth in the future. These degree programs retain current students for additional semesters as well as attracting students from other schools, thereby increasing revenues via additional tuition, room, and board income.

BETTER CURB APPEAL AND CAMPUS CLIMATE

When people come to our campus they pick up on a few important things right away. The first is that parking is a problem. This is a good thing. Adrian College now projects an image as the place to be. The frustration of trying to find a parking space is coupled with the idea that this is an active, vibrant campus. The second thing that people note during the school year is that students are everywhere, so you need to drive carefully. This, too, is a good thing. Young people like to be part of crowds. Visitors to campus note right away, of course, that the lawns are mowed and the flowerbeds are full and fragrant. You might think this is minor. You might think these are the kinds of things that are not important to how a campus functions, but you would be wrong. Remember how low campus morale was in chapter 2, during my first visit to Adrian College as a candidate? Poor curb appeal is not just depressing, it is a sign of a campus in crisis.

Visitors to Adrian College today will not see a campus that is just barely being maintained. Instead they'll see multiple new construction sites. In addition to new sports and academic facilities, we have added new terraces, fire pits, fireplaces, outdoor televisions, walking paths, picnic areas, hammocks, pavilions, grill areas, memorial gardens, and beautiful acreage. In short, Adrian College looks like the ivy-covered haven parents and students envision when they think of what a small private college should be.

RETENTION

Since Adrian College has instituted Admissions Growth, our retention numbers have reached extraordinary levels. Our 2011–2012 fall-to-spring retention was 93 percent. This statistic shows students are happy with their academic experience, with their social experience, with the cocurricular activities. They are happy with the sports teams, their musical performance activities, and their college-supported activities—the equestrian team, the student newspaper, the Model Arab League, and the like. This translates into returning the following year. This is happening even in a town that is really struggling by other measures—job losses are up, property values are down, city services are being cut, and municipal pay raises are nonexistent. This is happening in a state where families are less able to afford a private education than in previous decades due to stagnant wages. This is happening in an environment that makes it easy to transfer to another college and retain your credits. Michigan has many small private colleges that are easily accessible to transfer students. And yet our students are not moving to alternative schools, locales, or programs. At Adrian College, we keep our students because we create a unique experience through the Admissions Growth model, an experience that is not easy to find at other colleges, an experience that quickly immerses students in an identity group with others of shared interests. Friendships form, tight bonds are secured, and the idea of leaving for other colleges becomes much less attractive.

Adrian College still faces issues that *should* hurt our retention numbers. Our enrollment growth has been so successful that we need to build new residence halls quickly despite the capacity we've added in the past few years. We've added 348 new rooms, with capacity for 505 additional students since 2005. In spite of these facilities additions and improvements, we still need to add more residence halls quickly. We also need to continue to invest heavily in the modern amenities in these rooms that new students crave. In the past few years, Adrian College has added fourteen theme houses to campus, and one residence hall was renovated from a traditional dormitory to single suites with individual bathrooms. Yet we need to continue additional renovations to make more of these desirable residences available to more of our students. As I've mentioned earlier, downtown Adrian, itself, is relatively unattractive, not the type of place most students envision when they think about where they want to spend their college years: empty storefronts, dilapidated buildings, an ineffective local government all plague our downtown region. Honestly, students take one look downtown early in their freshman year and rarely return. All of these factors notwithstanding, Adrian College is seeing historically high enrollment that makes it easy for us to fill the college with strong, academically qualified students, and our retention has not been hurt—because Adrian College offers such a vibrant experience as a direct result of the Admissions Growth plan.

MEDIA COVERAGE EXPANDS

We have had good coverage. We have had bad coverage. In the end, nearly all coverage, good or bad, is good. People want to know what is happening at Adrian College. We are a source of activity. The media coverage of some of our recent commencement speakers, such as Tom Izzo and Pat Boone, was pretty widespread. We've also had notable convocation speakers like Temple Grandin and Senator Carl Levin.

Our Public Relations department blasts nearly everything that happens on campus to the media because our institution has a story to tell. And the media cover what's happening at Adrian College. Stories highlighting our tremendous growth have appeared in *US News & World Report,* the *Chronicle of Higher Education, Athletic Business,* and in Associated Press wire stories. Our varsity hockey events have been featured on Mitch Albom's radio broadcasts as well as on ESPN. Several Adrian College athletes have been featured in the pages of *Sports Illustrated,* and Adrian College athletics got a big media splash, nationally, during the 2007–2008 hockey season leading up to the NCAA tournament selection. Public Relations keeps media outlets informed about the events at our institution, but we also have made coverage of our campus easier for television outlets by hiring a full-time videographer who sends out B-roll footage (segments of film that can be used as background and transition shots during stories) on a regular basis. The college has also taken more control of public perception by creating professional-quality videos about campus activities and events and posting them on Vimeo as well as blasting them to friends and alumni. Admissions Growth has given us the financial resources we need to hire these people and promote our school. Prior to Admissions Growth, all of this effort simply would have been financially impossible.

MORE AND MORE SUCCESSFUL ALUMNI

I won't see the dividends from our recent and future alumni because those will come back to Adrian College many years from now. But these students *will* give back. They self-report as satisfied and happy with their undergraduate experience.

The recent and extensive media coverage of our successes at Adrian College creates a value-added education for our students. The improvements and expansion of our facilities and our faculty mean that our students are getting a superb education, but the media coverage ensures that others *know* of the excellent academic programs here. This means, of course, that in the coming years, our alumni will be in a better position to support their alma mater generously. Even though growth in alumni development is a long-term prospect, our donations have inched up during the few years since we implemented the Admissions Growth plan because alumni are excited by the growth of their college, and people want to give to a successful institution. Giving is a function of good feelings and satisfaction, and these are a direct result of the improvements our tremendous enrollment growth has funded at our institution. Even in just the past few years, overall giving to Adrian College has increased from $1.7 million in 2005 to $7.5 million in fiscal year 2012.

BETTER EDUCATION IN THE CLASSROOM

The core of the Admissions Growth plan is, of course, increased enrollment and what that brings to the college. The first thing it brings is additional dollars. These dollars fund faculty development, curriculum revisions, and explorations of new approaches to teaching and learning.

Our institution is currently expanding our focus on experiential learning. These experiences are as varied as quick outings to the city commission meetings for our journalism classes or extensive Global Health Experience trips to Central America, Guam, and other points around the globe for our students in the health professions. Our secure financial situation allows the school to fund vans for local travel as well as grants to cover fees and travel expenses for international experiences. Tuition income from added students also funds the hiring of more and more highly qualified professors and allows the college the opportunity to entice more experienced and well-known professors away from other institutions. The exceptional faculty members here take students on more field trips, encourage them to participate in better internships, and work harder to find paid summer research opportunities for students to further their studies in their fields.

Funding growth in our biology department is a priority, and our first-rate professors guide students in getting hands-on experience every year in a local wetlands area via a partnership with the Michigan International Speedway (MIS). Adrian College students and faculty regularly make field trips to this area to take part in a long-term research project identifying and tagging trees and plants along the walking trail on Graves Farm campgrounds at MIS. This project is part of research conducted by Adrian College faculty members on invasive species and will be part of a study on the ratio of invasive/native species in this eight-hundred-acre recreational area.

Experiences like these field research trips have garnered so much attention from the media and the public that the local public schools have begun asking our professors and students to share their expertise with area middle schoolers. Onsted Public Schools started the trend, asking if their students could join ours on research and tagging trips. The program has built up its own momentum as other schools asked to have their students join, and now twelve hundred middle school science students join Adrian College biology and teacher education students on their wetlands field trip experiences. This Track and Explore partnership between our institution, MIS, and the local schools has become so successful that the Teacher Education department has developed an entire program and website dedicated to reflecting the experiences of these students as well as showcasing the learning modules, lesson plans, and Michigan Department of Education curriculum benchmarks achieved during these activities.

Local schools and parents alike recognize the values of these shared explorations as these middle schoolers are at a developmental point where a noticeable decline in science test scores occurs across the nation. One hypothesis about this trend in declining scores recognizes that middle school is where most science classes become less hands-on and experimental and more theoretical and conceptual. Track and Explore turns Adrian College students into teachers and leaders, giving them a showcase for their knowledge and experience, and brings "hands-on" learning back to the science education experience for the middle school students who join them. These experiences help our students learn the value of science and aid them in developing the skills necessary to communicate their research to a less-knowledgeable audience. But it's not just our students this program prepares for the future. Track and Explore and all of the other partnerships our students and professors engage the community in are giving today's younger students a strong, solid education that will make them more capable, better-prepared learners in the future. We at Adrian College are creating stronger freshman classes for the years to come.

BETTER COMMUNITY RELATIONS

I detailed earlier in this chapter how the facilities you will build and renovate with the income from the Admissions Growth plan will draw community members in. Local residents, organizations, schools, and businesses will flock to your campus to utilize new and updated conference rooms, lecture halls, green spaces, auditoriums, and sports facilities. The new increased visibility Admissions Growth brings to your campus will continue to grow and build its own momentum in other ways as well. For instance, in almost any small community, it's the public librarian who knows best how to gain the most benefit from free and underutilized resources. Adrian and the small towns and villages surrounding it are no exception. Over just the past few years, Adrian College professors have hosted, facilitated, led, or assisted in literally dozens of events at local libraries on a truly impressive array of topics. The small public library in Blissfield, about thirteen miles from Adrian, has certainly made the best possible use of the expertise, experience, and capabilities of our professors on a regular basis. Professors Sarah Hanson and Thomas Muntean have hosted summer class presentations there on geology and volcanoes for learners of all ages, complete with displays of fossils, geologic timelines, and mineral identification workshops that young and old participants alike could participate in. Biology professor James Martin has been a guest speaker in the library's events series, keeping residents informed on important issues about the River Raisin watershed. Other professors have taught seminars on résumé preparation, hosted summer creative writing workshops for high school students, participated in Michigan Reads dinner and discussion events, and hosted book groups on topics as diverse as Jane Austen, Ernest Hemingway, Mark Twain's *Adventures of Huckleberry Finn,* and Amy Tan's *The Joy Luck Club.* English professors Dr. Jeffrey Berry, Dr. Richard Koch, Dr. Linda Learman, and Kristin Abraham have also served as judges and guest readers for the library's annual Middle School Poetry Contest. The director of the library, Dr. Bob Barringer, reminded me last year how much time our English professors have spent contributing to the poetry contest. The judges always take the time to respond to *all* of the young poets. Dr. Berry and Dr. Koch responded to each student's poem individually, taking turns reading famous poems that each submission had put them in mind of. Professor Abraham responded to every student as a poet, praising each poem, and giving advice for future poems. Other Adrian College faculty have baked cookies and volunteered their time for many events over the past few years, from the Christmas crafts and movie programs to the street festival Art at Your Feet. Supporting our local libraries is important to me, personally, so I was pleased when Dr. Barringer asked me to be the keynote speaker at the library's seventy-fifth anniversary celebration. As part of my duties that day, I led a formal rededication event during which local citizens pledged their responsibility to continue supporting the library that has served their village for generations.

You will probably remember that in its call to reform higher education in our country, the Kellogg Foundation charged colleges and universities with improving engagement with their home communities, but key to the foundation's definition of "engagement" is the understanding that it is not the place of a college or university to impose its knowledge or expertise on its neighbors. Rather, engagement results when institutions respond to community needs when called upon. It is completely possible that no one is better at calling on Adrian College and other nearby resources than Colleen Leddy, director of the Stair Public Library in Morenci, another small town library found just over ten miles from our campus. In just the past couple of years, she has asked for assistance from a number of our professors to make presentations, lead discussions, and participate in storytelling events. Before they will fund an event, many community and library foundations require that one of the participants or presenters be a scholar with academic credentials and demonstrable knowledge on the topic, so our local librarians often request time and assistance from our faculty. Philosophy and religion professor Dr. Melissa Stewart has assisted in the Stair Library's Prime Time Family Reading Time program three years in a row, now. Her participation required a substantial time investment before she even began. She and Leddy attended a two-day workshop in New Orleans to prepare for the six-week program, which involved using children's books to prompt discussions of various humanities issues and how they related to family members' lives. Leddy was enormously pleased with the results, saying, "It was a really incredible program," and adding that "Melissa was amazingly excellent at eliciting discussion from family members, from first graders to adults." Dr. Adam Coughlin, with our Exercise Science and Physical Education department, led a reading, viewing, and discussion series for adults at this library, called Pushing the Limits. This was a pilot program, funded by the National Science Foundation, intended to foster community reading and discussion on topics that might broaden our understanding of how science, technology, and research impact our lives every day. This particular program got coverage in the local newspaper after each program, and so Dr. Coughlin and the college received some very positive press for months during the spring of 2013. Professor Carman Curton (who contributed to this book) has also volunteered her time to the Stair Library, leading a dinner and discussion program with community members and a high school English class who came together to read and discuss the memoir *Stealing Buddha's Dinner,* and then participated in a conversation via speakerphone with the author, Bich Minh Nguyen. Another scholar who has shared his time and expertise with the library and its patrons is our history professor Dr. Michael McGrath, who was the discussion leader for the Muslim Journeys program. This National Endowment for the Humanities event brings together members of the community to read books on the Muslim experience and then participate in lectures and discussions by a local scholar. For this particular program, Dr. McGrath invested quite a bit of his own time, also: he first traveled to Denver to participate in an orientation workshop, then prepared a twenty- to twenty-five-minute presentation on five different books. He dutifully attended the "Meet the Scholar" kickoff event, showed up a few minutes before each program to talk with people, and then guided a discussion after each of his presentations. Dr. McGrath was committed enough to the program that he took the initiative to invite Corporal Tim Turner to participate as well. Corporal Turner is a marine veteran of two tours in Iraq and one in Afghanistan, a young man who has spent an academic year studying Arabic and Middle Eastern Studies in Amman, Jordan, and who is currently attending Adrian College via the Operation Education scholarship. Dr. McGrath invited Corporal Turner because, as he shared with me, "he can give accounts of life in two Muslim countries from very recent times, and he has the authority of someone whose response to the Iraqis and Afghanis is not hatred, but curiosity—he wants to understand them."

All of these professors, and many more, have responded to community needs when asked. Members of the public obviously recognize and appreciate the knowledge and experience our faculty bring to these events, but they also appreciate the attitude all of our professors share—a willingness to bring community members into a world of exploring and sharing knowledge, not a place where "wise old men" lecture to them. Another librarian, the assistant director of the Stair Library, Sheri Frost, has shared with me how much she appreciates that our professors "don't talk down to" to their audiences. The Kellogg Foundation recognized that colleges and universities have a responsibility to respond to community needs, and our professionals certainly do that. Leddy has said to me about our faculty at Adrian College, "Even though you all know so much, you don't make us feel stupid," and she and so many other librarians in the area have told me how impressed they are by the evidence that we take these chances to participate in such programs seriously. People recognize and respect how faculty members listen to comments, reflect carefully, and respond thoughtfully. They take the time to prepare for these commitments. Their care and professionalism shows, and members of the community talk about it and praise our professors, and that can only reflect positively on our institution. The momentum begun by the improved attitude that Admissions Growth stimulates at Adrian College creates a can-do sense of accomplishment. When faculty are involved in research that they are excited about, research that

Adrian College can fund with budgets for travel, for books, for conferences, then our faculty want to share their knowledge, and they are willing to spend time and effort in the community. All of this begins, again, with the increased tuition, that you, the institution's leader bring to your college through tuition income that is a direct result of the Admissions Growth strategy.

The enrollment growth generated by Adrian College's new admissions strategy is an important economic boost to our local and regional economy, too. In the six years between the implementation of Admissions Growth in 2005 and the 2011–2012 school year, Adrian College added thirty-three employees to its campus, bringing the total number of employees for that year to 370. (We are up to 480 now—a payroll increase of over $7 million yearly.) That year our institution spent more than $20 million on employee salaries, wages, and benefits. The professionals who have joined Adrian College recycle a huge percentage of their income back into our economy. They buy houses and cars and boats. They go to movie theaters, buy tickets to local live performances, support the symphony, shop, dine, and entertain in Adrian and the surrounding area. Using information gleaned from the Consumer Expenditure Survey and the U.S. Department of Commerce, Anderson Economic Group estimates that 89 percent of this payroll income, or $18.1 million, stays in our state in the form of spending on local goods and services (2013). When residents and employees spend money locally, then the local businesses they support spend additional funds, in turn, to support their businesses, and our college's influence on the economy in southeast Michigan grows even larger. Calculations using the U.S. Department of Commerce statistics show that Adrian College stimulates an additional $7.5 million in indirect spending from its payroll expenditures (Anderson Economic Group, 2013). Additional estimates show that Adrian College stimulates further economic expansion through indirect job growth as well. In fiscal year 2011, for example, payroll spending, nonpayroll spending, and student spending supported 370 jobs on campus and indirectly supported an additional 208 jobs in our state (Anderson Economic Group, 2013).

All of these numbers demonstrate that when your campus grows, you add faculty, administrators, and support staff. And when your payroll grows, it supports growth in your local economy. At Adrian College, our growth supports the community, and the community supports us. Local companies bring income to our campus when they use our facilities for conferences, our neighbors support our teams when they buy tickets to our games, people come from several towns over to patronize the WOW Café American Grill & Wingery, which a local Blissfield village official recently assured me serves up the best wings in the area.

Of course, our institution's recent growth has been the result of increased enrollment, and that enrollment means we are bringing more students to Adrian who spend money off campus as well as on it. People often overlook the impact of student spending, because students do not appear to have very much income at first glance. But students at small privates rarely pay all of their own tuition, which means, even though their personal income is small, nearly all of it is disposable. In fiscal year 2011, Adrian College students, spent a whopping $6.7 million dollars on off-campus rent, meals, and entertainment alone (Anderson Economic Group, 2013). This is in addition to the room, board, books, and supplies expenditures they make on campus.

When your Admissions Growth plan is successful, you're going to experience occasional growing pains, and your local city council or village government will be more willing to ease the way for your institution if it understands, as ours does, that our recent enrollment gains provide widespread economic benefits throughout our region. In just the past few years, the city of Adrian has helped our college in many, many big and small ways. Relaxing parking restrictions on certain days has been a major help for our campus. Nothing creates bad PR for an organization like getting a parking ticket while you're running a vital errand. Now our students and their families don't have to have that ridiculous worry hanging over them during move-in and move-out days. Similar exceptions to parking ordinances are enacted for short periods every year during Homecoming and Family weekends, too. And of course, the city leaders know that on days like these, thousands of people come into Adrian, and those people dine in our restaurants, they run to the local stores for last-minute and forgotten necessities like a soda or a disposable camera or a granola bar. They spend thousands of dollars in our little town. This is why Adrian helps on these days by having local city police officers put up barricades and close streets during our Bulldog Fun Run 5K in the fall and for Commencement in the spring.

The increased tuition income produced by the Admissions Growth plan at Adrian College directly funds local economic growth, and this tuition launches the momentum that continues to grow on our campus and will grow on yours as your vital and newsmaking institution draws in more and more impressive donations and grants. These, too, will contribute to the economy of your surrounding area, just as Adrian College has poured millions into our region. In the years since I arrived in 2005, Adrian College has utilized tuition income, donations, and grants from a variety of sources to spend over $70 million in construction projects. We have invested over $1 million creating an open recreation space in Caine Terrace, $1.7 million in dining hall renovations, nearly $2 million in the new Spencer Hall, over $8 million in new and renovated housing facilities, around $13.5 million in our spacious and expansive renovation to the Jones/Peelle math and science building.

These funds go directly to planners, architects, and construction firms in our region. Anderson Economic Group's (2013) recent analysis of Adrian College's economic footprint estimates that 74 percent of our nonpayroll spending directly supports Michigan vendors, and the indirect economic impact of our expenditures, that growth, which is spurred when our vendors purchase goods and services from other vendors, more than doubles the effect of our nonpayroll expenditures on the Michigan economy.

These investments, produced by our campus expansion, become income for local businesses and employees. Our city leaders recognize how Adrian College's growth boosts the local economy, and they step up when needed to ease the way for our institutional growth. Recently, the city of Adrian has helped forward our progress by revising sign ordinances, allowing us to install a sign over the WOW Café American Grill & Wingery, which can be difficult to find if you don't know where it is, and has also allowed us to change the electronic LED sign facing the adjacent highway with a new message every thirty seconds, instead of restricting it to a single change every five minutes as dictated by the old ordinance. Our institutional expansion has genuinely turned into a partnership with the city, as city leadership has expedited permits on numerous occasions to facilitate our many expansion, renovation, and construction projects. The city also relaxed parking lot regulations for one year so we could have a "staging area" for bricks, wood, steel, and construction trailers during the Peelle/Jones renovation.

THE PEAK OF THE PYRAMID

Many other benefits are difficult to quantify, but they are a positive side effect of this model. They are best summed up in a new culture that is clearly evident at Adrian College: improved morale, increased vitality, an abundance of smiles, a passion for teaching and learning, spirituality, friendliness. All of these attributes are the result of continuing momentum of the growth that can be enabled by only one thing: funding. And all of this funding started with the increased enrollment generated by following the six steps of the Admissions Growth model.

Key Takeaways

1. The Admissions Growth plan brings more than additional students and revenue to campus. It creates additional benefits that build a vital campus and a healthy

community. It creates momentum and builds on that momentum of its own volition.

2. A vibrant campus is a result of vibrant students. These students carry their positive experiences with them when they visit other colleges as well as when they return home. Students then self-recruit to your institution. Inquiries go up, and so do applications.

3. This generation of students is constantly logged on to social media. When students share their positive experiences via Facebook, YouTube, LinkedIn, and the like, your institution will benefit from their online enthusiasm.

4. Campus improvements, new activities, and added extracurricular and cocurricular activities will garner media interest, and that will only allow your institution's momentum to continue to build on itself.

5. Improved campus facilities will become revenue centers of their own accord.

6. Admissions Growth is designed to improve recruitment, but your revitalized campus and community will drive retention numbers up as well.

7. Improved recruiting numbers will drive up graduation rates and numbers, and will mean more alumni. Your alumni will be better prepared to be leaders of the future because of the superb education Admissions Growth has funded at your institution. These alumni will play a key role in future development of your campus.

8. Your improved income will increase the vitality that improves community relations. Better funded and well-supported faculty will continue outreach activities that will improve your campus, your students' education, and your community.

9. Admissions Growth tuition dollars will fund economic growth for your region. This income will help you build continuing and lasting partnerships with local community leaders.

Why Haven't Other Colleges Tried This Before?

Fifty-Three Athletic Teams: Extracurriculars Matter, Even at Williams College

When you look at *US News & World Report,* you will find that most people consider Williams College to be the best college in the country among the small privates. Williams College is a winner: it has over two thousand students, it's seen as a very strong academic institution, an institution that only brings in the best students, an institution that has very, very strict admissions standards, an institution that has attracted great faculty members for generations. Yet if you look at its website, Williams College doesn't have sixteen intercollegiate sports, as Adrian College did when I arrived in 2005; it doesn't have the twenty-four intercollegiate sports that we have now. Williams College currently has thirty-two intercollegiate sports. It also has twenty club sports, many of which actively recruit students. So I would suggest that Williams College is using many of the same recruiting enticements that we use at Adrian College. Athletics plays a major role in how this great American college procures its student body. One of the primary reasons that people are going to Williams College is in fact academics, and the primary reason that people are going to Adrian College is also academics. But they're going for another big reason too, and that is all of the on-campus activities for students both colleges offer in their similar admissions strategies.

Williams College figured out a long time ago that when you get into the minds of seventeen-year-olds, you know they live in a world where their priorities are about having a strong in-class experience as well as a fun, exciting out-of-class experience, and they're going to pick a college that offers both. Faculty and administrators alike can wish it were different, we can wish that the only reason young people choose a college is for academics, but the truth of the matter is the extracurriculars are important reasons, also. So the answer to the question of why other colleges have not tried this before is that some institutions *have* tried an Admissions Growth plan of their own. And some, like Williams College, find that the program has been hugely successful for them.

Not an Easy Plan to Understand

Another reason that many colleges have not implemented plans similar to Admissions Growth is that it is not an easy plan to understand quickly. Presidents and senior administrators do need to sit down and really put pen to paper and see how the numbers play out to comprehend why this fairly expensive model actually has a return on investment that more than pays for itself and certainly leaves plenty left over to funnel into academic affairs. The plan is not something that can be summarized in a twenty-second sound bite, and in a culture where people like to understand things very, very quickly, many just haven't taken the opportunity to grasp the possibilities of this model.

And, in fact, Admissions Growth is not an easy model to understand. I knew this when Rick Creehan and I first began to implement the model at Washington & Jefferson in 2002. Later, when I spoke to executive search firms, I gave them very few details. When I interviewed for the presidency of Adrian College in the early spring of 2005, I told the committee I had a plan, but I gave them very few details. I had a very specific reason for playing my cards so close. Unless you hear the entire model detailed over a two- or three-hour period of time, you don't hear the key concepts of frontloading, accountability, return on investment, increased admissions, greater selectivity. When you hear it laid out quickly, what stays with you are some very distracting buzzwords and phrases: "athletics not academics," "backlash from faculty," and "more" of everything a college doesn't really want to deal with during a crisis: "more debt," "more land," "more facilities," "more big, new construction projects," "more risk," and all of those other frightening phrases that dissuade boards from investing the funds needed for the plan.

In a world of elevator speeches it is not easy to request and receive three hours of lecture time with trustees, but this is absolutely essential to gaining the support you need from the top. I essentially offered only hints about the Admissions Growth process until I could spend two or three hours with the trustees at our first meeting after I arrived. I knew that if I had uninterrupted time to walk through the entire plan, then I could help them see how each piece of the plan, the large initial outlays, the expansion of facilities, the new accountability of everyone involved in recruiting, especially of the coaches, all worked together to produce specific, measurable enrollment and tuition income goals. Just as importantly, laying the entire plan out for the trustees all at once, showing how each piece of the process is linked to the others, helped them see how and why one-third of the model or one-half of the model or even three-quarters of the model simply would not provide the dramatic results that Adrian College needed in enrollment growth. Showing your audience the whole plan in one well-organized presentation demonstrates the coordination of all of the parts, allows them to see how necessary the entire plan is to reach the results that we have achieved right here at Adrian College over the past few years.

Focus on the Return on Investment

Again, Admissions Growth is very expensive, and it is very expensive for at least a year before the institution sees significant returns. Adrian College put $30 million into this model with the belief that there would be a return on investment. Some schools don't have that borrowing capacity, some don't have that fund-raising capacity, some can't combine borrowing and fund-raising to come up with that number, some have very conservative presidents or boards who don't want to take on debt. In addition, some presidents are risk averse, especially during times of falling enrollment. The key problem to overcome here is that most boards and presidents and their constituencies don't have confidence that Admissions Growth will bring in a sufficient return on investment. The significant investment required early in the plan makes it a frontloaded model. Even if presidents and trustees have considered using this model, their attitude may be that the possible reward is not worth the anxiety of waiting for the return on such a considerable investment. Schools that want to put this plan in place will have to invest a large amount of money first. Though all schools will not want to follow our lead exactly, Adrian College needed a large return early, so our institution funded a Multi-Sport Performance Stadium and a marching band immediately and began the Arrington Ice Arena the year after that, with baseball, tennis, and track and field facilities added in short order, as well.

Building and improving facilities are not the only parts of Admissions Growth that require heavy frontloaded investment, though. You need to spend a lot of money in many areas for at least one year before you will see any results. I have already detailed in chapter 5 how you must increase your investment in more coaches and in coaches who are full-time and who have clear recruiting expectations. You will have to give these coaches budgets for equipping their teams and making recruiting visits. Sometimes these expenses include leasing cars for coaches and other recruiters. If your Admissions Growth plan requires new facilities, you may have to acquire land, and then, in addition to the standard construction costs, you will have to commission traffic studies, finance geological site surveys, and pay for various legal fees, building permits, and the like.

Presidents may also hesitate when considering a plan like the one implemented at Adrian College not only because it requires a large investment up front, but it also carries significant time costs. Especially if the campus you're working with needs large capital improvements, the board, the president, and senior administrators will have to be prepared to invest time and effort commissioning traffic studies and hiring contractors, applying for rezoning, working with city officials, ensuring neighbors are informed, on board, and treated fairly, and winning over naysayers and detractors—both on campus and off.

Your particular version of the Admissions Growth process will probably also include investment in nonathletic extracurriculars and cocurriculars, and these can require significant up-front investments as well. A band will require a director, a symphony will need a conductor, not to mention music, practice rooms, and performance shells or gazebos, in addition to the standard recruiting and travel costs.

Even nonathletic investments require significant up-front investments if you expect them to produce results. Few schools take advantage of the opportunity to utilize their school newspapers and broadcast production facilities to aid in recruiting academically promising students. To make these activities more attractive to potential students, you will need to provide funding for computers, cameras, microphones, editing equipment, and broadcasting technology, as well as advisors. Not to mention that, if you follow the Admissions Growth model, you will also have to hire someone who will recruit for these activities.

Many presidents and boards of trustees may back away from this plan, not just because of the risk of investment, but also because of the yearlong—minimum—wait for returns. But the biggest risk is to do nothing at all, because schools that drop beneath one thousand students may be headed for extinction if they don't make some dramatic changes to their student population as well as to how they bring that population in and retain it.

Even so, schools are unlikely to try this model because they believe that going down this road de-emphasizes academics. Obviously the talk is about athletic teams and marching bands, or it can be about student newspapers—the list of possible extracurriculars is almost endless—but it is not always about what happens within the four walls of the classroom. So faculty and administrators look at Admissions Growth as something that emphasizes what colleges should not make priority one: namely the out-of-class experience. The face-value emphasis on athletics and other campus activities makes some people reluctant to jump into the Admissions Growth plan.

Lead from the Top

Related to this reluctance to execute the Admissions Growth plan are situations where presidents fear backlash. On many campuses presidents might be apprehensive that the faculty will begin to get vocal by objecting to this model. If they do, then faculty members might take a vote of no confidence or go to the board of trustees to argue that the president does not place appropriate emphasis on academics, and this can create problems for presidents. So if the administration does not start with enough faculty "buy-in" at the beginning of the program, it does take a certain amount of courage to implement Admissions Growth. Of course, this program also requires a president who can articulate its requirements and benefits clearly to all constituencies: trustees, faculty, administration, and in some cases, the community at large. Some presidents just cannot communicate the plan accurately with enough emphasis on long- and short-term benefits, and some presidents simply may not have an adequate forum or platform for reaching all of these constituencies effectively. However, Admissions Growth is a model that requires leadership from the top to be successful. From the very beginning at Adrian College, the Board of Trustees and administrators had considerable confidence that there would be a return on such a large frontloaded investment or the college would have been in trouble very, very quickly. Grassroots support is important over the long haul, but not at the beginning. Remember, *you* are the one who has the vision of the long-term gains. The president is the one who must guide the vision and direct the plan for the vision. But you must have the support of the trustees or your governing board to implement this plan. If you don't, it doesn't matter what you want to do, you won't be able to do it.

Head Off Faculty Backlash

Clearly the most frequent and serious likelihood of backlash will come from faculty members. This is why the board must support the president 100 percent from the beginning. Faculty concerns usually fall into two categories: The first is the initial focus on extracurricular activities. Faculty, especially faculty who have been enduring cuts and substandard conditions and below-average pay scales will see money being spent, and they will resent it. Admissions Growth often requires heavy investment in land and facilities that need to be built or significantly improved. Faculty will see many new people being hired, at a time when they are feeling overworked and have likely been seeing cuts or hiring freezes in their own departments. They will see budgets being prepared and funds being spent on travel and equipment when their own travel funds have been drawn down or are nonexistent. Faculty will see that very little of the initial investment is directed toward them and their departments, and they will feel left out of the new growth. If faculty members believe that the priorities of the institution have changed, they will push back.

Constant communication with faculty will soften backlash and associated problems. One skill a president who implements the Admissions Growth strategy must have is the ability to help professors see the long-term payoff for the college and for them. One of the president's jobs is to help them see that future academic investments will be prioritized when the campus has experienced just a few years of enrollment growth and rising tuition income. At Adrian College, as soon as we implemented the Admissions Growth plan, which we termed Renaissance I, we immediately began planning for Renaissance II, those changes and improvements that the college's new growth would fund: more support staff, renovated academic buildings, improved Internet networks and wireless access, state-of-the-art video and radio production facilities, and of course, new lines for faculty funding as well as increased budgets for faculty salaries, travel, and professional development. The president must help faculty members understand that the success of the Admissions Growth plan will allow the institution to prioritize future academic improvements and that these investments will benefit them in a concrete manner after just three to five years of enrollment growth.

Enrollment First, Not Sports First

A second reason faculty may push back against the Admissions Growth method is an understandable fear of change and the belief that such change is going to lead to further cuts in the academic budget. At this point, the president absolutely must disabuse professors and other constituents on campus of the notion that this plan will make their institution a "sports first" college. Constant communication and transparency with faculty will show them that new funding for extracurricular activities is *not* coming from current academic budgets.

A president can cut down, combat, or even eliminate faculty pushback against the Admissions Growth method by reminding faculty members that the plan will produce more students. Adrian College's application pool, for instance, grew by over 300 percent in the first year. Having more students to choose from in admissions means that you can very quickly become much more selective, and of course, that means better students. Faculty members inherently understand that better students raise the quality of all interactions on campus. Having academically stronger students on campus frees faculty from teaching semester after semester of remedial courses as well as from turning their office hours into extended tutoring sessions for underprepared students. The president's primary communication goal while waiting with faculty to see the first results of the Admissions Growth system is reminding all audiences that it is not a "sports first" model, it is an "enrollment first" model. This is why the board of trustees must support the president 100 percent, from the beginning. If the board is not behind the plan, then faculty members can push back against a plan they fear is making the college academically weak. These are the types of fears that can begin a movement toward a no-confidence vote.

Some presidents don't see their problems as fundamentally enrollment based. As American inventor Charles Kettering said: "a problem well-stated is a problem half solved." The problem for at-risk small private institutions is *low enrollment*. The problem is not lack of fund-raising, not lack of gifts and pledges, not lack of money from summer camps and conferences. The problem is low enrollment. Enrollment makes up over 90 percent of the budget at small baccalaureate institutions, with the exception of a very few elite colleges. So the formula is really very simple: If you need more money, then grow the largest part of your budget.

One way to be sure that you are ignoring the best method of increasing your institution's income is to hold out hope for a few pipe dreams to prosperity. Presidents and boards can hope for one big gift or one huge bequest. They can believe it might be possible to profit from patents on pharmacological research or new technology produced on their campuses, when the fact of the matter is that the institutions that benefit from such research belong to a very exclusive club. Just a handful of R&D universities earned 95 percent of patents attained by institutions of higher education in the past decade (National Science Foundation, 2010). Sitting back and hoping for these outcomes is like playing the lottery. Any or all of these fortunate events *may* happen at your college, but they *probably* won't. Holding out hope for such windfalls is just another way of refusing to see that low enrollment is the problem and the Admissions Growth plan is the solution.

So Obvious, Few People Ever See It

This is also the place to say some small colleges have never embarked on a plan such as Admissions Growth simply because their leaders have never thought of it. It just never occurs to them. Presidents and senior administrators rarely consider following a much more quantitative approach to their student enrollment and admissions process. Key to the Admissions Growth model is the process of assigning accountability to more than just admissions counselors, namely to coaches, band directors, and the like.

Presidents and trustees might also conceive of their own version of the Admissions Growth model but end up avoiding or discounting its obvious benefits and ability to bring in motivated students because they are reluctant to bring more student athletes to campus. As I discussed earlier, there are some pretty unpleasant stereotypes floating around in higher education, and these perpetuate the idea that having too many athletes reduces the diversity of student interests on campus. Connected to this notion is the belief that a campus with more than a few athletic teams is a very homogenous place, one that doesn't encompass a diversity of ethnicities, of religious affiliations, and of academic and extracurricular interests. Plenty of people in secondary education hold the unfounded belief that all athletes are of the same mind and that if an institution brings in too many of them, they will overwhelm a campus with one set of viewpoints and opinions. So some administrators and faculty, and perhaps even trustees, are reluctant to embrace this model.

As I covered earlier, Williams College clearly has utilized a version of Admissions Growth to increase and stabilize enrollment, and that stability and the tuition revenue it brings has helped it to fund an academic program that is excellent by almost any measure. In fact, many colleges with superior academic reputations leverage their athletic teams to grow enrollment. Again, they just choose not to highlight that particular strategy when they discuss enrollment plans or promote their academic distinctions. Clearly, the Massachusetts Institute of Technology (MIT) has utilized a version of the Admissions Growth model, at least in part. MIT has thirty-two intercollegiate sports teams as well as thirty-four club teams.

The campus has an ice arena, football stadium, and baseball stadium, separate fields for track teams and for field hockey, tennis courts, and facilities for squash as well as for swimming, diving, and water polo, a boat house, and a sailing pavilion. MIT certainly has a reputation that would suggest it doesn't need a model like Admissions Growth, but perhaps undergirding that reputation of strong academic credentials is a model that partially funds academics through the tuition that student athletes contribute to the budget. Even if MIT didn't use this model to grow, it clearly sees the benefit of fielding sports teams, even on a very academically respected campus.

Admissions Growth Stabilizes Enrollment

Presidents who do not see their problems as fundamentally enrollment based will not see the need to make the necessary investments to grow their enrollment. The beauty of this model is that it stabilizes a college's enrollment over the long term. However, leaders at institutions that would truly benefit from the Admissions Growth model may not understand the investments required to grow enrollment. Matriculation fluctuates a great deal in higher education. A small school may have strong enrollment one year and low numbers the next, and it is easy to see your tuition income fall extremely rapidly with just a few down years. Presidents might plan to increase income by lowering the discount rate and hoping to enroll the same number of students. But lower discount rates don't help schools that bring in a strong freshman class each year and keep losing students through attrition, year after year. Admissions Growth solves this problem by bringing onto campus students who are actively engaged in teams and other activities that will bring them back for four years. Many colleges focus on growing enrollment through traditional first-contact methods. They host more college fairs, arrange more high school visits, hire more admissions counselors. All of these channels are important, but none are the answer to falling enrollment. Making initial contact with students, bringing students and their parents to visit campus, and getting them to fill out admissions forms is just the first half of the equation. The second half is extracurricular activities that are unique to your campus and offer a vital sense of identity, belonging, and engagement to students.

If presidents are distracted by ineffectual ways of raising money or inefficient recruiting methods, they will take their eyes off the ball. Presidents of small private institutions must be focused on the root of their problem, and the root of their problem is falling enrollment. Enrollment is their source of a school's income, and income provides students with a quality education by funding investments in professors, in facilities, and in infrastructure such as Internet access.

Few institutions have tried this approach, and those that do don't publicly address it in terms of enrollment growth. It is clear that some colleges have instituted a type of Admissions Growth plan similar to the one outlined in these pages. They simply don't label it Admissions Growth, and they certainly don't publicly credit the plan for their successes. The kind of leader who can understand the potential of such a plan and introduce it successfully is what your small baccalaureate institution needs. That is the kind of person I describe next, in chapter 9.

Key Takeaways

1. Many great schools use this enrollment model to get strong and stay strong. Honesty should compel all of us to admit that today's students pick a college for many reasons. Academic offerings and scholarly reputation are only two of these reasons.

2. Trustees and administrators must take time to fully understand how the model works before making a decision to implement Admissions Growth. The strategy and process cannot be captured in a twenty-second sound bite.

3. In understanding the model, your focus must not be on "costs to implement." Your focus must be on "return on investment."

4. Presidents and administrators must be willing to commit significant time to implementing the model. Quality implementation requires significant oversight and diligence.

5. For most small privates with dwindling enrollment, the biggest risk is to do nothing.

6. This model requires leadership from the top. Presidents must be ready to lead with boldness and confidence, or the forces aligned against the changes this model requires will prevail, and enrollment will continue to fall.

7. Constant communication with the faculty will mitigate resistance.

8. The president's message to faculty should emphasize the academic improvements that can be implemented once Admissions Growth—and the resulting financial windfall—takes place.

9. Remind all involved that Admissions Growth is not a sports-first plan. It is an enrollment-first plan.

10. Pipe dreams are not strategies. Unexpected institution-changing gifts as well as other sources of major revenues probably won't appear. Hope is a wonderful

emotion but a poor strategy. Admissions Growth is the sure and steady approach to financial security.

11. Admissions Growth stabilizes enrollment, and thus, revenue. This allows your institution to have a stable financial plan with which to fund a quality education for students.

CHAPTER 9

Who Will Implement Admissions Growth Successfully?

I consistently tell people on my campus that the most important thing that happens at Adrian College every day is the teaching and learning process that occurs in the classrooms throughout campus. Education tops everything else in importance. It is the way out—the way forward—the answer to most of the problems facing our country.

Lives are transformed in the classroom. The wisdom leading to everything from medical advances to breakthroughs in information technology is gained through education. The role higher education plays to advance modern society can't be overstated. Small private colleges are a critical asset and an important option for all students. But, as I've pointed out earlier in this book, it does not matter how many excellent professors you have on your faculty or how many peer-reviewed articles they produce. If you don't have students sitting in front of these professors each time they teach class, the educational process falls apart, and nothing can be taught or learned.

All of this serves to underscore the importance and value of Admissions Growth. It clearly illustrates how all of us—professors and administrators—can benefit from a well-implemented plan. The plan, however, won't just happen because a president or a leadership team on campus says that it should happen. A particular type of leader is required, one with specific skill sets in important areas.

Leadership

Bookstores are full of books that spell out the essential elements of leadership. But these books are not focused on the particular type of leadership that is required to implement this plan from the corner office at a college or university. Presidential leadership that seeks to implement a "sea change" in how we generate enrollment in higher education has some similarities to leadership in other professions—business, church, politics—but it requires some differences as well. This chapter spells out the most essential leadership qualities that will serve college presidents who attempt to grow their institutions via the Admissions Growth model.

Willingness to Confront Reality

In order to garner the courage that is required to implement this model on most campuses, presidents need to confront reality. In October 2011, the U.S. Department of Education released a list of colleges that failed its financial responsibility test, and 150 of the 180 schools on the list were small private, nonprofit institutions. Many small colleges are in trouble, perhaps only two or three slow recruitment years away from extinction. Our budgets are built on enrollment. Unless we figure out how to grow enrollment quickly and then stabilize larger classes for many years to come, we could be on the endangered species list.

Our institutions are expensive. There is a reason why public universities teach classes of five hundred students: it is far less expensive to do so. In order for us to provide personal attention with tenured professors in classes of fifteen to thirty students, we need significant resources, resources that are nearly always provided through tuition, room, and board. It is absolutely true that we are "tuition driven." If fewer and fewer students select small private liberal arts colleges because we are perceived to be too expensive, then we may be riding a business plan that cannot sustain itself much longer.

This is not conjecture. Consider data from a 2012 Lawlor Report on college affordability and the marketplace realities that confront educational leaders:

- 89 percent of prospective college students' parents said "paying for school" was a primary concern.
- 62 percent of students entering college in 2010 agreed that the "current economic situation significantly affected" their choice of college.

- 55 percent (of 2010 first-year students) said that being able to afford college was "challenging" (Lawlor Group, 2012).

It is time to face these facts and it is time to worry. This is our reality and we must confront it.

Transparency

All you have to do is look at the state of many small private colleges in this country to see that big changes are required to fashion a new model that can give us the resources we need to not only survive but to flourish. These changes must be bold and aggressive, as well as far different from how we have attracted students in the past. Leaders should make these changes openly and without apology. They should articulate to alumni, students, faculty, and staff that our future depends on significant investments inside and outside the classroom that will attract new students. In doing so, they not only build trust and a clear vision of the future, they also unleash creativity in those who can offer suggestions on how the model can be tailored to fit the needs of a particular campus community. If leaders try to implement this Admissions Growth model quietly because they fear faculty backlash or board disapproval, then they will quickly be seen as less than transparent, and a whole new set of problems will arise.

Impatience

Conventional wisdom would suggest that campus leaders must implore various constituencies to be patient as new facilities are built, recruiters are hired, and programs are put in place. But this model requires leaders to push ahead at lightning speed in order to experience the enrollment growth that will justify the investments and yield results that are so badly needed on many of our campuses. Leaders need to be impatient. For example, at Adrian College, once we decided to build a new stadium for football, lacrosse, and soccer, we moved ahead with a justified sense of urgency. We hired an architectural firm within a few weeks, we began construction soon after, and we were playing games on our new field less than nine months after we broke ground. This required impatience. Despite calls to slow down, to form additional committees, and to consider why "we've never done it this way before," we pushed ahead quickly because we knew we would only see a return on that investment once that facility could be used to bring enrolled students to campus. The same is true for our campus ice arena. Less than one year after I presented the plan to our trustees, the facility was open, and we had over 180 students waiting to enroll and play ice sports at the college. We were impatient. If people don't feel the urgency of the moment at small liberal arts colleges, then they are probably the wrong people to have on your staff.

Creativity

Leaders must be creative and tweak this Admissions Growth model to fit the culture on their campuses. In other words, the model outlined in this book is only a *template*. Presidents must consider their college's history, its location, and the programs that have worked well in the past in order to identify what can work at their schools. For example, Adrian is in Michigan, a Midwestern state with cold weather and a deep history of successful hockey teams. The Detroit Red Wings play seventy-five miles from Adrian, and they are one of the most successful professional teams in the history of team sports. There is a culture of hockey in Adrian that made it an easy sport to implement at the college. But hockey may not work in southern Florida. Perhaps sport fishing is the extracurricular program to build in southern Florida. In southern California maybe a surfing team is the program you should leverage. In Maine you might be able to leverage an outdoor activity (e.g., kayaking) to grow enrollment. If your campus culture is historically rooted in social justice and activism, could a program in Peace Corps preparation be developed to enroll students who would not normally attend your college? If your college is strong in culinary arts, can you cultivate a program that competes in national cooking competitions? The possibilities are as endless as the creative mind can conceive. It is up to bold, creative leaders to lead the way and inspire others to help them with new ideas. A quick search of the Web can give you some unique ideas that have worked at other schools, ideas that attract qualified, high-achieving students who would not otherwise attend your institution. For example, the University of Florida has won the Collegiate Bass Fishing Tournament two years in a row: 2012 and 2013 (Collegiate Bass Fishing, 2013). I suspect they are attracting academically excellent high school graduates who also share a love of bass fishing. Recently, Trinity College in Connecticut lost its first squash match in fourteen years after setting an NCAA record of 252 wins (Bello, 2012). I am sure that Trinity attracts squash players from around the world who would not normally apply to the college without this unique niche sport.

Ingenuity

Ingenuity is a close cousin to creativity. If creativity is "the ability to transcend traditional ideas, rules, patterns" and the like, as the dictionary tells us, then ingenious people take creative ideas and cleverly refine them to better meet the needs of particular situations. For example, at Adrian College we "tweaked" the marching band by adding a drum corps and several baton twirlers to refine an already good idea. This added approximately ten more students to the band—to the list of positions for which we could recruit—without changing the basic structure of a strong and popular extracurricular activity. And remember, when your return on investment per student equals $20,000, then adding ten students is significant. As I've mentioned a few times already, small privates such as Adrian College only need about four hundred students in each freshman class to maintain a thriving campus, so every activity does not necessarily need a recruiting goal of two or three dozen undergraduates.

Trust

Two types of trust are essential in order for the Admissions Growth model to be successful. First, board members, faculty, staff, and other campus constituencies must trust that their leader will hold people accountable for recruiting students. If recruiting does not take place, then the investments in facilities and programs will not provide a return. It goes without saying that the leader must do his or her part to hold people accountable and to terminate those individuals who are not doing their jobs. Second, people must trust the model itself. The model will produce, the model will work. It does take time, but ultimately, your college will see a huge return in students. While it is nerve-wracking to spend millions of dollars on facilities, staff, and related program costs one full year prior to seeing a return, the results ultimately make the investments more than worth it.

Risk-Taking Abilities

It is true that the greatest risk brings the greatest reward. This model is built on a risk-reward continuum. If you risk a small amount of money, you will get a small number of students. If you risk a large amount of money, you will get many more students.

For example:

Build an ice arena (expensive) → attract 175–225 students

or

Start a bowling team (inexpensive) → attract 10–12 students

Remember: nothing is cheap; nothing is free. Even if you decide to start low-investment activities such as bowling, cheerleading, or a student newspaper, you still must spend money and do it right. Recently at Adrian College, we started men's volleyball. This is a relatively low investment for a relatively small reward. But it still required a cash investment. Men's volleyball requires uniforms, a net, balls, a coach, and travel money. It does not require a stadium, an ice arena, or even expensive equipment. Volleyball teams generally field a roster of twenty-four people. They do not bring in hundreds of students like football teams or multiple-team hockey programs. And yet, for a relatively small amount of money, colleges can see a reward of approximately eight new students each year. The same is true for golf. Men's and women's golf teams recruit four men and four women each year. These students purchase their own equipment. We simply provide a coach and a course and travel money. Supporting the team year after year is fairly low in cost. Even with apparel, travel, and tournament fees, the team costs under $14,000 a year, not including the coach's salary. Low investment on our end leads to low return in our student population. Eight new students each year is not a significant number in our student body. And yet if you add golf recruiting to volleyball recruiting to tennis recruiting to other low-investment sports, you ultimately can grow your freshman class by a significant number of students.

Focus

Once you decide on the activities you want to leverage, you need to remain focused on bringing these to fruition before embarking on several additional ideas. The tendency to become unfocused is a problem because, once the model starts working, many, many individuals will encourage you use it to leverage their own area of interest. For example, at Adrian College I was encouraged to start a rowing team by a group of staff members who rowed during their college years. They made this suggestion even though we don't have a suitable river, lake, or reservoir for practices anywhere close to campus. In addition, there are only three collegiate rowing teams within 160 miles of our campus, so the frequent long-distance travel would make such a team hard to manage and even harder to recruit for. I was encouraged to start a rifle team, even though we have no indoor location for such an activity and the campus is surrounded by residential areas. I was encouraged to start a curling team even though curling simply is not part of the culture in this area of Michigan.

Now, the people who presented these ideas were deeply passionate about their activity and made convincing arguments about potential student popularity. However, the problem was that these activities were not a good fit with Adrian's geography, location, and culture. It was important for me to remain focused and to not be susceptible to every proposal that followed the introduction of Admissions Growth on our campus.

Willingness to Hold Others Accountable

Leaders of the Admissions Growth model *must* hold people accountable. There is no other way to implement this model effectively. If recruiters are not held to account for their results, everyone will see that results don't truly matter in terms of job security, and the college will quickly slip into old and bad habits. Each recruiter must have a numerical goal to achieve. If he or she cannot achieve this goal in one or two years, then that person must be terminated and replaced by someone who can get the job done. Take a look at table 9. Recruiters, coaches, and administrators track inquiries, applications, acceptances, and deposits weekly and know that they are accountable for their results.

Results-Oriented

This model is built on results . . . period. Implement this plan only if you will expect and demand results. *To fall short of accountable results risks the entire investment.* Know the goal of each team and each activity and hire coaches and advisers who will get the results you need.

In order to get results, we provide constant feedback to coaches, admissions counselors, and administrators regarding their efforts. Each Monday every person responsible for recruiting students to our college receives a report on the number of inquiries, applications, "accepts," and paid deposits that they generate in their area. When people fall behind, we talk to them about it. The report compares each recruiter's results to those from previous years and to a three-year rolling average. This means that no one is surprised at the end of the year if they do not get the results we expected and agreed to when they took these positions.

Table 9. Weekly Report Generated Week Thirty-Two of Our Fifty-Two-Week Admissions Cycle for 2013

SPORT	GOAL	INQUIRIES	APPLICANTS	ACCEPTANCES	DEPOSITS
Women's Bowling	6	223	67	50	9
Baseball	10	270	81	61	11
Men's Basketball	7	197	59	44	8
Women's Basketball	7	197	59	44	8
Men's CC & Track	9	346	104	78	14
Women's CC & Track	9	346	104	78	14
Cheer	6	167	50	38	7
Dance	10	270	81	61	11
Women's Equestrian	8	124	37	28	6
Football	50	1,353	406	305	55
Men's Golf	4	124	37	28	5
Women's Golf	4	124	37	28	5
Hockey Club ACHA (4 teams)	32	617	185	139	25
Men's NCAA Hockey	8	223	67	50	9
Women's NCAA Hockey	8	366	110	83	15
Men's Lacrosse	8	270	81	61	11
Women's Lacrosse	8	270	81	61	11
Men's Soccer	8	223	67	50	9
Women's Soccer	8	223	67	50	9
Softball	7	197	59	44	8
Synchronized Skating	8	167	50	38	7
Men's Tennis	4	124	37	28	5
Women's Tennis	4	124	37	28	5
Volleyball	7	197	59	44	8

Ability to Work with Foundations

To work successfully with foundations, you need to understand a few things about the mind-set of the people who manage them. Foundations want to plant seeds. They don't want to provide operating funds into perpetuity. They want to see a plan, support a plan, and then move on to other projects. Admissions Growth is a plan that provides foundations a perfect opportunity to support a college, to fund initial growth and then to step back and move on to other needs. For example, if a foundation elects to support a rink or a stadium or a track & field complex, you will only need to build that facility once. This substantial, one-time investment by the foundation will bring in students continuously for generations without any additional cost for the locale, itself. To secure additional funds from foundations, a college president has to be able to communicate not only how such a one-time investment will benefit the institution, but also how the benefits will continue to accrue, year after year, even without additional funds from the foundation.

Agility

No one bats a thousand. You will probably pick an activity, sport, or program that simply does not work. For us, that was women's field hockey. We hired a women's field hockey coach shortly after we built the stadium, gave her a recruiting car and a credit card, and asked her to start a team by the following year. After three months on the road she returned to campus and told us that it just would not work. Too few high schools in Michigan have women's field hockey teams, and students in the areas of the country that do have several teams (Maryland, Massachusetts, Connecticut, etc.) simply would not travel all the way to Michigan to play at the college level. We thanked her for her honesty, gave her a small severance package, and ended the program. But we had to be nimble, agile. We had to let that part of the plan go and then find something to replace those students. We launched a bowling team, instead, and it has been a smashing success: by its second year, the team was ranked twentieth in the nation by the Collegiate Bowling Coaches Association, and seventeenth in the nation by CollegeBowling.com's Power Rankings (Adrian Bulldogs, 2012).

Our experience with the bowling team could not have been more different from ours with field hockey. About 339 Michigan schools have girls' bowling teams. Bowling is an indoor sport, sheltered from the harsh Michigan winters and growing in popularity throughout the state.

My point is this: leaders must be willing to admit failure, they must know when to cut their losses, and they must be nimble enough to change direction quickly when they need additional students to complete their model. Remember Admissions Growth is not about following the plan to the letter, it is always *only* about bringing in students. It is about *enrollment*.

And Finally . . . Courage

Courage inspires. Especially when it produces visible results. Presidents who have the courage to implement this model will see great results. These results will inspire others to pitch in, get involved, be creative, and work harder. On your campus, morale will improve, revenue will increase, visible change will take place, and a great sense of momentum will overtake your institution. Once you build it up, momentum is hard to lose. It will perpetuate itself through new students matriculating at your institution for many, many years. You only have to find the courage to follow this plan for the first, front-loaded year. When your institution starts seeing the results of Admission Growth in the second year, courage won't be necessary. This plan's successes will continue to show results. And your plan to grow enrollment will provide so many clear, easily quantifiable benefits that continuing to follow it won't be courageous, it will be clearly in the best interests of your institution and the many constituencies it serves.

American Education *Needs* Admissions Growth

A large part of my job, and the job of all college presidents, is to travel the world in search of donors, new ideas, new markets for students, and any link, connection, or person who can make our campus better in some way. As I travel to distant lands, one thing becomes increasingly clear to me with each passing year: America's higher education system is the envy of the world. I have yet to visit a country whose families who value education do not want to send their children to America. While outsourcing has negatively impacted nearly every area of manufacturing and many other areas of business and commerce in our country, higher education remains a strong magnet for insourcing from other countries Our product is not only fine, it is excellent. We should acknowledge this and be proud of our industry.

But a large part of our allure in other countries and a large reason why we educate students so well is the plurality of our institutions. The diversity of institutional options that students can select as they consider their own learning styles, personal likes and dislikes, and the type of institution that will give them the best opportunity to enter adulthood is outstanding. For some students, large public universities work best. These institutions graduate capable people year after year. For other students, colleges with strong religious convictions serve their educational needs very well. And still other students want to enroll in colleges and universities that offer strong preprofessional programs (engineering, computer sciences, aviation, aeronautics, etc.), colleges that will craft a student's four-year experience around a narrow field of study.

All of this is good and all of this is as it should be. Overall, we are a healthy industry, but part of the body is beginning to get sick, and until we recognize that we have a problem and begin to treat the problem of declining student enrollment at small liberal arts colleges with new ideas, strategies and approaches, we will get worse and worse. Additional institutions will close, and the great plurality of colleges that have dotted our landscape since before our country was founded over two hundred years ago will be diminished. This will be sad for us, sad for our faculty, but most importantly, sad for many students who simply need our type of education in order to complete a college degree.

I hope I am wrong. I hope the concern I see on the faces of my colleagues at presidential conventions is mistaken and that my intuition is simply in error. I hope our colleges are strong, enrollment is assured, and we are all wonderfully healthy. If this is the case, great. Our colleges will remain strong for generations to come with few changes, few investments, and very little need to think or act differently.

But if I am right and we are already seeing signs of significant problems in the long-term financial viability of our schools, then the Admissions Growth model outlined in these pages is important and worthy of consideration and discussion. I hope it is helpful to you. I write this book not as an advertisement for the school that pays my bills, but instead as a way to help *your* school become better, more robust, more financially secure, and on solid ground to enter the future offering the greatest gift any young adult can enjoy . . . a college education.

Key Takeaways

1. Successfully implementing the Admissions Growth plan requires specific leadership skills.

2. Before all else, leaders in higher education must be realists—not optimists, not pessimists—but realists.

3. And reality suggests that many small private colleges in this country are in trouble financially.

4. Increasingly, small private colleges are perceived to be too expensive, and this perception isn't getting better, it's getting worse.

5. Boldness and transparency should guide all leaders who decide to implement this plan. Without these two characteristics leading the way, the plan will not succeed.

6. Patience is not a virtue. A firm decision to move forward quickly and to make big changes immediately is the key to success.

7. Leaders must be willing to transcend traditional ways of growing enrollment and commit themselves to this model in order for it to work.

8. Leaders must be willing to trust the model, trust the plan, before beginning implementation. If you don't trust the plan, it is easy to discard before real results are appreciated.

9. If leaders are not willing to terminate nonperformers, they should not implement this model.

10. Admissions Growth relies on accountability and results. People who cannot get results need to be dismissed from the college.

11. This model requires leaders who take risks. It is not for the faint of heart

12. Leaders must be focused doers. Real change is required with this model. The only way to utilize the Admissions Growth model successfully and increase your enrollment is to be willing to be an agent of change.

13. Small private four-year institutions are worth saving. Admissions Growth is a plan that is worth pursuing. It can help your school become strong, vital, and financially secure.

Afterword

Mike Rogers, U.S. Representative, Michigan, 8th District (R)

I graduated from Adrian College in 1985, during a time when enrollment had been increasing after some lean years. It was a great undergraduate experience for me with the faculty-student relationships providing personal attention and small class sizes, the comparative advantage that small liberal arts colleges offer over their large public counterparts. Because of these relationships, I, like alumni of many small liberal arts colleges, kept an eye on my old school even as I pursued my own career.

For twenty years, I read the alumni magazine to stay abreast of my friends from college as well as news from campus. Though I did not return to Adrian College often, when I did I would stop in to see old professors or say hello to my former football coaches and observe what had changed since my undergraduate days. Over time, with another decline in enrollment and tighter budgets, deferred maintenance appeared to be an issue, and the people I spoke with seemed concerned about the college's future. Clearly my alma mater was enduring a down cycle with fewer resources. That alone made it difficult to attract outstanding professors and create new programs to captivate prospective students.

As I learned about the challenges facing Adrian College, I realized through my committee work in Congress that many other small private colleges are facing these same pressures. The similarities between these small colleges are striking. Though most have enjoyed storied histories and loyal alumni bases for hundreds of years, this history does not indemnify them against the economic realities that now confront families with college-age children. Even if families want to enroll their children at these colleges, it is questionable whether they will do so given cost and student debt load.

In 2005, when Adrian College welcomed a new president with a very unique business plan to grow enrollment and balance the budget, I was cautiously optimistic. He promised to fund this plan through private donations and new enrollment revenue. As a conservative in Congress, this made me very happy.

Like many alumni, it took me a while to see the "method to Docking's madness" when he quickly spent $35 million on new facilities—most of it going to athletics—and faculty were asked to be patient for two or three years until classrooms could be filled with new students. But the "build it and they will come" strategy worked admirably, and I could soon see the changes everywhere on campus. Hundreds of new students filled the sidewalks, and new academic programs soon followed. New dining halls, dormitories, and classrooms were needed to accommodate the growth, and the feeling of momentum and vibrancy on campus was palpable.

Now nine years later when I visit campus, I see a thriving institution with a secure future and outstanding students walking across the commencement stage ready to assume their leadership role in our society. This is a good news story, and I'm proud to be part of it as an alumnus and someone who cares deeply about education and the transformative role it plays in the life of our nation.

While I am impressed with the results, I am also impressed with the role private foundations, individuals, and families played in Adrian College's ascension. He and his senior team on campus combined the power of ideas with an entrepreneurial spirit and a lot of hard work to completely transform a struggling institution. I hope that other college leaders throughout the country will copy this template to elevate their own private colleges to new levels of growth and excellence.

There certainly needs to be a place on the educational list of options for young people to choose colleges that place teaching first and that fulfill the promise to guide each student personally in pursuit of their educational goals and aspirations. The continuing story of Adrian College is a model for many other small colleges to ensure that quality liberal arts education remains a highly valued option and its life-long benefit for future success impacts thousands of graduates for years to come.

Keeping College within Reach: Improving Access and Affordability through Innovative Partnerships

Testimony of Jeffrey R. Docking, Ph.D.
President, Adrian College
Adrian, Michigan
Hearing before the
Subcommittee on Higher Education and Workforce Training
Committee on Education and the Workforce
United States House of Representatives
September 18, 2013

Chairwoman Foxx, Ranking Member Hinojosa, and members of the Subcommittee, I thank you for the opportunity to appear here today to discuss a unique business model that Adrian College created eight years ago to reverse a downward spiral in enrollment, revenues, and the academic quality of our students. This entrepreneurial approach to saving our College ultimately gave us the revenues we need to create innovative partnerships with businesses and enhance access to students throughout the Midwest.

Let me explain.

In 2005 Adrian College dropped below 900 students and was saddled with a $1.3 million annual operating deficit. Three of our dorms were closed, our deferred maintenance bills reached several million dollars, and leaky roofs and dandelions were a constant sight on campus.

The academic quality of our students also suffered. We attracted only 1,100 applications in 2005 and rejected only 71 students. Essentially it was open enrollment.

Many freshmen were not prepared academically to attend a private liberal arts College so they either failed out or quit before they graduated; our retention rate stood at 59 percent.

Our problems were compounded by our location in southeast Michigan. Adrian College is located 60 miles southwest of Detroit, a city currently undergoing bankruptcy protection, and our major local manufacturing base is in automotive parts, a very troubled industry during those years. The perfect storm descended upon families that wanted to send their children to college, especially a private college. People openly questioned whether Adrian would survive these circumstances.

But Adrian did not close, it thrived. During the past eight years our enrollment doubled to over 1,700 students and our annual budget increased from $28 million to over $64 million. Our retention rate stands at 85 percent and our freshmen classes grew from 263 in 2005 to 665 last fall. We built over $60 million in new facilities and started five new graduate programs, eight academic institutes, and nearly doubled our endowment. Each year we have given raises to our employees, hired additional workers, and expanded benefit coverage.

At Adrian, we like to joke that we skipped the Great Recession.

How have we done this? How under these circumstances were we able to attract more students and make college affordable to the families in our state?

We did it through a unique business model that relies on strategic investments, measurable results, and accountability. This model, which I can discuss further during the question and answer period, responds to the needs of students and the job market in Michigan. It requires us to listen closely and respond quickly to the voices of employers and families, and it works very well as you can see from the story I just recited.

•   •   •

When Adrian started to flourish we looked for innovative partnerships with businesses that could advance the College's educational mission while cultivating talent needs in our business community.

Let me list a few here.

In recent years we allocated money for students to conduct micro-research studies with local businesses leaders. Several students have worked with businesses who want to optimize social media and web-content marketing to expand their operations.

In addition several other students worked with the Michigan International Speedway to test pond water, catalog indigenous flora, and develop statistical modeling methods to control invasive species on 1400 acres at this important business in our community.

Other examples include psychology students working with local doctors to gain a broader understanding of the Placebo Effect. Students conducting research with businesses on potential hydrocarbon reserves in our area, and a student working with an startup apparel company to build a business plan.

In addition to micro-research we recently finished construction on three campus incubators that students use to start businesses in our small town of 23,000 people.

These incubators will not be limited to our students. If local residents want to use our business professors and facilities to incubate an idea, we are open to having them on campus at no charge.

My third example of innovative relationships occurred two months ago when, under the leadership of the Michigan Colleges Foundation, 11 small college presidents in Michigan organized a two-day retreat with major business leaders to discuss *the talent gap:* The gap between the skills business leaders say they need when they hire recent graduates and the skills these graduates actually bring to their new jobs. Forty-five CEO's and high-level executives from companies such as Dow Chemical, The Kellogg Corporation, Amway, and Stryker joined the presidents to exchange ideas on this important topic.

Finally, we restructured our entire internship office to place students in businesses that openly express a desire to hire new workers. Students are told that their internship is actually a three month interview. If the company likes them they will be hired.

I could provide you with many more examples of how innovative partnerships with our local business community have helped our region. But in the interest of time let me end by saying that these partnerships have given us the resources we need to expand our financial aid offerings and provide greater access to higher education for many young adults.

This emphasis on making education more affordable reached its climax at Adrian College last week when we announced a new guarantee to all incoming freshmen: Beginning in the fall of 2014 all freshmen will be guaranteed a high-paying job of at least $37,000/year or part or all of their student loans will be paid for them.

I thank you for the opportunity to share some of what we've done at Adrian College and I am open to any questions you may have.

Memorandum: Economic Scope Analysis for Adrian College

Memorandum

Date: November 26, 2013

To: Dr. Jeffrey R. Docking, President, Adrian College

From: Samantha Superstine, Senior Analyst, Anderson Economic Group

Re: Economic Scope Analysis for Adrian College

Cc: Robert LeFevre, President, AICUM

Purpose of Report

On behalf of Adrian College, the Association of Independent Colleges & Universities of Michigan (AICUM) commissioned Anderson Economic Group (AEG) to estimate the economic footprint of Adrian College in the State of Michigan.

Overview

We define economic footprint as the total economic activity in the region (in this case, in Michigan) that is associated with or supported by an institution. The economic footprint analysis in this memorandum includes all spending, employment, and earnings associated with Adrian College operations and student spending. Adrian College and students at Adrian contribute to the Michigan economy in two ways:

- The direct spending that enters the Michigan economy in a variety of industries; and
- The indirect, additional economic activity that occurs as a result of the re-circulation of the direct spending in the Michigan economy.

We present the total spending, earnings, and jobs by taking the initial direct effects, and adding the indirect effects. See "Appendix A. Methodology" on page 6 for details of our estimation methods.

In this memo, we describe and calculate the components of Adrian College's economic footprint in Michigan for fiscal year 2011 (FY 2011). The total economic footprint of Adrian College in terms of spending, earnings, and jobs is summarized in Table 1 on page 2.

Table 1. Economic Footprint of Adrian College, FY 2011

	Direct	Indirect	Total
Spending (millions)	$54.8	$39.8	$94.7
Earnings (millions)	$18.1	$12.8	$30.9
Jobs	365	208	572

Source: Adrian College, IPEDS, Consumer Expenditure Survey, College InSight, BEA RIMS II Multipliers
Analysis: Anderson Economic Group, LLC

Spending by Adrian College and Students

We began by estimating Adrian's spending on payroll, goods, and services, as well as spending by Adrian's students. The spending that goes to vendors and employees in Michigan contributes to Adrian's economic footprint in the state, which is discussed in the following section.

Spending by Adrian College

Payroll Spending. In fall 2010, Adrian College employed 370 employees. In FY 2011, Adrian spent over $20 million on salaries, wages, and benefits for employees. Most of this spending remains in Michigan.

Non-Payroll Spending. Adrian College spent over $19.5 million in FY 2011 on goods and services for the college. This includes spending on:

- Instruction;
- Academic Support;
- Student Services;
- Institutional Support;
- Auxiliary Enterprises;
- Athletics; and
- Construction.

Figure 1 on page 3 shows spending by Adrian College by function, highlighting that payroll expenditures account for the largest proportion, followed by student services, institutional support, auxiliary expenses, and other expenses.

Figure 1. Adrian College Expenditures by Function, FY 2011 (thousands)

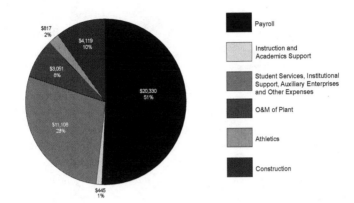

Source: Adrian College, IPEDS
Analysis: Anderson Economic Group, LLC

Student Spending

Adrian College enrolled 1,670 students for the 2010 fall semester. These students spent nearly $23 million in FY 2011. This estimate includes spending on the following:

- Room and board;
- Off-campus rent and food;
- Books and supplies;
- Apparel and basic needs; and
- Off-campus meals and entertainment.

Figure 2 below shows student spending for Adrian College, highlighting that the majority of which is on room and board.

Figure 2. Student Expenditures by Function, FY 2011 (thousands)

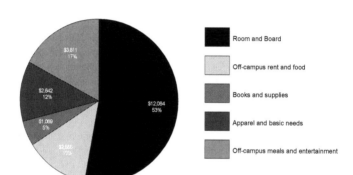

Source: : Adrian College, Consumer Expenditure Survey, College InSight
Analysis: Anderson Economic Group, LLC

Adrian College's Economic Footprint in Michigan

Adrian College contributes to economic activity in the state by adding direct and indirect spending, earnings, and jobs in Michigan. Below, we provide an overview of the scope of these three components of Adrian's footprint.

Spending

We quantify both the direct and indirect spending by Adrian College in Michigan. Many local vendors rely on spending by Adrian College for business. Additionally, local businesses rely on student and employee spending on goods and services in the area. Direct spending results from money spent in the Michigan economy by Adrian College and its students. Indirect spending is a secondary effect of this direct spending. As Adrian and its students pay Michigan vendors for goods and services, these vendors in turn spend more at local suppliers. Similarly, Adrian's Michigan-resident employees spend earnings on goods and services in the state, supporting additional spending to fill the need for those goods and services.

The direct portion of Adrian College's economic footprint includes three sources:

1. Payroll spending;
2. Non-payroll spending; and
3. Spending by students.

Adrian Payroll Spending. We estimate that $18.1 million (89%) of the $20.3 million in payroll spending remains in Michigan. These employees then purchase goods and services from local vendors, who in turn spend additional money in Michigan to support their businesses. We estimate that the additional indirect spending from Adrian's payroll expenditures is $7.5 million.

Adrian Non-Payroll Spending. We estimate that $14.5 million (74%) of the $19.5 million spent by Adrian in FY 2011 was spent on goods and services from Michigan vendors. Once we consider the additional spending on goods and services that is supported by Adrian's non-payroll spending, we estimate that total Michigan spending associated with Adrian's purchases from Michigan vendors is $31.2 million.

Spending by Students. Of the $22.7 million that students spent in FY 2011, we estimate that $22.2 million went to Michigan vendors. Once we account for the additional economic activity supported by student spending in the state, we estimate direct and indirect student spending totals $38.0 million.

Table 2 on page 6 shows the spending footprint in Michigan for Adrian's payroll and non-payroll spending, as well as student spending.

Table 2. Spending Footprint of Adrian College in Michigan, FY 2011 (millions)

	Direct	Indirect	Total
Payroll Spending	$18.1	$7.5	$25.6
Non-payroll Spending	$14.5	$16.7	$31.2
Student Spending	$22.3	$15.7	$37.9
Total	**$54.9**	**$39.8**	**$94.7**

Source: Adrian College, IPEDS, Consumer Expenditure Survey, College InSight, BEA RIMS II Multipliers
Analysis: Anderson Economic Group, LLC

Jobs and Earnings

All of this spending in the state results in indirect job creation in addition to direct employment by the university. The footprint for Adrian College in Michigan is 572 jobs, and $30.9 million in earnings. Table 3 below shows the direct and indirect jobs and earnings supported by Adrian College.

Table 3. Jobs and Earnings Supported by Adrian College in Michigan, FY 2011

	Direct	Indirect	Total
Jobs	364	208	572
Earnings (millions)	$18.1	$12.8	$20.9

Source: Adrian College, IPEDS, Consumer Expenditure Survey, College InSight, BEA RIMS II Multipliers
Analysis: Anderson Economic Group, LLC

Appendix A. Methodology

We define economic footprint as the aggregate spending, jobs, and earnings in Michigan that are associated with Adrian College.

Direct economic activity includes spending and employment by the college, while indirect and induced impacts stem from the recirculation of dollars within the defined geographic region. As Adrian College makes expenditures, the money is then re-spent throughout the Michigan economy, resulting in a "multiplier" effect. These indirect effects are also a significant contributor to Michigan's economy, and are thus included in the total footprint.

Direct Economic Footprint

Direct spending includes the following categories.

Payroll Spending. In order to determine the amount of payroll spending in the State of Michigan, we relied on data from the Integrated Postsecondary Education Data System (IPEDS) for FY 2011. Adrian College provided us with payroll spending by zip code, which we used to determine the amount of payroll for Michigan residents.

Non-payroll Spending. We obtained data from IPEDS on spending by function for FY 2011. We then relied on data from Adrian College to inform what proportion of this spending went to Michigan vendors.

Student Spending. To estimate student spending in Michigan, we used data provided by Adrian College on the number of students that lived on- and off-campus at Adrian College. We then estimated the student spending for several categories of living expenses:

- Room and board;
- Off-campus rent and food;
- Books and supplies;
- Apparel and other basic needs; and
- Off-campus meals and entertainment.

For each category, we estimated total spending for the total number of students, with the exception of books and supplies, which we calculated on a FTE-basis. Data for books and supplies is from College InSight.[1]

We obtained room and board costs for on-campus students from Adrian College. Spending on apparel, basic needs, and off-campus meals and entertainment are taken from the 2011 Consumer Expenditure Survey (CES) on annual expenditures by educational attainment.[2] We multiplied each of these annual values by 75% include expenditures that occurred during the time that students spend on campus. For students living off-campus, we assumed that spending was 10% higher for rent and food, apparel, basic needs, and off-campus meals and entertainment.

---

1. College InSight is an initiative of the Institute for College Access & Success, and provides data sourcing from IPEDS, Pell Grant files, Fiscal Operations Report and Application to Participate files, and Common Data Set files. Data can be found at college-insight.org.
2. Spending for "all consumers" is lower than for those with a bachelor's degree. We assume undergraduate students do not yet have a bachelor's degree, and therefore used the value for all consumers.

We assumed all room and board spending was in Michigan. For the rest of the categories, we assumed that some spending took place outside of Michigan, allowing for vacations, trips, and online purchases. We assumed that 35% of books and supplies were purchased online, and therefore the spending related to these purchases would not remain in the state.

Indirect Economic Footprint

We calculated the indirect economic effects of Adrian College expenditures by multiplying the direct expenditures listed above by final demand output multipliers based on those released by the U.S. Department of Commerce Department's Regional 2010 Multipliers (RIMS II) for the State of Michigan. We allocated spending to the following industries:

- Salaries and wages: Households;
- Employee benefits: Insurance carriers;
- Instruction & academic support: Educational services;
- Student services, institutional support, auxiliary enterprises, and other expenses: Junior colleges, colleges, universities, and professional schools;
- O&M of plant: Facilities support services;
- Athletics: Spectator sports;
- Construction: Construction
- Housing and food: Combination of accommodations and households;
- Books & supplies: Retail trade;
- Apparel & basic needs: Retail trade;
- Off-campus meals and entertainment: Food services and drinking places.

References

Adrian Bulldogs. 2012. Women's Bowling. Http://www.adrianbulldogs.com/sports/w-bowl/2011-12/releases/20120112gzc77n.

Anderson Economic Group. 2013. Memorandum: Economic Scope Analysis for Adrian College. East Lansing, MI: Anderson Economic Group.

Barker, M. M. 2011. Manufacturing Employment Hard Hit during the 2007–9 Recession. *Monthly Labor Review* 134 (4). Http://www.bls.gov/opub/mlr/2011/04/art5full.pdf.

Bello, Anne. 2012. Yale Men Defeat Trinity Squash, Ending Record Breaking Streak. College Squash Association. Http://collegesquashassociation.com/2012/01/18/yale-men-defeat-trinity-squash-ending-record-breaking-streak/.

Brown, R. n.d. List of Colleges and Universities That Have Closed, Merged, or Changed Their Names. Westminster College. Http://www2.westminster-mo.edu/wc_users/homepages/staff/brownr/ClosedCollegeIndex.htm.

Carbasho, T. 2005. W&J Enrollment Climbs as More Projects Take Shape. *Pittsburgh Business Times.* Http://www.bizjournals.com/pittsburgh/stories/2005/06/13/focus.5html.

Carnegie Foundation for the Advancement of Teaching. 2013. Size & Setting Classification [Data file]. Http://classifications.carnegiefoundation.org/descriptions/size_setting.php.

College Board Advocacy & Policy Center. 2011. Family Income. Trends in Higher Education Series. Http://trends.collegeboard.org/college-pricing/figures-tables/enrollment-and-income#Family%20Income.

College Board Advocacy & Policy Center. 2012. Tuition and Fee and Room and Board Charges over Time in 2012 dollars, 1972–73 through 2012–13, Selected Years. Trends in Higher Education Series. Http://trends.collegeboard.org/college-pricing/

figures-tables/tuition-and-fee-and-room-and-board-charges-over-time-1972-73-through-2012-13-selected-years.

Collegiate Bass Fishing. 2013. Tournament Results. BoatUS Collegiate Bass Fishing Championship. Http://www.collegiatebasschampionship.com/2013-tournament-results.html.

Fairbanks, A. M. 2011. For Recent Graduates, Starting Salaries Declined over Past Decade. *Huffington Post*. Http://www.huffingtonpost.com/2011/09/02/college-graduates-salary_n_946759.html.

Field, K. and A. Richards. 2011. 180 Private Colleges Fail Education Dept.'s Latest Financial Responsibility Test. *The Chronicle of Higher Education*. Http://chronicle.com/article/180-Private-Colleges-Fail/129356.

Gallup. 2013. Americans Unsure If Best Times for U.S. Are Past or to Come. Http://www.gallup.com/poll/159596/americans-unsure-best-times-past.aspx.

Gayles, J. and S. Hu. 2009. The Influence of Student Engagement and Sport Participation on College Outcomes among Division I Student Athletes. *The Journal of Higher Education* 80(3), 315–33.

GDA Integrated Services. 2010. Dwindling Interest in College Characteristics. Three Cues. GDA Integrated Services. Http://gdais.com/resources/newsletter/2010-fall.html#versus.

Gillen, Andrew. 2008. A Tuition Bubble? Lessons from the Housing Bubble. Center for College Affordability and Productivity. Http://www.centerforcollegeaffordability.org/uploads/Bubble_Report_Final.pdf.

Hart Research Associates. 2013. It Takes More Than a Major: Employer Priorities for College Learning and Student Success. *Liberal Education* 99(2), 22–29.

Irving, C. 2001. Muskingum College's Gutsy Move. *National CrossTalk: A Publication of the National Center for Public Policy and Higher Education.* Http://www.highereducation.org/crosstalk/ct0101/muskingumcollege.shtml.

Kawamoto, D. 2011. Financial Benefits of a College Education Are Smaller Than You'd Think. Daily Finance. Http://www.dailyfinance.com/2011/05/24/financial-benefits-of-a-college-education-are-smaller-than-youd.

Kellogg Commission on the Future of State and Land-Grant Universities. 1999. *Returning to Our Roots: The Engaged Institution.* Association of Public and Land-Grant Universities. Http://www.aplu.org/page.aspx?pid=305.

Kellogg Commission on the Future of State and Land-Grant Universities. 2001. *Returning to Our Roots: Executive Summaries of the Reports of the Kellogg Commission on the Future of State and Land-Grant Universities.* Association of Public and Land-Grant Universities. Http://www.aplu.org/page.aspx?pid=305.

Lacy, S. 2011. Peter Thiel: We're in a Bubble and It's Not the Internet. It's Higher Education. TechCrunch. Http://techcrunch.com/2011/04/10/peter-thiel-were-in-a-bubble-and-its-not-the-internet-its-higher-education.

Lawlor Group. 2012. Trends for 2012: Trend One: College Is Becoming Unaffordable. Http://www.thelawlorgroup.com/pov/more-intelligence/lawlor-trends-2012-trend-one.

Moody's Investors Service. 2013. Moody's: New Survey Finds over 40% of Universities Face Falling or Stagnant Tuition Revenue and Enrollment. Https://www.moodys.com/research/Moodys-New-Survey-Finds-Over-40-of-Universities-Face-Falling-PR_287436.

National Association of College and University Business Officers. 2011. U.S. and Canadian Institutions Listed by Fiscal Year Endowment Market Value and Percentage Change in Endowment Market Value from FY 2009 to FY 2010. Http://www.nacubo.org/Research/NACUBO-Commonfund_Study_of_Endowments.html.

National Center for Education Statistics. 2011. Projections of Education Statistics to 2019. Http://nces.ed.gov/programs/projections/projections2019.

National Center for Education Statistics. Back to School Statistics. 2012. Http://nces.ed.gov/fastfacts/display.asp?id=372.

National Center for Education Statistics, IPEDS Data Center. 2013a. Fast Facts: College and University Education: Enrollment. Http://nces.ed.gov/fastfacts/display.asp?id=372.

National Center for Education Statistics, IPEDS Data Center. 2013b. Generate Pre-defined Reports, Total Enrollment, Selected Years, Washington & Jefferson College [Data file]. Http://nces.ed.gov/ipeds/datacenter/reportdraw.aspx.

National Science Foundation. 2010. Academic Research and Development. Science and Engineering Indicators: 2010. Http://www.nsf.gov/statistics/seind10/c5/c5s4.htm#s5.

NCAA. 2011. NCAA Participation Rates Going Up. Http://www.ncaa.com/news/ncaa/article/2011-11-02/ncaa-participation-rates-going.

NSSE (National Survey of Student Engagement). 2012. Promoting Student Learning and Institutional Improvement: Lessons from NSSE at 13: Annual Results 2012. Bloomington, IN: Indiana University Center for Postsecondary Research.

Sander, L. 2008. Athletics Raises a College from the Ground Up. *Chronicle of Higher Education,* September 19, A1.

Schultz, M. 2008. MSU Awarded $550M Isotope Lab. *The Detroit News.* Http://www.detroitnews.com/article/20081212/SCHOOLS/812120373.

Sevier, R. A. 2010. Have College Brands Delivered on Their Promise? *University Business.* Http://www.universitybusiness.com/article/have-college-brands-delivered-their-promise.

SimpsonScarborough. 2013. In-Depth Interview Findings. Report Presented to Michigan Colleges Foundation, Lansing, MI.

Acknowledgements

Am I allowed to list a thousand names that truly deserve to feel the love? I suppose not. Pity, because this book is really the collective work of sales professionals all throughout the United States that I've had the privilege to know, observe, manage, coach, train or partner with over the past twenty-plus years.

Of course, a few names stand out, people who inspired me in one way or another to write this book. Jim Suth, one of the truly gifted sales minds and a truly great friend. Cassandra Grauer, one of the greatest people on the planet and a marketing wiz. Jason Forrest, one of the brightest sales leadership minds in the nation today. JoAnne Williams, whose very presence inspires me. Ruth Schwartz – thanks for pushing (and pushing, and pushing!). Tim Weeks, my Saturday morning advisor. And Wade Mayhue, whose assistance on this project was invaluable.

And saving the best for last… I thank God each day for His incredible blessings, and right at the top of that list is my wife, Karen, who knows me well and loves me anyway. I love you more each day, baby.

To the Author and Perfecter of my faith.

Introduction

This book is written for sales professionals who are looking for an added edge in earning the extra sales – the tough sales. This is not a sales "how-to" book nor is it a comprehensive work on sales theory. It is a resource book, a reference of answers to tough sales situations designed to help top performers in handling the most difficult of sales situations.

While I believe the ideas herein will help any sales professional to some extent, "Deal With It!" was written primarily for sales professionals who sell directly to consumers (or B2C, if you will). If your selling environment is primarily business-to-business I would suggest you peruse the Table of Contents to determine whether you might benefit from this work. Many business-to-business salespeople have told me that they found the principles insightful and applicable to their selling environment.

HOW TO USE THIS BOOK

For Sales Professionals:

If you are on the "front lines" of customer interaction you can use this book in three different ways:

1. Read it through from cover-to-cover and highlight as you go along. Then go back and put to use the things that struck you the most. Read it actively, take notes in the margins, and record your application ideas while they are fresh in your mind.

2. Look at the Table of Contents and flip ahead to the chapter that will make the greatest impact on your performance today. However, I urge you not to skip the opening segment on "The Mindset of a Top Performer". It is imperative that you understand the philosophical approach of great salespeople in handling the toughest of situations.

3. Keep the book on your bookshelf in your office and use it as an ongoing self-training manual. Pick one new skill to work on each week and really nail it down. Great sales counselors are notorious for driving their own self-improvement.

For Sales Managers and Coaches:

One of the most important roles you play in your position as a sales manager is that of performance coach. You can use this book to gain ideas on how to handle the situations that salespeople bring to your attention. Keep the book on your shelf and use it as a resource.

You might also find that the book makes for useful **sales meeting material**. You can go through a chapter each week and discuss the issues and suggestions. I have heard from countless sales managers over the past several of years who have used this book to enhance their sales meetings, with reports of riveting and highly applicable group discussions.

(If you would like to order multiple copies for your sales team we happily offer bulk discounts. Please send an e-mail to cassandra@ jeffshore.com.)

THE CHALLENGE TO...*ME*

At the risk of sounding arrogant, I consider myself to be an expert in sales. But while I claim a certain knowledge about the sales business, I do not claim to know every answer for every problem. You might disagree with some of the counsel I offer in these pages. *That's good!* Someone once said that if two people agree on everything, only one of them is thinking.

I challenge you to *challenge me* on these ideas. Try them on for size. Work with the concepts and put them into practice. It just might solve your problem. Or it might get you thinking of a different solution altogether. That's great - either way you win!

Ultimately, I want nothing more than to be a resource for the tens of thousands of people I hold in such deep respect: the sales professionals whose job it is to help people fulfill their dreams. Master the tough challenges and you'll find yourself amongst those who can prove that they are, indeed, GREAT!

The Mindset of a Top Performer

Everything can be taken from a man except for
the last of the human freedoms; the ability to choose
one's attitude in any given set of circumstances.

Victor Frankl

Many intelligent adults are restrained in thoughts, actions and results. They never move further than the
boundaries of their self-imposed limitations.

John Maxwell

ARE YOU GREAT?

I'm going on the assumption that you are a great salesperson. Not
"good" or "want to be great" – but *great*! It is important that you see
yourself as a great sales counselor, because your actions and behaviors
will always be dictated by your self-image. If you see yourself as mediocre, you will do mediocre things. If you see yourself as great, you
will do the things that great salespeople do. I'm not talking about arrogance and self-importance, but about the quiet self-definition of top
professionals that says, "I do what top performers do because I am a
top performer."

**Your actions and behaviors are always consistent with the way
you see yourself!**

Great sales counselors are positive energy people. They are driven
to goal achievement and they carry tremendous amounts of empathy

for their customers. They constantly seek to refine their skills, never being satisfied with "good enough". Great salespeople know that, at the end of the day, they are accountable to themselves for their own performance. They take pride in the job they do and they consider how they will improve all the more tomorrow.

Mostly, great sales counselors are inspiring. They maintain wonderful relationships with their peers, their friends and certainly with their customers. They experience success in the broadest sense of the word – financially, of course, but also in their relationships, their job satisfaction and their quality of life. People gravitate to these top performers because they see a confidence and assurance that they themselves often lack. Great salespeople have a way of drawing others to them and those who are drawn are better off for the experience.

I must say, parenthetically, that this belies the long-considered vision of a salesperson known for loud jackets, power handshakes, quick winks and schlock-y closing lines like, "What's it gonna take, little lady, to get you to move forward today?!" The fact is that today's prospects simply won't stand for this approach. They long for professionalism, empathy, and mostly to deal with real and authentic positive-energy people.

GREATNESS IN THE TOUGH TIMES

Again, I'm going on the assumption that you are a great salesperson and that, since you are great, you will do the things that great salespeople do. Like mastering the tough selling situations, for example. Your aptitude in facing down sales office challenges is one of the hallmarks of your own proficiency.

Over the years I've met many salespeople who see themselves as "successful". But they tend to base that success on the commission pace they are on, the car they are driving, or the pricey outfit they are wearing. In other words, they've made a lot of money so they must be successful. In fact, they must be *great* salespeople.

Not necessarily. In my opinion, greatness in sales means effectiveness and success *in good selling and conditions and bad.* I am not interested in those who are only successful given strong market conditions. In fact, if you need a great market in order to be a great salesperson, what does a weak market make you?

If you are looking for a real-life example look no further than the real estate meltdown of the late 2000's. The bursting of that bubble sent tens of thousands of real estate professionals – Realtors, mortgage brokers, builders, appraisers, etc. – rushing for the exits. Many of these people drew six-figure incomes for years, only to find that a dramatic market turn left them broke and looking for answers. Some left the business simply because they saw the writing on the wall. For others the business left them – their companies shut down or cut back to a skeleton crew. But for thousands of salespeople, the real estate crash was an awakening moment, a realization that circumstances will carry us for a time, but that the true and top performers find a way to sell *regardless* of market conditions. Their skills are sharp not by some genetic coding that inclines them to be great salespeople, but because they understand that constant and consistent growth is the only job security they really have.

Great sales counselors hone their skills in the strong markets in order to prepare themselves for the tougher markets. Moreover, they are both strategic and flexible in their approach to the sale. Like soldiers before a battle, they know both the strategy *and the contingency plans.* They have in their minds the picture of the perfect sale and they are prepared to deal with the difficult situations that they will undoubtedly face.

> There is one quality that one must possess to win,
> and that is definiteness of purpose, the knowledge of
> what one wants and a burning desire to achieve it.
>
> **Napoleon Hill**

Top performers understand that the difference between greatness and mediocrity is not identified when the wind is at our backs and the stars have lined up. What makes top performers great is how they perform in times of adversity – in the most difficult of days and the toughest of situations. Top performers embrace these challenges because they know that there are lessons to learn in times of adversity that cannot be learned in times of prosperity.

> The end of the matter is better than its begin-
> ning, and patience is better than pride.
>
> **Ecclesiastes 7:8**

It stands to reason that improving your ability to handle the tougher sales challenges should be a part of your professional success strategy. After all, we are not judged as successful based on how we handle the best of situations, but rather by how we stare down adversity. Anyone can sell when people are lined up and already motivated to purchase. It's those who excel in the challenging situations that stand apart.

As a sales trainer, I am frequently approached by sales professionals who say to me, "The customers just don't have any urgency." Here's a news flash: the customers aren't *supposed* to be urgent when they are considering a purchase. It is your job as a salesperson to help them create that urgency. What that salesperson is really saying goes something like this: "Unless the customers come to me already urgent to buy my product, I'm just not a very good salesperson." Great salespeople create urgency.

PREPARING FOR THE TOUGH SITUATIONS

So we have work to do, because dealing with adversity comes through knowledge, strategy, practice, preparation and attitude. Dan, a good friend of mine, is a pilot for a major airline. He flies 747s from the U.S. to Asia. As you might imagine, there is plenty of "down time" when the plane is flying through fair weather on cruise control for hours at a time. Dan is required to head to Denver on a regular basis for ongoing training and certification. And what do you suppose the training focuses on? For the most part the training is all about how to handle the tough situations – mechanical problems in flight, severe weather, terrorism threats, etc. What makes a great pilot great? Not the soft landings or the time it takes to get from point A to point B. A top-performing pilot is distinguished based on his or her ability to handle adversity, and to do so on the fly (pun intended). Dan prepares not for the best of situations but for the toughest, and when they come about he is more than ready. His training prepares him to handle the tough times with a cool head and a considered strategy.

Are you equally prepared? How much time do you spend preparing for adversity and for the difficult challenges you face? Top performers will tell you that having your presentation down solid will make all the difference when the rough situations come along.

The payoffs in preparation are fantastic. When you improve your capability for mastering the tough selling situations you...

- **Increase Your Skill**

  When you do something and it works, you find a natural desire to do it again – only better. Every time you face down a sales challenge and overcome adversity you prepare yourself for the next and bigger test that comes along. We become more skilled not by attending a training class that never moves beyond the basics, but by learning from the challenges and improving each time we face a tough situation.

- ## Increase Your Value

  The best salespeople in any industry get their fair share of sales…
  and someone else's fair share as well! They get the sales that mediocre
  performers miss, not based necessarily on better product or lower
  pricing, but on superior sales skills when the challenges are particularly difficult. In this way you increase your value – to you, to
  your customer, and to your company.

  Moreover, sales managers don't want the constant phone call from
  the salesperson who needs to be rescued out of every difficult conversation. The leadership of your company will greatly appreciate
  your expertise in deftly handling these tough situations. You'll find
  that others on the sales team look up to you, and you will become
  the "go to" professional who is rewarded with the best opportunities.

- ## Increase Your Longevity

  The discomfort associated with failure has a way of taking its toll
  on salespeople. If you are continually frustrated whenever a challenging situation arises you will find that you burn out far more
  quickly.

  Great sales counselors simply last longer because they see these
  situations as opportunities to grow and excel all the more. They
  take pride in their skill and they carry a tremendous confidence,
  knowing that they will get sales that mediocre salespeople will not.
  In fact, top performers come to embrace the tough challenges, seeing them as the opportunity to really shine. The tough challenges
  lead to deep psychological rewards in addition to the financial returns of being a superstar (I happen to believe that the former is a
  more powerful motivator than the latter).

- **Increase Your Boldness**

  Finally, when you stare down adversity and you come away with the sale, something amazing happens internally. You begin to learn that when you shrink *away* from the challenges you *lose* and when you *face* the challenges you *win*. This simple yet profound lesson causes you to be bolder the next time around. You have your strategy in place and you have the confidence that the strategy works. You can picture success in your mind, and you see the conversation play out exactly as you had planned it.

  Look at is this way. Boldness is very much like a muscle group. Neglect the muscle and it atrophies. It shrinks away to nothing and when you need to do some heavy lifting you cannot. But if you exercise that muscle group it becomes stronger. Work it more and it becomes stronger still. When you become an expert at diffusing the tough situations, your boldness muscle can do amazing things!

WHAT THEY DON'T TEACH YOU IN SALES TRAINING

> Ideas are great – they make us interesting. Decisions are great – they make us bold. But it is action alone that makes us the best.
>
> **Jeff Shore**

If you're like many sales counselors, your initial "training" consisted of the following instructions: "Here's the policies and procedures manual – here's your product – try not to get us sued." When I was first hired as a sales counselor I was simply told to head to my assigned territory and start selling.

Fortunately, I had an excellent partner who showed me the ropes (thanks, Pam!), but I soon discovered that the majority of what I needed to know I would have to learn on the fly. I faced various sales situations and I improvised as best I could. The learning curve was tremendous in those first few months (and I got my hand slapped more than a couple of times), but over time I learned the basics.

What I did *not* learn in those first months was how to master the more difficult situations that I faced in my sales encounters each day. When it came to things like dealing with difficult people, closing early in the process, or even remembering peoples' names, I struggled.

I thought I might find the answers in the sales training sessions that my sales manager provided from time to time. It didn't work out that way. Don't get me wrong – sales training is absolutely essential and I'm a big advocate. Effective training teaches new skills, and it keeps you fresh and motivated. But for the tougher challenges the learning comes by doing. Most of the difficult selling situations don't fit neatly into the "Critical Path" training module. In fact, veteran sales counselors will tell you that they learned 10% of what they know in a sales training program, and 90% through trial and error.

It has been said that experience is the toughest teacher because you get the test first and the lesson later. That is definitely true in sales. So much of our "training" comes from what is learned on the job, and the greatest of those training sessions come through dealing with tough situations. Each time we conquer a difficult challenge it prepares us for the future.

The good news is that you don't have to experience all those challenges yourself. You can (and should) learn from the experiences and observations of others. You are not the first person to deal with the tough negotiator, or with the person who only wants the product that has not been released for sale. Others have gone before you and have learned how to master these situations, turning them into fantastic selling opportunities.

LESSONS IN ADVERSITY

I was hired as a new home sales representative in February of 1987 in the Bay Area of Northern California. The market was strong in the mid-1980's and it would only get stronger for the remainder of the decade. I never lacked for sales in those early years. In fact, a good part of my job was handling campouts and managing long waiting lists.

I would have told you at the time that I was a great salesperson – and I would have meant it. I was driving a brand new BMW. I bought a new home. There was food on the table and a decent pair of shoes on my feet. By 1989 I was making more than my parents had ever made in one year – *combined*. Oh sure, I was highly leveraged and in debt, but with my income there was certainly no need to worry, right?

For those of you who are familiar with California economic history you know where this story is headed. In early 1990 the real estate market began its rapid decline into a deep slump. The downturn was sudden and unexpected. The decline was head-spinning.

At first there was denial. "This is a temporary thing. The market is bound to correct itself at some point." After that came excuses. "The problem is we just aren't getting good quality traffic. We need better ads." After a short while the confidence began to erode. And then the desperation began to set in. I had to face the reality that I was not prepared for a market downturn. I did not have the skills and I certainly did not have the mental toughness.

And that is when I first learned to sell. That was, in fact, the beginning of this book, though I didn't realize it at the time. I recognized that in a strong market I could blow off the customers with the tough situations. After all, there were always more (and easier) prospects just outside the door. But in a tough market I needed to embrace the difficult challenges that my customers raised.

One of my early mentors in sales was a gentleman (and I use that term with all its best meaning) named Bill Kinnaird. He was a veteran who had already seen tough markets and had lived to tell about them. Bill had a way of counseling his customers through their concerns with grace and ease. He was self-confident without being the least bit arrogant. The most important thing I learned from Bill was that it shouldn't matter what is happening in the market – a sales counselor should always be prepared to handle the challenges of any customer in any market condition. Bill taught me that handling tough situations in a strong market means you will maximize the opportunities that come your way, and that handling the tough situations in a weak market means you will get the sales that others will not.

I was a successful salesperson right out of the gate. But I was only an *effective* salesperson when I learned how to handle some of the more tricky aspects of sales in challenging conditions.

A WARNING

Dealing with difficult situations can be uncomfortable, at times extremely uncomfortable. It's been said that top performers do those things that mediocre performers find uncomfortable. I disagree with that assessment. I think top performers do the things that they themselves find uncomfortable…*but they do them anyway!* A tough situation to you might not be so to me, and vice versa.

Top performers are winners because they stare down their discomforts and refuse to allow their own uneasiness to dictate their actions. If you want to master the tough situations you will need to train yourself to embrace discomfort. You'll need to "flex your boldness muscle" as I stated earlier.

PRACTICING PERFECT

As in any discipline, be it sales, sports, theater arts, etc., practice makes perfect. Actually, that is only partially true. *Perfect* practice makes perfect. You will never become proficient in the discipline of mastering tough situation by reading a book. Your skills improve when you get outside your comfort zone and practice the techniques – *out loud!*

For some of you, the very words "out loud" make you uncomfortable. My advice: Deal With It! This is not about your quest for comfort but, rather, about your journey to greatness. For the sales professional, a large part of the process centers on presentation skills. Sales is a performance business. So like all performers, you must practice, and you must do so in such a way as to simulate the actual environment.

Actors are quite accustomed to dress rehearsals, where opening night is simulated from beginning to end. Football teams practice by donning pads and hitting each other – offense vs. defense in game situations. Sales professionals practice by presenting their arguments out loud over and over again, until the presentation is well rooted in the second nature. That's what great salespeople do. And you are, of course, a GREAT salesperson…right?!

The Faux Bluetooth

I am in the car a fair amount and I have the now-ubiquitous Bluetooth earpiece that I wear when I drive. You'll often see me driving down Highway 49 gabbing away. But you need to understand that I often wear the Bluetooth just so the other drivers don't think I'm crazy. You see, when I'm talking in the car I'm typically not on the phone!

I talk to myself incessantly. Why? Because I am a public speaker – I talk to people for a living. And I think it disrespectful to my customers if I just show up and wing it. No, I'd rather take the time to think through what I want to say and how I want to say it. And I'd like to practice over and over again so that I can get it down solid so that when I walk onto a stage I am not making stuff up. Public speaking can qualify as a tough situation at times. I want to know that I've practice perfectly, and that I am really ready for what I'm about to do.

FAILING SUCCESSFULLY

If you have as your goal to be a truly great sales professional, there is one uncomfortable reality you'll need to deal with – you'll need to learn how to fail successfully. Let me explain.

Failure is, in my opinion, an underrated virtue in business today. C-level executives brashly state that "Failure is not an option" at staff meetings and in company rallies, but the fact is that failure is a vital part of the growth process. In fact, failure is a constant reminder of an important fact: you're pushing toward greater levels of achievement!

Several years ago my wife put some juggling bean bags in my Christmas stocking. I took them out and read the tip sheet to get some ideas of how to juggle. The first of those tips read as follows: "Practice over a bed." At first it made no sense to me, but then I began to practice. I soon discovered that the bed was a lifesaver for my back! I was dropping bean bags right and left and picking them up off the bed was far easier than picking them up off the floor.

That tip sheet might as well have read, "Step One: Fail....repeatedly." That is a reality of juggling. In fact, it is a requirement of any performance art – music, athletics, theater... or sales. And, yes, sales is a performance art. As such, it requires diligent practice that follows a pattern of failure, finding the problem, fixing it, improving, and repeating that process over and over again.

Failure is not comfortable, but it is an incredibly powerful teacher if you choose to embrace the lessons, if you choose to fail successfully.

WHERE DO WE GROW FROM HERE?

Get used to this principle: when we stop getting better we start getting worse. There is no "stay the same"; it simply isn't an option. You stay the same and the rest of the world will run right over the top of you. Great sales professionals understand that being the best is not a matter of luck, nor timing, nor DNA. Being the best is about commitment – daily commitment – to improving both the skills and the attitude.

Embrace the challenges, enjoy the difficult situations, and smile at adversity. If you are well prepared for the tough encounters, you will have both the aptitude and the confidence to land the sale and you will do so with the knowledge that you are getting more than your fair share of the orders. Why? Because you are doing more than anyone else is either able to do or willing to do. That is, you'll get more sales because you *deserve* more sales. And that, my friends, makes you a GREAT salesperson!

DEAL
WITH
IT!

MASTERING 21 TOUGH SALES CHALLENGES

I.
"We Need to Think About It"

Salesperson: *"Is this is a great car, or what?"*
Prospect: *"It certainly is. We really like it a lot. You bet. This is exactly what we've been looking for. Why, we couldn't ever hope to find anything better. In fact, this car is perfect in every way, and there is no reason not to buy."*
Salesperson: *"Well, what do you say we draw up the paperwork and make it yours?"*
Prospect: *"Wow! Hold on a second, cowboy. It's a big decision. We need to think about it."*
Salesperson: *"Arggh!"*

You've heard it again and again. You're deep into the sales process and you believe you have a prospect who truly loves your product and seems very close to a purchase decision. But just when you are thinking it's time to pull out a purchase order the prospect blind-sides you with the most famous of buying lines, "We need to think about it for a while."

As Charlie Brown used to say, "Arrrrgggh!!!" You had that prospect in the palm of your hand. It was a *sure deal*. You were ready for the accolades from the boss, you were looking forward to writing the name on the sales report and you even had ideas about a nice dinner to celebrate the victory. "What do you mean you have to think about it?!"

Let's get into the "why" of the situation before we try for the "how to". Why is this such a common objection in sales? It's as if people come out of the womb with this one phrase already embedded in their mind. The truth is that most people operate from what I call a "script of life", things we often say reflexively to deal with certain situations. (The most prominent example: "Can I help you?" Response: "No, thanks. I'm just looking.") These internal scripts are drawn upon whenever there is discomfort, and they represent an escape mechanism to get us out of trouble.

Want to know why these script statements are so common? Sadly, it's because they actually work! Far too many salespeople are more than ready to roll over when they hear things like, "We want to think about it." The mediocre response to this comment is, of course, "Oh, that's fine. This is a big decision. Why don't you take my card and call me with any questions you might have." My friend, if that is your go-to tactic, you might as well put them in your car and take them directly to your closest competitor!

The critical (and painful!) truth is that once the customer leaves your sales environment they move beyond your influence and into the influence of other salespeople who might be more adept in the area of closing technique. You must see this visit as your only shot at the sale, and you must progress the sale as far as the customer will allow. If they truly love the product (and why would they still be there if they didn't?) they will thank you later for your persistence in leading them in the right direction.

Before we get to the "how-to's" of overcoming this objection I have some advice for you: structure your conversation so that the "think about it" objection doesn't come up in the first place. You see, this objection is always in response to a closing line, correct? ("This boat looks right for you. Would you like to buy it?" "We have to think about it.") And so we start with an important principle: if your sales conversation leads to undesired responses from the customer, *change your conversation!*

In this case, you might consider a summary close before asking the final closing question. If your product is a ski boat, it might sound something like this:

Salesperson: *"You had initially described a mid-price range ski boat with a canopy that would comfortably seat six. Does this look like what you were hoping to find?"*

Customer: *"It is. This is pretty much what we had in mind."*

Salesperson: *"And you said you wanted to keep the price under $30,000. Correct?"*

Customer: *"That's right."*

Salesperson: *"Great, so we found what you were looking for. Are there any other concerns before we proceed?"*

Customer: *"Can't think of any."*

Salesperson: *"Great. You're going to love this boat. The paperwork process will just take a few minutes."*

In this case we are simply repeating back everything we've already heard from the prospect. And because we are framing this discussion according to the customer's own requirements, we are taking advantage of an important sales principle: It is impossible to argue with yourself!

OVERCOMING THE "WE NEED TO THINK ABOUT IT" OBJECTION

When a customer tosses a "We need to think about it" at you, consider these steps:

- ## Revisit the Dissatisfaction

  Remember that prospects buy for a reason, and that reason comes down to overcoming what is wrong with their current situation. There is a hole, a need, a desire to better their life experience, and by this point in the transaction you should know well what that is. There is dissatisfaction with the current situation, and the sooner the prospects move forward the sooner they can put that dissatisfaction behind them.

  So we start by getting right to the source of the issue and we place that back in the prospect's mind.

  > *"I understand. Let's make sure we're thinking about the right things here. You said that the car you are currently driving is killing you on the fuel costs, and that you are just plain worried about it's reliability now that you're at 150,000 miles. Is that correct, and do you believe that the car you are looking at will alleviate those concerns?" (Wait for response) "So is it safe to say that you're not entirely thrilled driving back home in the car you arrived in?"*

  I'm not suggesting that this approach will overcome the "think about it" objection – it won't. But it provides a great starting point from which you can move on to the next steps. It isolates the dissatisfaction *in the customer's mind* and allows you to narrow down to the real issues.

- ## Smoke Out the Objection

  Whenever a prospect is slow to make a purchase decision, you can safely assume that there is an objection left in the way. You are not performing at your peak until you can determine the specific objection and offer an agreeable solution. Ultimately, you'll want to flush out the objection before you ask for the order, but this is not always possible. Often times the prospect will hide something from you.

If you have not established a trust relationship with the prospect, this part of the process will be very difficult indeed. But if mutual trust has been established it is time to play the role of counselor. The conversation might look like this:

> *"Mr. and Mrs. Gutierrez, I know this is a major decision and it requires a great deal of thought. I respect that. But I also know that you came to see me because you had a real need, and that this particular policy meets that need better than anything else. So that I can help you in this process, would you mind sharing with me what it is that you still have to think about?"*

This approach will only work when there is sufficient trust established, such that the prospect sees you as an advocate for their interests and not a greedy sales hound. Approach this in a consultative manner and see where it leads. Make sure your body language is comforting and passive. Sit back, slow down, and be sincere in listening to their concerns.

- **Create a Risk of Loss**

  One of the classic blunders of a mediocre sales counselor is to let a strong prospect leave the sales presentation without sensing a risk of loss. Underachievers fail to promote the idea that there is only *one* specific product that will best meet the needs of the prospect and that, as soon as the prospect walks away, that particular product *will* be sold to someone else. It is poor sales technique and a tremendous disservice to the customer *not* to inform them of the perils of "thinking about it".

  > *"I understand your need to think about it, I really do. This is a big decision and you want it to be right. But it is my job to make sure you know that there we have just one car that will fit your needs perfectly, and if you were to leave without buying there are no guarantees. It could be sold this afternoon. I don't want some-*

one else to buy the car that is right for just you, so let's talk this through..."

• Control the Environment

Should the customer persist in their desire to "think about it", your next step is to attempt to control the location of this deliberation. You must do all in your persuasive power to keep the prospect from leaving. If they "want to think about it", that's fine, but persuade them to do so on the premises.

The principle is simple: once the prospect leaves, all bets are off. They could lose the best choice in product to another customer, or you could lose the prospect to another salesperson. Once the prospect leaves the sales environment, you have ceded control. Emotion wanes and fear fills the vacuum. The prospect begins to consider the hassle of associated with buying today. Soon the fear becomes a powerful *deterrent* to action. And you have no influence on this thought process, because you are not in the picture.

Try saying to the prospect:

> *"Jack and Barbara, I understand. This is a major decision and I understand why you would want to give it some thought. But you also don't want that perfect diamond ring ending up on someone else's finger. Tell you what. You want to think about it and I understand. Why don't you head back to the lounge area and do just that. Have a cup of coffee, relax for a little bit, talk as long as you need to. I'll be right here if you have questions. In the meantime, I'll make sure we don't sell this to anyone else, as long as you're on the premises."*

• Control the Timing

Alas, many a prospect will refuse your suggestion and insist that they need to "sleep on it". There is yet one more opportunity to retain some control over the decision making process by suggesting a deadline on the time they will take to think it over.

"I understand and I respect that. I think you are aware that when you leave we could sell that recreational vehicle to the next person who walks through the door, but it sounds like that's a risk you're willing to take. You say you want to sleep on it and think it over. You do that. I'll call you tomorrow morning at 10:00 and get your answer. In the mean time if you have any questions please call me."

This tactic removes the false sense of security that causes prospects to think they can take as much time as they want to make up their minds. It also lets the prospects know that they are accountable to you for their answer at a certain time.

This approach is inherently logical. When a prospect is leaving and is truly "thinking about it", when are they most likely to do their thinking? On the drive home…over dinner…at two in the morning when they can't sleep. Providing the prospect with a specific deadline helps them to sort through the issues with far less brain damage.

The call on the following morning, by the way, sounds like this:

"Jack, I know you and Barbara probably talked a great deal about that gorgeous DreamLiner. It is still available – shall I put a sold sign on it for you?"

- ## Keep them Involved

When possible, try to direct precisely *what* the prospect will be thinking about after they have left your sales office. Offer something that will keep them emotionally involved when the scary details begin to overwhelm them. Photos of product work well, as do testimonials from other customers. You can also keep them involved by offering a specific task related to the purchase. Direct them to your company's website, or send them to a website that endorses your product. Have then draw up a list of reasons why they should buy, and why they shouldn't, and make an appointment to review the list the next day.

Finally, if a customer does leave the sales office under the banner of "we need to think about it", it probably means you have some soul-searching to do as a sales counselor. After all, you thought you had them. You still believe you have the right product for them. So why didn't they commit?

The answer will be found in one of three buying factors. When we make a purchase decision there are always three important elements that have come together:

1) The product meets my needs
2) I trust the organization and sales counselor I am dealing with
3) I sense an urgency to buy the product today

If any of these three elements are not in line you need to discover what is lacking and seek to plug that gap. Do you have relationship work to do? Are they not really all that excited about the product itself? Do they sense a risk of loss by walking away? Any of these questions could lead you to discover where their head is at and how to best move the sale along during the next conversation with the prospect.

2.

Dealing with Abusive and/or Argumentative Customers

Salesperson: *"I think you'll love our product."*

Customer: *"Why don't you let me decide that, will ya'?"*

Salesperson: *"Right. So, have you seen anything out there that you like?"*

Customer: *"Yes. I like quiet salesmen."*

Salesperson: *"Gotcha. Well, I'd like to help in any way I can. Do you have any questions I can answer?"*

Customer: *"Look, we don't need you to play nice-nice with us. Just let us look around and we'll somehow manage to find our way <u>without</u> a tour guide."*

Salesperson: *"Alrighty, then. I guess this would be a bad to time to ask you for your contact information, wouldn't it?"*

Here's the situation. You're in love with the 1986 Corvette Stingray. T-top, of course, and it's gotta be red. It's not like you've got $10,000 burning a hole in your pocket, but if you saw the right car you'd be all over it. You're driving down the street and you pass a used car lot. You know the place – multi-colored triangular flags draped from light pole to light pole; helium balloons off the antennas; placards on the windows of the cars that say things like, "A Real Beauty" or "Sweet Ride". In the back of the car lot is a trailer – the sales office.

And there it is – the exact car that you've always dreamed about. Up to this point, the placard that says "A Real Looker" just makes you roll your eyes, but when the placard is on the window of the 'Vette, it makes perfect sense. So you really want to look at the car, but now you have a dilemma. Do you really have to talk to the salesperson?

Is there anyone besides me who would be willing to admit that they are not as charming an individual on a used car lot as they are at a cocktail party? When you walk onto a used car lot do you instantly engage the sales representative? Do you look forward to learning from his keen insight and being entertained by his quick wit? Or do you clam up, fearful of what some schmuck is going to try to pull over on you?

It is not at all unusual to display a certain "attitude" when you walk onto a car lot. Such a posture is one of self-defense, likely based on previous negative experiences or stories heard from others. You do not wish to be abused, so you strike first with a subtly abusive buying approach. The key question: *Does this type of approach make you a bad person?* NO! It makes you a car buyer. You are about to spend thousands – even tens of thousands – of dollars on this purchase and all you can think about are the bad experiences with used car salesmen in the past. And your approach is not even directed at this one particular salesperson – you haven't even met that person yet! You are simply carrying the weight of your fears when you walk into a potentially threatening environment.

To some degree your customers are dealing with these same issues and perceptions. They are contemplating an important and difficult decision, perhaps one of the major deliberations of their lifetime. The decision, they fear, will be followed by pain – pain associated with finances, change, family concerns, choices, etc. Now layer on top of that a general tendency not to trust salespeople. You end up with a customer who must take self-protective measures in the form of curt, cold, or even rude demeanors. *The degree of their "attitude" will depend upon the depth of their fears.*

My overriding message to you: give 'em a break whenever you can. You don't need to put up with abusive language, threats, personal attacks, etc., but try to listen through the negative emotions, the sarcasm and the attitude to see whether their approach is simply rooted in fear. Fear is a normal part of the buying process, and a good indication that you are dealing with a strong prospect.

Let's suppose a customer comes into the sales environment and is demonstrably irascible in their demeanor. Let's also suppose that you were just listening to a Zig Ziglar recording and you are nothing but positive. What do we have? Well, we have something of a stand-off. The fact is that someone is going to change. Either they are going to end up positive or you are going to end up negative, but there is no way that ten minutes down the road will retain your original demeanor.

From that perspective, there is something of a game that is being played in many sales encounters. The game is called, "Who Will Set the Emotional Tone"?

So what would it take for you to go negative? Nothing, really. That's right – all it would take for you to mirror the negative tone of the snarky prospect would be for you to *not* have a specific agenda to stay positive. In the absence of a commitment to positive energy on your part, negativity is almost a certainty.

> We awaken in others the same attitude of mind we hold toward them.

> **Elbert Hubbard**

> I am an optimist. It does not seem too much use being anything else.

> **Winston Churchill**

This is a defining attribute of great salespeople (and you are a *great* salesperson, aren't you?!?!). Top performers make a <u>unilateral</u> decision towards a positive environment, and they do so *before* the sales encounter begins. As part of the preparation process, great salespeople make an important decision: "I commit to a positive environment, even if my customer has other ideas at the start. I will stay positive, and I will guide my customer along that same positive path."

Many salespeople have described this as something of a game, and I can see that point. Someone will change. Who will it be?

Here are some specific methods of calming down that agitated customer:

• **Stay Emotionally Neutral**

The irate customer will be looking for the opportunity to attack. When you confront an emotional customer with an emotional response *you will lose*. You cannot win an emotional argument with a customer – you are outgunned. The difficult customer is on the purchasing end, meaning there is a greater emotional commitment to the process. It's business for you, but it's personal for them. Because they are more emotional they have more ammunition to work with. Joining them in a negative emotional environment will win you the sale exactly zero percent of the time.

One effective method for maintaining an emotionally neutral position is to listen right through the negative delivery and instead focus solely on the facts and the logic. Stay away from the customer's desire to lure you into an emotion-based confrontation.

You might consider taking notes right from the start. Why? Because you tend to write the facts, not the emotions, and that keeps you in that left side of the brain where you need to be. Further, particularly emotional customers might just tone it down a bit if they know that their words are being recorded. You want *everyone* on the logical side before you're done with the conversation.

- ## Take Control of the Environment

  When you have someone who is visibly disconcerted you first need to isolate that person from all others who might be affected, particularly from your other prospects. There is nothing worse than an unhappy customer on a rampage around other customers. Even if the customer is dead wrong, the new prospects cannot help but be affected and uncomfortable by viewing the confrontation.

  Get them into a more neutral setting if at all possible. A negative conversation in a sterile sales office can make the customer even *more* aggravated, since they are fighting you on your own "turf" (at least that's how they see it). Take them outside, into a lounge area, or to some other neutral place. The only exception here is if the customer is so irate that the sales counselor would fear for their own safety – that's a different subject altogether.

- ## Listen into Logic Mode

  When people are angry they are emotional, correct? The problem in dealing with emotionally-driven people is that you cannot solve the problem until the customer moves over to the *logical* side of the brain. The remedy is to let the customer vent – and keep on venting – until the emotional statements are exhausted. By default, the customer must then turn to the logical in order to proceed.

An example: A particularly upset customer says something really out there, such as, "This is the worst organization on the history of the planet." This is, quite obviously, an emotion-based statement, clearly without logic. (After all, it's a big planet with a long history, right?!) There is no appropriate comeback to this statement. Looking at the customer and saying "Is not!" will fail to win you the argument. On the other hand, after the customer has had the chance to vent some steam you are in a position to query for specifics, and the specifics come from the logical side of the brain.

• Offer an Apology

Understand that you can offer an apology without admitting that you were in the wrong. For example, "I apologize. It is never our desire that any of our customers feel the way you are feeling right now. I want to help, so let me understand this more fully so we can find a resolution." That response is both respectful and solution-oriented.

Of course, if you or your company is, in fact, in the wrong, you must apologize at once. You cannot solve the customer's concern by hiding behind your mistake.

• Delay the Conversation

There are times when a customer is so utterly disturbed that there is simply no way to hold a conversation with them in their agitated state. You might need to find a way to defer the conversation until they have had some time to cool off.

> *"I want to help you with the concern but I need to do some work on this. Can I call you at 2:00 this afternoon? By then I should have some answers for you."*

Not only does this buy you some time to solve the problem, but when you do call them back at 2:00, they are likely to have calmed down from their highly emotional state. They have since gone back to work or to some other activity and have stepped out, at least temporarily, of their emotional tirade. Given some time to consider the manner in which they spoke to you, the customer will often become contrite and even embarrassed by their tone. You might even gain an apology when you talk to them later in the day.

Of course there are limits. You do not have to put up with cursing, threats, verbal abuse, etc. There is a time to tell a customer, "I cannot have a conversation with you if you choose to talk in that manner. Why don't we talk later in the day. Or I could give you the number of my manager."

• Hand Them Off

As much as we might not care to admit it at times, not *everyone* will like us. Let's face it: you are likely to talk to hundreds (in some cases thousands) of people each year in your sales environment. The chance that every one of those people will like you is pretty slim. It might make more sense to hand the prospect off to another sales counselor for a "do-over".

> *"You know, I fear we've gotten off on the wrong foot, and that perhaps I've given you some reason to not want to work with me. That's fine. My principle regard is for you to accomplish your goals. Let me propose this: that you consider working through this transaction with my partner, Linda. Linda is great and I think you'll enjoy working with her. Would that be acceptable to you?"*

As a salesperson I wanted everyone to like me – everyone. It just didn't always work out that way. When I figured out that sometimes the personalities will clash for some unexplained reason, and that I had a safety valve in a peer, I was liberated from the pressure of trying fix problems that were both beyond my control and not in the best interest of the prospect. Set your ego aside and hand them off!

- **Suggest They Go Elsewhere**

  There are times when a customer, despite your patient efforts, can simply not be turned around. They are not happy now, and it is doubtful that they ever will be. It might be necessary to suggest to that customer that they should consider some other vendor. Make the offer politely, as it will often lead to even more agitation from the customer. But if the prospect is this difficult to work with *before* they've taken ownership of the your product, imagine what they will be like after they move in. Talk to your sales manager about this one – but it might be time to move on.

  One of my favorite stories comes in the form of a letter than was sent to Herb Kelleher, then-CEO of Southwest Airlines. An irate customer had sent vitriolic letter to Kelleher complaining about her experience, skewering the employees she met, and vowing to never fly Southwest again. Kelleher investigated the situation, and wrote this brief note to the complaining ex-customer. "I think you've made a wise choice."

  When you do find resolution to the customer's concerns you'll want to make certain the situation is fully and permanently resolved. Ask them directly, "Are we okay now?" Thank them for their honesty and reassure them that you are there to help with their concerns.

3.
Handling Multiple Prospects Simultaneously

Salesperson: *"Welcome to Jewelry Outlet. I'm Jeff. So, you're out looking for jewelry. How's the shopping coming along?"*

Customer: *"Well, we..."*

Salesperson: *"Excuse me. Hello and welcome to Jewelry Outlet. I'm with someone right now but I'll be with you shortly. I'm sorry? Where were we?"*

Customer: *"Well, nowhere actually. You were asking how our shopping is..."*

Salesperson: *"Will you excuse me for a moment? Hello and welcome to Jewelry Outlet. I'm with someone right... excuse me. Hello and welcome to Jewelry Outlet. I'm with...huh? Hello and welcome to... Hello and ..."*

Customer: *"We'll just show ourselves around."*

Salesperson: *"But I... excuse me..."*

It's the weirdest thing in the sales world. It doesn't matter if you only see five units of traffic a day – you'll see four of them between 1:30 and 1:40, then be dead the rest of the afternoon. This is one of the strangest of all the sales laws: customers visit in bunches. Perhaps they're all on the same bus, or maybe they all got out of the same movie at the same time. Whatever. Inevitably you're stuck trying to deal with multiple prospects simultaneously.

For some sales environments this is a common occurrence. As a new home sales counselor in Northern California, for example, I routinely saw between fifty and one hundred traffic units per week. With a sales conversation that often went 90 minutes in length, there was a whole lot of customer juggling to do.

It seems like the phenomenon of the "rush" is a natural part of just about any retail business. That's a good thing. Crowds bring energy, and energy brings about sales! In fact, the best retailers in the world diligently focus on how to create a positive energy experience for their customers, and the customers respond by adopting that energy as their own. Think about the Cheesecake Factory on a Friday night, a Toyota dealership on a Saturday afternoon, or Best Buy at Christmastime. The energy is palpable, and people flock to that.

The fact is that no one wants to shop where no one else wants to shop. So the top professional will leverage off of this group energy and use it to his/her advantage.

Whether you are in a high traffic or low traffic environment you need to be prepared at any given time to deal with a rush of traffic. Here are a few techniques to keep in mind:

- **Know Thy Customer – and Fast!**

  One advantage for salespeople in high-traffic environments is that they are forced to speed up their discovery process with every customer. They know that time is at a premium, that at any moment the door could swing open and another new visitor could come in. Therefore the effective sales counselors strive to learn *as much as they can as fast as they can.* They think through the order and content of their investigation questions. They don't wander off on pleasant but unnecessary tangents. They stay focused on questioning, listening and understanding.

This is a healthy mindset for *all* sales counselors, regardless of the traffic volume. Even in a low-traffic sales office it is always possible that your next visitor is driving towards your store. Consider coming up with four rapid-fire questions that you can commit to memory. These questions can teach you important information about the prospect right out of the gate. For example:

✓ *"Have you been shopping all day? How's the search coming along?"*

✓ *"So what happened? What got you out looking for _____?"*

✓ *"What's most important to you about the _____ you are looking for?"*

✓ *"What is right and what is wrong about your current situation?"*

Tweak those questions to match your style and your product, but come up with some opening questions that will give you a quick understanding about your customer.

• Spend Your Time with the People Most Likely to Buy

Inevitably you will find yourself in a situation where you need to make an important choice: there are two customers and only one of me – whom should I spend time with? The answer: spend your time with the person who is most likely to buy. This is one of the most important truisms in sales. And how do you know who is most likely to buy? By learning as much as you can as fast as you can through focused discovery questions (see above).

In the absence of a fast and focused investigation a sales counselor is forced to make a decision as to whom to spend time with based on…what? What kind of car they're driving? How they are dressed? Whether they are "nice"? All of these are poor criteria for making such an important determination.

• **Hold Group Presentations**

Got four buying parties on the sales floor at the same time? Why not talk to them all at once through a group presentation? Not only can you save time by sharing key information just once, but you build a sense of urgency when customers see that there are others who are considering purchasing. Everyone wants to buy where everyone else wants to buy. Group presentations provide a great sense of validation that this is a "happening" place.

When you have several buying parties arrive at your office at the same time, simply raise your voice a bit and share information that will be beneficial to all concerned.

> *"Folks, welcome to the RV SuperStore. I'm Jeff and I thought while you're all here at the same time I'd give you a general overview of our company before you start browsing. After that I'd be happy to answer specific questions and show you around. The RV SuperStore is the only store that…"*

The only downside to group presentations is that it limits your ability to discover what is specifically important to the different parties you are addressing. Since there is still only one of you and four of them you will eventually need to determine whom to spend time with *first*. Be attentive to the body language during your discussion, noting which customers are showing the most interest. From time to time ask if anyone has questions. Those with the questions are more likely to be the most interested buyers.

- ## Schedule Future Appointments

  If you suspect you have two strong prospects in your store and you can only spend time with one of them you'll want to offer a specific one-on-one appointment with one of the parties at a later time. Pull them aside and inform them of your dilemma, and ask if they can come back later in the day or first thing tomorrow – but make sure you designate a specific appointment.

  > *"I'm sorry for any inconvenience but we're pretty busy right now and my attention is divided trying to handle several visitors at the same time. I'd really like to offer you my full and undivided attention. Is it possible we could schedule an appointment for later this afternoon or first thing tomorrow so I can help you without interruption? I'd be happy to stay after hours today or come in early tomorrow if you need me to."*

  The offer to stay late or come in early is a sign of respect and care for the prospect's schedule, and will likely go a long way towards an agreement for a future appointment.

- ## Send the Prospect out for Coffee or a Sandwich

  When I was working in a sales office we had a favorite sandwich and coffee house just a few blocks away. I got to know the owner fairly well and I set up an "account" at the place. From time to time I would send a customer over to that sandwich shop while I was busy working with another prospect, informing them that they had great sandwiches and excellent coffee. "Tell them Jeff sent you." The store employees would then put their charge on my tab and I'd pay it later.

  By buying the prospect lunch I bought myself some time to finish up with my other customer and to prepare for the appointment. I also bought a commitment to return. I never had a customer take me up on the lunch offer and then fail to return to my sales office.

Further, psychologists will tell us that people are far more likely to do something for use if we've first done something for them. Your action in buying lunch will lead to a reciprocal act – in this case the agreement to return to the sales office.

Finally, consider investing in a stack of Starbucks cards, providing you have a Starbucks fairly close by (and these days, who doesn't?). Hand a card to a strong client when you are busy and set an appointment for 30 minutes later.

4.

Closing on the First Visit

Salesperson: *"Well, this looks like a great car."*

Prospect: *"We sure like it."*

Salesperson: *"How about that. You found a car you love in just a few minutes."*

Prospect: *"How about that."*

Salesperson: *"Yep. Uhhh…. How about that, huh?"*

(Awkward pause, kicking the dirt, looking down)

Salesperson: *"Well, here's my card. Why don't you call me with any questions."*

Sales Manager: *"Can I please see you in my office – NOW!?"*

We all know – we've seemingly always known – that closing is the name of the game. We've heard the ABC of closing (thanks to Alec Baldwin), and the advice to "close early and close often". In the worst case, testosterone-laden sales "experts" bark about closing via any means whatsoever, no matter how manipulative or abusive the techniques may be. Many advocate introducing a closing question very early in the process, as early as in the initial greeting, even at the risk of offending a prospect.

One sales closing book on the shelves in stores all over the world espouses nothing short of intimidation and abuse as a legitimate part of the sales process. The closing approaches are set up with statements like, "This close is intended to embarrass and shame the prospect into buying, and it does just that." Small wonder then that so many prospects enter into the sales conversation in a frightened or cynical frame of mind.

The problem, of course, is two-fold. First, today's customer does not wish to be treated in such way and is far more savvy in spotting such blatant manipulation. And second, most salespeople are (fortunately) not cut out that way. The very techniques that sales professionals are trained to use are inconsistent with their moral values and belief systems. As a result, many salespeople will abandon the closing attempt altogether, or wait for the "perfect" moment (which, of course, rarely presents itself). I've seen salespeople say things like, "I'm more of a 'let the sale happen' type of guy. The customers will let me know when they're ready to purchase." Really? Since when did closing notification become the responsibility of the shopper? Did I miss that memo?!

Knowing when to close is an age-old problem for sales professionals in all industries. Close too early and you risk alienation. Close too late and it doesn't happen at all. There has got to be a way to balance these issues out, and I think we can find it if we follow this simple rule-of-thumb: Ask for the sale as early in the process as you can, *without damaging the trust relationship*. You have to ask – that's your job – but if you're going to damage the relationship, you're probably not ready to close.

Our quest, then, is to build the relationship quickly by taking a keen and sincere interest in the prospect, and then using that information to pose a closing question relatively early.

For example, let's suppose that in a three-minute discovery you determine that your car-buying prospect is in the market because their old car is bleeding them on maintenance costs. You also discover that, while they like the SUV they've been driving, they are aghast at the cost to fill the tank. And with their children now nearly grown, the need for an SUV is not as strong as it was. Finally, you discover that these prospects are really into the cool gadgets that come with today's cars – back-up cameras, navigation systems, etc.

Now we take that information and summarize it back to the prospects. "So you're telling me that if you keep driving your current car you'll be paying a small fortune both to maintain it and to put gas in it, and that you'll have to put up with a car whose features don't really thrill you, is that correct?" Of course, you know that is correct because you are simply restating what they've told you in the form of a summary question. And now you offer a solution close. "So if we could show you a car that was incredibly reliable with amazing quality ratings, that could double your fuel efficiency over what you are getting now, and also has the kind of features that will make driving a pleasure again, would you be interested?"

At the most fundamental level, closing is about framing a solution around a future promise so that the customers see themselves and their new lives in a new and exciting light. In other words, I don't ask closing questions for my own benefit – that would be nothing more than manipulation. I ask closing questions for my customer's benefit – and that is a part of the customer care I provide. I ask closing questions to provide clarity to my prospect, so that they can narrow the options in their own mind and settle in on the best possible choice for them.

If that is indeed my perspective and my motive, then asking closing questions early in the process does the customer a huge favor. Note that in the example above, a strong closing question was asked in the first few minutes of the conversation, and well before the product demonstration. But consider how much better the product presentation will be if the customer has already agreed to the solution!

From here we have a second principle. Not only do we want to close as early as possible in the conversation, but we also want to make the close specific to the needs of the prospect. The more the close is based on the customer's stated needs the more effective the close will be. Are you starting to see how the discovery questions and the closing questions go hand-in-hand? You cannot get the closing right if you do not truly understand the prospect.

Here are a few mindsets that will help you achieve a successful first visit close.

• Don't Stop the Sale

Any time a new visitor comes into your sales office, the sales conversation will eventually end in one of two ways: either they will buy or they won't buy. If the prospect does *not* buy it means that someone stopped the sale. It is only a question of who the culprit was – you or the customer.

For any number of reasons the customer might stop the sale. But *you* must *never* stop the sale. Keep that sales process moving forward towards a close. Adopt the mindset that the purchase decision is the last logical step, and that everything you do works towards that step.

One great way to check yourself on this is to take a few brief moments after every single sales conversation to digest and dissect what went right and what went wrong. Before you move on to your next task on the to-do list, take some time to replay the conversation in your mind and ask some of the critical questions that will help you to learn on the fly:

✓ Did I ask them to buy? If not, why?

✓ Who stopped the sale? If it was them, why? If it was me, why?

✓ What could I have done differently to extend that conversation?

✓ What can I learn from that last encounter that will make me a better sales professional on my next encounter?

This discipline of learning from every sales experience will go a long, long way towards dramatically improving your closing proficiency.

• Stop Relying on Buying Signals

I'm a contrarian compared with most sales trainers on this issue. Sales trainers will suggest that you should look for specific buying signals from your prospects – heightened energy levels, move-in or drive-off questions, etc. It is one thing to ascertain the customer's intentions and to determine where they are in the process, but it is quite another to rely on buying signals in order to get *you* into selling mode, in order to get *you* excited about asking a closing question.

Let me use this example. I don't know whether you have ever been "secret shopped" – where a mystery shopper comes in with a hidden camera or microphone to record your sales presentation. These recordings are used as a training tool to evaluate and improve sales performance. I've seen hundreds of video shops in my career – I believe they are invaluable training tools. But when I'm watching a video shop I play a little game: I try to determine the exact moment that the sales counselor suspects they are being shopped. The conversation is proceeding along when the shopper says something that tips off the sales counselor that this might be a secret shopper. Suddenly, the sales counselor's energy level spikes up. The pace quickens. They start talking about product benefits in glowing terms. They share the company story with energy and enthusiasm. They start using soft closes and they become more urgent about moving the sale along. In short, they start doing everything they were trained to do!

What's wrong with that picture? Whether the sales counselor is tipped off that they are being shopped, or whether their energy level excels based on some juicy piece of urgency information given to them by their prospect, it only proves that the salesperson's energy level *was not where it should have been in the first place.* Why did it take the shopper or prospect to "perform" in order for the salesperson to give them the benefit of their positive energy and best presentation? Shouldn't they have already been there?

Folks, there is one, that's right, *one* legitimate buying signal: the prospect came through your door. You must overcome your addiction to buying signals. Top professionals see buying signals not as a surprise but as just another confirmation of what they have already determined: this person is here to purchase today.

• You've Got Nothing to Lose and Much to Gain

The absolute worst-case scenario on a first-visit close is that the customer will say "no". Big stinkin' deal. If you can't handle a simple "no" then you're definitely in the wrong line of work. (Sorry to be so blunt on that, but sales is about asking for the order. If you can't handle rejection – and many people can't – that's no problem. Find something else that you excel at, but it won't be sales.)

You really have nothing to lose by closing on the first visit. You won't offend the customer because they *expect* you to close. After all, you are a *salesperson*, and this is a sales environment. This is what you do and the customer knows it.

And in fact you have everything to gain. What are the benefits of first-visit closing attempts? First of all, you get the customer seriously thinking about the purchase. They think about it now; they think about it later. Your request for a decision accelerates their decision-making process. That's good!

Second, you determine exactly where your customer is at in the sales process. If they say "no", it is completely logical for you to follow-up with a question as to where they are in the process. "That's fine if you're not ready at this time. I want to help you throughout this process, so can you tell me where you're at in your decision-making and what issues still need to be resolved?"

Third (and most important, in my opinion), you make the *next* closing attempt a lot easier. The customer already expects a follow-up attempt, and both you and your customer know that the presentation is geared towards resolving the customer's lingering issues so that they can buy. In other words, the second close is far easier than the first. (And the third is easier than the second, and...)

Finally – and stay with me on this 'cause I'm going to get radical on you – *they just might say "yes"!* Really, it happens. That is, if you allow it to happen.

5.

Closing on the Fifth Visit

Prospect: *"Hello, Jeff!"*

Salesperson: *"Hello, Mr. Rodriguez."*

Prospect: *"I'm back again to look at that home on lot 24."*

Salesperson: *"I noticed. Do you need the key again?"*

Prospect: *"Nah, I've been here so many times I had a key made on my last trip."*

Salesperson: *"Smart. Do you need anything from me?"*

Prospect: *"Nope. I'm going to make my decision any month now."*

Salesperson: *"Wake me when you do."*

You know the type – pleasant, interested, responsive....and slow! They give you all the right signals; they have a clear need, financial capability and a love for your product. They say all the things that get you to believe they are a whisker away from a purchase decision. In fact, they love you personally and have made it clear that they respect your talent and ability. They even refer to you as "my salesperson" when talking to others. They just can't pull the trigger.

Be clear on this: the strong relationship you've built in all their previous visits won't give you any comfort when they finally decide to proceed…*with a competitor.* For the frequent visitor or reluctant purchaser, you have to do some important and urgent soul-searching. You must ask yourself whether the cause of the delay is your lack of assertive closing?

This leads us to one of the more important questions a sales counselor can ever ponder: "Is closing something I do *to* someone, or is it something I do *for* someone?" How you answer will determine your course of action with this prospect. Why is the question so important? Because if you see closing as something you do *for* rather than *to* a prospect, you will actually close this type of buyer more assertively. Why? Because the longer they wait the harder the decision becomes. You are not doing them any favors when you elongate the process by not closing as strong as you should. In fact, you are likely adding to their brain damage.

Moreover, you need to face an important fact: the longer this process goes on, the further removed is the prospect from the initial emotional attachment to the product. That emotion that was so strong at the onset of the process wanes as the customer shifts into a more analytical mode. The urgency lays in the emotion, and in the absence of emotion there is little urgency and, thus, little chance of a sale.

As time goes by your customer falls into a pattern of delay, and they find no loss in doing so. Eventually that initial positive emotion subsides and they are left with a jumble of facts. In other words, the longer the process goes the more logic-oriented it becomes. That is not good if you are trying to sell an emotion-driven product to an emotionally-driven customer.

This discussion goes hand-in-hand with Chapter Four – Closing on the First Visit. If you ask for the order on visit one, you will find that ultimately you'll have fewer fifth visits. You can speed up the process by closing early on.

There is one other very significant danger that we face when dealing with this drag-the-feet type of customer. In sales, we constantly face a prevailing belief in the mind of our prospect and, if we do not address this paradigm we are doomed to failure. I believe that one of the most dangerous perceptions that a prospect can hold is this: *Waiting is Safe.*

This notion is deadly to a salesperson and counter-productive to a buyer with a want. But be clear: your number one competitor is not the dealer down the street or the salesperson who sells a similar product as you. Your number one competitor is whatever the customer currently has. Do you sell cars? Your #1 competitor is the car they pulled up in. Do you sell vacation homes? Your #1 competitor is whatever they've been doing for the last 10 years. Do you sell life insurance? Your #1 competitor might be their desire to live on the edge and invest that money in car payments rather than insurance, thus never moving forward.

Remember that the prospect always has this option at her disposal: to do absolutely nothing. To sit on her hands and delay in making a decision, all the while staying with her current situation, as flawed as it might be. If she believes that waiting is safe, she will continue to put up with her dissatisfaction and you will continue to be frustrated.

An important part of your role as a salesperson then is to clarify on the prospect's behalf why waiting is, in fact, *not* safe. To do this you must feed back the customer's current dissatisfaction in such a way that there is no confusion but that moving forward is a must. "So you're telling me that you really can't drive your current car much longer – it's not reliable and you don't know when it's going to break down at night on the freeway, is that correct?" Or, "So you're telling me that you really can't go on with the unsettled feeling that if something happened to you, your family would suffer financially, is that right?" Or, "So you're telling me that your current vacations are getting more and more expensive, and that you're tired of never knowing exactly what your accommodations are going to be, is that what you're saying?" This approach is entirely respectful, because it simply feeds back that which I have already learned from the customer.

So what are we going to do about it? Here are three approaches to consider:

- ## Put on the "Counselor's" Hat

  I favor the title of sales counselor instead of salesperson because this is the most important role we play. You must counsel your customer into a buying agreement. Your very job is to give the information and guidance that they cannot come up with on their own.

  As a counselor, you must first determine the root of the hesitation. Principally, you must discover whether the delay is based on fear-based (emotion) or event-based (logic). Fear based delays include concerns about making a commitment, indecision between two similar products, or financial unease. Event-based delays are easier to deal with once you discover the cause of the inaction: gathering funds, getting someone else's approval, getting qualified, etc.

  If the customer has come in several times without purchasing (despite your persistent efforts) you'll need to ask some pointed questions in order to determine the root cause of the procrastination. By this point you should have built enough of a trust relationship with the prospect to be blunt and direct.

  > *"Mark, you've come in several times and you've indicated that you like our product, yet you haven't purchased yet. I need to understand what's going on in your decision-making process. Tell me why you haven't moved forward with a purchase decision on the product that you clearly love."*

  Then listen attentively and respectfully to the customer's concerns. This is not the time for judgment on the merits of their delay. Rather, it is time to counsel them into a breakthrough moment.

- ## Tie Back to the Emotion

  You need to come to terms with this unpleasant reality: the longer a customer stays in the "buying cycle" without making a decision, the less likely it is they will eventually purchase from you. This is the case because the majority of consumers are emotionally motivated in their purchase decisions, and the longer they stay in the buying cycle the farther removed they are from their initial emotional impression.

  Think about the customer's third visit to your store without making a decision. At this point, are they asking questions that indicate emotion or logic? In all likelihood they are asking technical questions. At this point the questions are about specifications, terms, etc. That's a problem, because it indicates they are traveling away from their emotional connection. This is especially true with big-ticket purchases.

  The key then is to keep the prospect emotionally engaged in the product they are considering by revisiting the reasons they fell in love in the first place. Even if the customer is bringing up technical points they must constantly be reminded of what caused the emotional appeal at the outset.

- ## More Closes Means Stronger Closes

  I'm going on the assumption that you are a professional, and therefore you are not satisfied with having asked for the sale just one time. The true sales expert will take advantage of closing opportunities throughout the follow-up process. The good news is that once you've asked the customer for the sale the first time, they'll expect that you'll ask again. The closing process becomes easier with each close.

  But with the slow-mover, you must be more assertive with each of your closing approaches as you move through this process. You have permission to become more frank with your closes on each subsequent attempt. Not rude – but right to the point. By the fifth visit there is no need to soft-pedal the question.

"Jose and Sabrina, this is the fifth visit to look at this car so that you clearly love. Most people would have long-since bought this. You know you love it. Why not make today the day?"

"Mandy, you know you love this ring and you know that we will eventually sell it to someone. You don't want us to sell your ring to someone else, do you?"

- **Force a Final Decision**

The longer this process goes on, the more your chances of getting a sale diminish. Eventually the customer will simply wear out under the weight of the decision-making process and stop coming in altogether. You've got nothing to lose by forcing the customer's hand and asking them for a *final* decision: yes or no. The reality is that you'll be doing this customer a favor. They don't need the mental anguish of delaying the decision. They need to decide to purchase or decide to move on. They might just need someone to put it to them that succinctly.

"My friends, I'm going to do you a favor. The longer you wait, the more difficult this process becomes. I'm going to ask you to make a final decision in the next 15 minutes – yes or no on this particular RV. Either way, I will support your decision. But you're giving yourselves a migraine by waiting too long. Either you're going to buy this RV today or you're willing to walk away and let someone else own it. 15 minutes. I'll be right here."

That might sound abrupt, but you'll find that your customers are liberated when they know they've made the final decision. By letting them know that you'll support them either way, you are telling them that in your heart you want them to make the right choice.

6.

Closing When a Decision-Maker is Absent

Salesperson: *"So, you like the car?"*

Customer: *"Yes."*

Salesperson: *"And you think Sheila will like the car?"*

Customer: *"I'm sure she will. And she trusts me. In fact, I bought our last car without her there and she loved it."*

Salesperson: *"Great. Bring her out to take a look and we'll see what she says."*

Sales Manager: *"CUT! Your line is, 'Great – let's write it up!'"*

———————————

In all my years in the sales business, I've rarely seen anything that will cause a sales counselor to bail out of the closing process quicker than the discovery that one of the decision-makers is not present. This sole piece of information will cause more than a few salespeople to reach for the eject button, reasoning that the decision is too monumental to take place in the absence of the significant other.

This thinking is extremely dangerous because the salesperson's assumption becomes self-fulfilling. That is, if you truly believe that a person will not make a purchase decision under these circumstances then you will alter your presentation to match your belief. The sale will never stand a chance. This is particularly frustrating to sales *managers* given the fact that big-ticket purchases are made in the absence of a decision-maker every day across the country.

Now, you might be thinking to yourself, "I would never buy a (car, home, RV, etc.) without my significant other present, nor would I want my significant other to buy without me there." Fine, but who said *you* were the buyer? Plenty of people see things differently, and it is *their* opinion that counts.

Look for a moment at the potential prospects who might buy unaccompanied:

- **"Whatever makes you happy" buyers.** She has her ideal dream car in mind. He couldn't give a rip as long she is happy. She buys and lets him know. This is actually quite common for many couples, and it actually makes the sales process easier. If you are selling an emotion-based product, you don't really want competing emotions if you can help it. Being alone means a greater chance of a sale.

- **Out of area shoppers.** People from out of town can be great impulse shoppers. Some are just killing time while on a business trip but have surprising emotional responses to products they love. Others are relocating to the area and are shopping as a part of an entire life adjustment.

- **"Know what they want" buyers.** Sometimes two people have been looking for a long time and they just know how the other thinks. When they come across exactly the right product at exactly the right price, it is not necessary to have the significant other present. This is a done deal. Write it up.

- **Dominant buyers.** In many cases, there is one dominant decision maker and that's just the way it is. This person will make the call when they see the right thing. And to assume otherwise is to offend this type of personality!

- **Impulsive buyers.** Some people are mildly impulsive. Some are radically impulsive. I have a friend who got shut out on the purchase of the home he really wanted. After leaving that sales office he passed by a different new home community. He went in, saw a home he wanted, and bought it on the spot, without so much as a phone call to his wife. Now, for some of you men that might be "a little troubling" to your wife. But once again, you are not the buyer. If the prospect wants to buy, by all means sell!

- **Internet shoppers.** You're in the market for a diamond ring, or a boat, or a new life insurance policy. Ask yourself, "How much information is available on the web that can help me with this purchase decision?" The answer, of course, is TONS! Today's consumer is incredibly well informed even before they walk through your door. So what could be holding them back if they already have the information they need to make an informed decision? Forget about decision-makers – ask for the order!

Here are four ways to approach this situation:

- ## Assume the Sale

First and foremost, assume that this person is going to buy whether the significant other is present or not. This is one of the most fundamental principles of successful salespeople – they fully believe that *everyone* who comes in the door is there to buy. Top performers take the mindset that says, "You are here to buy until you prove to me otherwise." Don't give them the opportunity to bail because of *your* bias against selling in the absence of a decision-maker.

- **Determine Their Authority**

  When you get to the closing questions, be direct in determining the limits of authority of the prospect in front of you.

  - *"Are there any other decision-makers in this process, or are you prepared to move forward by yourself?"*

  - *"Does your (husband/wife/other) need to be here to make a purchase decision, or is he/she comfortable with whatever your choice is?"*

  - *"Are you making the purchase decision on your own then?"*

- **Explain the Risk of Loss**

  This is the most effective way to sell when someone is absent, by explaining that the *absent* person will miss out on the perfect product if the *present* person does not proceed today. Building a risk of loss leads people to get off the fence and make the difficult (but proper) decisions.

  - *"I understand your discomfort in making this decision on your own, but you need to understand that there is only one _____ available at this price. The next person through the door could buy it."*

  - *"You know your (husband/wife/etc.) better than anyone. Ask yourself whether he/she would say 'yes'. If they would buy if they were here, then why do you want to risk having them miss out on owning this product?"*

- **Close on a Change of Plans**

  If you need the other person present in order to secure the sale, and if this is a big decision where the prospect is considering hundreds or thousands of dollars (or perhaps hundreds of thousands of dollars!), wouldn't it make sense to get the absent party to change their plans and pay a visit right away?

  Close on that idea. "This is obviously a big decision. Perhaps it makes sense to get Robert over right now. How far away is he? Can he take a short time off of work so that you can get this right?"

- **Close on Something!**

  We always want to get the sale firmed up, but there are times when we have to settle for something else. In this case, attempt at the least to close the party who is present, even if they won't purchase alone. "Can I just ask, if it were up to you alone would you purchase it today?" This question confirms that the present party is fully engaged. That might encourage a greater level of persuasion in that night's dinner conversation.

7.

Dealing with Language Barriers

Salesperson: *"This home has a spectacular entry foyer with a cathedral ceiling and a sweeping staircase that speaks only of elegance. I think you'll agree that the towering volume as you enter is stirring yet graceful, harkening back to classic architecture from a by-gone age."*

Prospect: *"I no understanding this word: home."*

Salesperson: *"This could take a while."*

Let's put this one in perspective. Your spouse has been offered the perfect job doing exactly what they've always dreamed of (and making *huge* money). It's the perfect opportunity – and the only sacrifice on your part is that the job is in *Guadalajara, Mexico*! So off you go on a house-hunting journey. (All right, I can hear the retort of "So long, honey. Don't forget to write" – just go with me on this!). You're feeling mighty confident when you walk into that new home sales office, aren't you? This is where those three years of Spanish One will really pay off, right? And you know all about the purchase process in Mexico, and the financing process, and how to determine good quality, and how to know if you're getting ripped off…

Welcome to the perspective of so many people in the United States today. So many customers have not mastered the English language. They are not comfortable with the oddities of the American culture. There is a lack of trust based on a lack of familiarity. Bluntly, they are scared – just as you would be if you walked in their shoes.

Buying any expensive product is tough enough, but without really knowing what you're doing it becomes ten times more difficult and one hundred times scarier. Now throw in a less-than-perfect under-standing of the language and you have a recipe for buyer paralysis… unless a helpful sales professional can help relieve that stress.

This makes for a wonderful and untapped opportunity for you - a hidden market, if you will. What do these prospects need from you more than anything else in the world? Think about that question for a moment and try to come up with an answer.

What these prospects need more than anything else is a sales counselor they can trust – one who truly cares about who they are as individuals, and who is willing to patiently work through the communication gaps. You can cement their loyalty (and the sale) with a little bit of patience.

My advice is to specialize in this buyer. Establish yourself as the one sales counselor who will go out of the way and take a little more time to make this customer comfortable.

Here are a few techniques to consider when dealing with this prospect:

- **Slow Down!**

  I took four years of Spanish in school and I felt I knew a few things about the language. I could conjugate verbs like a madman and I had no trouble ordering food in a Mexican restaurant. Later I got the opportunity to use what I had learned while working with a number of Spanish-speaking people. And I quickly determined that I was totally lost! I could pick out perhaps one quarter of what I heard. I learned Spanish at a slow speed, not the way it is spoken natively.

This is absolutely the case with so many of your customers. They cannot trust you if they do not understand you, and they often cannot understand you until you slow down and allow time for mental interpretation to take place. We don't realize how quickly we speak our native language, but if English is your only language then spend a few minutes watching Telemundo or an Asian channel. The words blow by you like a high-speed roller coaster, leaving you to wonder what is being said.

Slow down! Better yet, give them *permission* to slow you down. Tell them to stop you whenever they don't understand. One way to do that without offending them is to take a self-effacing approach:

> *"You know, I have a tendency to talk too fast at times. If we ever get to the point where I'm talking to quickly for your comfort, please let me know. It's something I'm trying to work on."*

- ## Take an Interest in Who They Are

A couple of years ago I was in a taxi in Denver, Colorado and I struck up a conversation with the driver. I wasn't expecting anything more than casual banter, but I discovered within 15 minutes the following details about his life: that this man was a guerrilla fighter in Ethiopia in the 1970's; that he trained guerilla warriors both in Ethiopia and Sudan in the 1980's; that he escaped Ethiopia leaving everything behind – including his family; and that he now drives a cab only to save enough money so he can go back to Ethiopia and Sudan as often as possible, sneak in and out, and plant churches in those two countries.

What an amazing story! I was enraptured and humbled to hear his life story. And to think I almost didn't bother to ask anything about this fascinating man. The key to this story is that despite his difficulty with the English language (I had to fill in the gaps from time to time), my interest in his life and in his experiences made for an unusual and enjoyable bond between us.

The mediocre sales counselor seeks only to *tolerate* those who struggle with the language. The great salesperson reaches to a deeper level than the language, seeking to discover something about this visitor's soul that will spark a trust relationship. Your customers have incredible stories to tell, stories of success, failure, heroism, war, travel, poverty, personal endeavor, family values and much more. All they need is for you to take an interest. Do it – and be prepared to be surprised.

I almost hate to say it for fear of encouraging manipulation but, when you reach out to those who speak English as a second language, you increase the trust level so remarkably that you greatly increase your chances of getting a sale. So many sales counselors will not go out of their way to take the time with these customers; this becomes an untapped buyer resource for the caring sales counselor.

- **Check in Frequently During the Conversation**

  Consider memorizing a simple, four-word sentence and using it frequently throughout the encounter. The phrase is, "Does that make sense?" You should be constantly checking in with the prospect to make sure they are tracking with you. Many customers are self-conscious about not being able to keep up and are therefore unwilling to let you know that they've missed something. When you ask them if what you are saying makes sense you are giving them permission to slow you down.

Keep in mind that this technique is not limited to those who struggle with the English language. This is a good habit for any salesperson to use with any customer.

- **Eliminate "Industry Speak"**

  Consider for a moment how difficult the English language is. It's tough enough without throwing in all the industry terms that are entirely unfamiliar to your customers, especially to those from other cultures.

  For example, your product requires financing and you start talking about APR. Can I suggest that the average American-born U.S. citizen can't get their brain around APR – consider how much more of a problem would this be for someone still learning the language.

  It is far too easy to lose a customer while we rattle off our presentation in industry-ese. It is imperative that we stop and check in on a regular basis to allow the customer to ask questions and slow us down.

  "Does that make sense?"

  "I know that can be a complicated issue; are you clear on all this?"

  "Do you have questions about that?"

  Keep in mind that this principle does not only apply to those who struggle with the language, but to anyone who is unfamiliar with terms that you and I might consider to be common in the industry. In home sales (my background) this is a common problem with terms that describe the elements in the home: landing; pony wall or knee wall; soffit; PUD; Good Faith Estimate (are other estimates in "Bad Faith"?), and so many more. You don't want your customer to feel stupid; be careful with this.

- ## Worst Case: Ask for an Interpreter

  I'm not in love with this idea, simply because it requires that any interpreter convey not only the message but also the trust I am attempting to build. But this is preferable to having a customer who simply does not get it, nor is likely to *ever* get it. You might want to talk to your sales manager first, but when you sense that your words will not be understood you must be aware that the customer will inevitably end up with a confused version of the process. This is a good time to call for help.

  There is one more consideration that shouldn't be overlooked. The network of people who come to the United States from other countries is stronger and wider than you might think. In most cases Vietnamese-Americans, for example, know other Vietnamese-Americans in their geographic areas. The referral possibilities are incredible. If you can get your customer to share the message that there is a great opportunity being offered by a trustworthy sales counselor, you can corner that referral business.

  That said, spending extra time on buyers for whom English is a second language is what you should do simply because – well, it's the right thing to do. These people need your help and your patience is your gift of customer service.

8.

Helping a Customer Through "Buyer's Remorse"

Salesperson: *"Hello, Frank. Hi, Marcia. How can I help you?"*

Prospects: *"We had a question for you."*

Salesperson: *"Shoot."*

Prospects: *"When you said the payment was three hundred – did you mean three hundred <u>dollars</u>? Like, three hundred American dollars?"*

Salesperson: *"Uh, yeah. What did you think I meant?"*

Prospect 1: *"Well, that's what we thought you meant. But then we got home and started thinking, if we take that from our eating out budget, that means we can't eat out again for another 12 years."*

Prospect 2: *"And five months."*

Salesperson: *"We'd better go back to square one here."*

————————————

Just how real is buyer's remorse? Is it a natural occurrence, or have we projected this fear into the customers' minds? Is this something that needs to be addressed up front, or should we wait until we see signs of a possible cancellation?

There are a number of opinions on these questions, so let's look at what the customer is going through in the process making a buying decision to see if there are some clues as to the validity of this phenomenon.

THE CUSTOMER'S FEARS:

✓ **Fear of change.** This is one of the most serious issues that a customer will ever deal with, and it can have a crippling effect for some people. This explains why so many people don't move forward at all, rather than dealing with their discomfort.

✓ **Fear of commitment.** There is no such thing as an independent financial decision. Every financial decision we make affects every other financial decision we make, and your customers know this at some intrinsic level. Once the decision is made it rules out all other choices, and remorse is an immediate sign that the comfort level is not as strong as it needs to be.

✓ **Fear of a bad choice.** There are so many decisions out there. Buy or lease? Cash or finance? New or used? Company 'A' or Company 'B' (or 'C' or 'Q' or 'Y')? Blue or green? Basic or Deluxe? Or Super Deluxe? I could go on – we've only scratched the surface of the number of choices to be made. The shear volume of choices makes for a difficult night's sleep, with plenty of time in the dark to reconsider each decision.

✓ **Fear of being taken advantage of.** No one wants to look the fool. No one wants to find out later that the smooth-talking salesperson was actually a shyster. They trust you now, but will you still be there for them down the road?

✓ **Fear of the unknown.** This might be the most disturbing and distressing of all the concerns of a prospect. The issue is not whether the customer has all the right answers. The real concern is that they don't even know the right *questions*. So much of the purchase decision is a great mystery. Within this understandable ignorance lies a great deal of apprehension, and left unattended these fears can lead to a cancellation.

To fully understand buyer's remorse we must first acknowledge that purchase decisions tend to be emotional. We fall in love with an item and get that dopamine rush that is associated with anticipation of an event. We imagine the ownership and we look forward to how our lives will improve.

Because we tend to be emotional creatures making emotional decisions, we must also understand that emotions can be fleeting. As soon as the transaction takes place the emotion starts to wane and we are left with our fears (see above). Unless we have a sales counselor who can help us deal with this problem *in advance*, the issue will cause otherwise successful transactions to unravel, particularly if you sell a product that has some form of "think about it" clause (in many states, for example, the law states that you have several days to reconsider a real estate purchase decision).

If you want to get your hands around this issue, you need to put yourself in the customer's shoes. Buyer's remorse is a very real malady that must be dealt with. Here are a few suggestions:

• **Educate the Customer**

Your customer needs to know how common buyer's remorse is. Let them know that they are not alone in what they are experiencing, and that all customers go through this to some degree. Then share a third-party story about another customer that experienced remorse but decided to hang in there and buy the product they love.

You can also use the opportunity to remind them of all the positive reasons why they decided to purchase in the first place. When they made the decision they were in love with the product. Why? Connect them back to that point and remind them of what it was about this particular solution that was so appealing.

It's okay to warn your customer at the time of contract that buyer's remorse really happens, just as it happens with every major decision we make in life. Most everyone who gets engaged, for example, has at least *some* second thoughts about the permanency of marriage. The decision to purchase a big-ticket item is one of the most important choices we will make in our lifetime – of course there will be second-guessing. That evaluation time allows us the opportunity to further cement into the logical side of our brains the conviction that we have made a good choice.

> *"I want to warn you that some – not all – but some people deal with a questioning period just after the sale has been made. This is a natural and even healthy occurrence. Don't fight it. Just do two things. One – remember why you bought this in the first place: You love this product and you know it's right for you. Two – call me and share your concerns – it's helpful to talk through whatever is on your mind. Don't be surprised and don't worry about it. It's natural."*

- **Inform Them of the Consequences of Backing Out**

    (This segment is only for those who sell with a transaction period that lasts days or months – homes, pre-ordered cars, etc.).

    If you have an "all sales are final" policy it is your responsibility to let the customer know this at the time of purchase. Too many sales counselors make the mistake of threatening to keep the customer's deposit only after the buyer has threatened to cancel the transaction. Sorry, but that's too late. By the time the customer is threatening to walk they have already become emotionally detached from the product, and once that happens there is little to be done.

The secret is to firmly instruct the customer as to the consequences of a cancellation *while they are emotionally tied to the product,* that is, at the time of the contract. Don't be wishy-washy and don't give them a hint that they can walk away without recourse. You are trying to instill this consequence into their minds so that, in the event they consider backing out, they will immediately consider the financial risk.

> *"All right, folks. You love the home and that's great. We're glad you love it, and we're going to build you a wonderful home for your family. You are committing to buy it, and we are committing to build it for you just as you instruct us. We are moving forward with the full intention of building you a quality home. That's our commitment and we are putting it in writing. Your commitment in writing is that you will go through with this purchase. Should you at any time decide not to go through with the purchase, you would be going against your contractual obligations, and I want to go over with you now what the financial loss would be in that event."*

Warn them regarding keeping the deposit before you have to do so. Bringing up the deposit after the final decision to cancel rarely leads to the customer "un-making" that call since, by that point, the emotional tie has been severed.

- **Reconnect with the Emotions**

When a customer hints that they are having second thoughts over the purchase you'll want to take them back to the emotional place where they were when they decided to buy. That decision was made at an emotional high point in the interaction – they had fallen in love with your offering. Try to recreate that in a description. Refresh their minds as to why they made the decision in the first place.

> *"Thanks for sharing your concern with me. I really appreciate you bringing it up and I want to help you through this very normal process. You say you're concerned about the financial commitment, and I understand that. Can we for a moment go back and revisit the reason why you chose this RV in the first place? Tell me some of the key reasons why you decided to purchase…"*

> *"Thanks. So, you'll agree that those things that attracted you to this motor home have not changed, right? And the financial issues have not changed, right? Yes, I understand it's a lot of money, but you need to consider the fact that you are buying a home away from home – a <u>home</u> that is just right for your family. When you go through with this decision, you are reaffirming that you've done something wonderful today that will positively affect you for years and years to come. Tell me how you're feeling."*

- **Buy Some Time – (Give them a chance to fall back in love)**

Your customer made an emotion-based decision to purchase. That's good. What you don't want is for the customer to make an emotion-based decision to *cancel* the transaction. Fear-based cancellations are painful because the customer rarely makes a good decision under negative stress.

Try to get your customer to take the time to allow the emotion to subside and balance it with logic. This is where the Ben Franklin approach is so powerful.

"You don't want to make a long-term decision based on a short-term concern. This is too big a dream to give up over something temporary. This is what I'm going to suggest you do: Sit down with a piece of paper and draw a line down the center of the page from top to bottom. On the left side list all the positive reasons you should go through with this purchase as you had originally decided. Then on the right side list all the logical reasons why you should not. I think you'll find that the positives far outweigh the negatives."

You've probably noticed by now my affection for the title of "sales counselor" as the most apt description for salespeople. Nowhere is this title more appropriate than in dealing with people who are thinking about walking away. This is where our role of counselor comes in to play and helps us to act in the best interests of both our company *and* our customer.

- ## Stay on the High Road

  If they are destined to renege on their purchase decision, don't burn bridges. Ask for permission to stay in touch so that you will be their company of choice when they decide to go ahead with a purchase. If they are going to walk away for legitimate reasons, you want them to walk away with a favorable impression about you and about the company. They're going through a difficult time as it is. They don't need the added guilt trip on their way out.

9.

Breaking Through to the Under-Communicator

Salesperson: *"So tell me what you're looking for in a watch."*

Customer: *"Something nice."*

Salesperson: *"Yes…well…we'll see what we can do. Are there any features that are particularly important to you?"*

Customer: *"I want it to keep the time accurately."*

Salesperson: *"Right. Fortunately our watches do that. Let's do it this way. Would you like a gold tone or a silver tone?"*

Customer: (*Shrug*)

Salesperson: *"Is there anything you can tell me that would help me to help you?"*

Customer: *"I think I've made myself pretty clear."*

We would love it if all of the visitors to the sales environment were warm, engaging, gregarious and easy to communicate with. The reality is that the sales floor is an often-intimidating place, or at least it is perceived as such by the wary shopper. When the customer fears a negative environment they often strike a self-protective pose that can be seen in any number of portrayals. They might seem passive, quiet, disinterested and even mean at times. Does this make the shopper an unfriendly *person?* No! It makes them a shopper.

To illustrate the point let me take you back to one of the least favorite locales for many people: the used car lot. The majority of people experience anxiety when approaching a used car lot, fearing that they are about to be confronted by an unscrupulous salesperson whose only goal is to take advantage of them. Is this always the case? Of course not. But the fear is real and the reaction to that fear is also very real.

I like to think of myself as a good guy. I don't have a lot of enemies (of which I am aware!) and as much as possible I like to get along with those around me. However, when you see me walk onto a used car lot I get quiet, reserved, disinterested and unsocial. You might even read me as a bit mean. Does this make me a mean person? No! It makes me a car buyer. I know the pain of buying cars from people who have purposed to take advantage of me, and I have no desire to become the victim of another manipulative smooth-talker. My biases and perceptions control my actions. I recognize that a great many salespeople in that business are trustworthy and ethical, but I don't yet know that when I walk through the door and at this point I fear the worst.

That's how I get when I walk onto a used car lot – and I am a normally outgoing person. Imagine how this response is multiplied with someone who carries these same fears *and* can be described as an introverted personality. Small wonder that customers will choose to under-communicate. This is simply a defense mechanism.

The solution will be found in one overriding concept: unilateral respect. Many salespeople will offer respect only after they receive it, but in the sales conversation we must understand that respect is earned, not handed to us. The great sales counselor will make a decision – even before the customer walks through the door – to offer unilateral respect and appreciation for this visitor. If the respect is not immediately reciprocated, the mature sales counselor responds by saying to herself, "That's fine – I have work to do to build the trust with this customer and earn their respect, but I will not allow my respect for them to wane in the meantime."

Respecting someone who does not (yet) respect you takes a great deal of maturity and confidence, traits that Daniel Goleman describes as "emotional intelligence" (in the book of the same name). Emotionally intelligent sales counselors practice unilateral respect, friendliness and kindness. They understand that what the customer needs above everything else is an advocate who truly understands what they are going through, and who will go out of their way to meet the customer's needs.

How do we do this? A few suggestions…

- **Respect the Need for Control**

  One of the greatest fears of any shopper is the fear of losing control to a manipulative salesperson. This customer wants to be in control, but they don't always know how. They fear that if they tip their hand and share too much information they will weaken their position.

  Under-communicators need to be talked to in the language of esteem. Don't be afraid to take a submissive posture in your desire to help.

  "It is my job to give you the information you need to make an intelligent decision."

  "I promise to provide the best service I can throughout this process."

  "I want to be a resource for you, regardless of where you eventually purchase."

- ## Match Their Analytical Side First

  Under-communicators don't need sales counselors who are fresh out of a Zig Ziglar seminar and desire to carry the entire transaction on their own emotional shoulders. They need a chameleon, someone who will adjust to their style and their communication preferences. Does that mean we take all the emotion out of the sale? No way. It simply means that we start with the logical and factual and then transition to the emotional when the customer reaches a comfort level that allows them to do so.

  Do this by sharing information early and immediately asking questions about whether you have what they are looking for. For example,

  > *"We have everything from single beds to California Kings. What size were you interested in today?"*

  > *"We are located in the town of Orange Park. Are you familiar with this area?"*

  > *"Our pens start around $50 and go up to several hundred. Is there a price range you were hoping to find?"*

  Once it appears that your product might fit their needs, begin transitioning to confirming statements such as, *"Wow, this sounds like it meets your needs exactly."*

- ## Use Your Tools

  Most sales environments are full of wonderful and positive distractions that will temporarily take the focus off of the one-on-one relationship between buyer and seller and instead direct the prospect's attention to something more tangible and analytical. Give the customers a tour of the area and let them get comfortable with their surroundings. All the while you are giving them reason not to fear you. This will encourage them to open up and share information.

(For extra credit, visit a CarMax and go through the early portion of the sales presentation. The initial tour is well-structured and comforting, exactly what the nervous prospect needs when entering a car dealership.)

- **Appeal to Their Intellectual Ego**

  The cynic would respond, "Do you mean I should patronize this buyer?" Well, yes – if patronizing means meeting them at their level and understanding what they are going through. Tell them you appreciate their style, and that they obviously know what they are doing. It's okay to say to an under-communicator, "You're in charge. I'll give you information, but you will make the decision."

10
Bringing a Once-Hot Prospect Back to Life

Salesperson (call one): *"Hey, it's Jeff. Just wanted to check in with you and see where you're at. You can still get that model in Cobalt Blue if you call me today. I'll hold it until you can get here. Let me know."*

Salesperson (call two): *"Hello, it's Jeff Shore. I didn't hear back from you guys yesterday and I've got someone else looking at the Cobalt blue. I know you want it, huh? Whadaya say? Give me a call."*

Salesperson (call three): *"Hi, this is Jeff Shore, you know – from Carroni Brothers. You visited my office last week and I showed you that Cobalt Blue model, and you really seemed to like it. I um...I don't know how to tell you this but I already reported it as a sale to my manager, so I really need you to call me back."*

Salesperson (call four): *"This is Jeff Shore from Carroni. We've notified the authorities and we're sending out search dogs. We're even talking to scientists who believe the planet is rotating slightly faster since you fell off! By the way, I got written up – thank you very much."*

Go ahead – admit it. You were already calculating your commission and deciding on where to spend it. You already told your sales manager that the Cobalt Blue was sold – you just need to do the paperwork. You even told another interested party that the sale was as good as done. And now the customer won't return your phone call. Your red-hot buyer is apparently ice-cold.

To start, you might consider asking some introspective questions as you think back on your conversations. Self-examination can be difficult but it can also provide outstanding learning opportunities. In this case you might want to take some to consider whether you did all you could to move this sale along. Were there clues that came up during the sales conversation that would have led you to believe these prospects were not as serious as you thought? Did you allow them to leave without making a commitment when they really could have done so? Did you fail to build the urgency that would have caused them to buy while they were here? What can you do to bring this buyer back?

Some thoughts on what to do now...

- **Don't Assume They've Lost Interest**

  Sometimes people just get busy or distracted with other issues in their lives. Perhaps they are involved in a big project at work, or their children are consuming their time over a school issue, or they have a medical concern. Remember that the whole time they are considering a purchase, life goes marching on. The decision might be delayed for some reason, but that does not mean they are not going to purchase at some point.

My wife and I were thinking about reworking the deficient heating and cooling system in our house, a high-priced endeavor to be sure. But at the time we were mulling over this very expensive proposition, we were also planning my daughter's wedding (another very costly endeavor, by the way!). The salesperson might have thought we had lost interest when we were not urgent in making a decision. The fact is we were just busy with other things.

The strategy, then, is to outlast the prospect. That is, to still be interested in them when they are finally interested enough in you and your product to move forward. Lesser salespeople will give up before that happens. Will you be the one who is still a part of their lives?

- ## The Strategy: Don't Get Eliminated!

Smart sales professionals believe that the prospect will buy from them sooner or later. In fact, I advise that as soon as you connect with a prospective purchaser you adopt the following mindset: "You are now my customer, and I am now your salesperson." This mindset gives you tenacity, as the owner and steward of this prospect. It also assures you will serve that prospect's interest to the fullest extent possible.

Why is this mindset so important? Because shoppers are constantly in elimination mode. In most cases the modern consumer simply has too many choices at his or her disposal – there is too much to look at and too much to take in. So the consumer of today utilizes a very powerful tool in the arsenal of shoppers: elimination. Think about it for a moment. You don't look at every shirt or every pair of shoes at the department store. You eliminate entire sections, entire colors, entire brands. You sift through a rack of shirts on the fly, systematically eliminating choices until you land on one that catches your interest. This is also true for cars and jewelry and insurance policies. Elimination as a means of smart shopping is as common as the sunrise.

This elimination comes about in two ways: actively or passively. Active elimination takes place when a customer knowingly and deliberately passes over your offering for any number of reasons: price, style, function, features, etc. Passive elimination occurs when the shopper simply forgets that you exist. This is why we follow-up diligently with our visitors, to prevent the passive elimination that occurs when we slip out of the shopper's memory after not having stayed in touch.

Other sales counselors will allow this to happen – you must not. Call them until they tell you to stop calling them. This is the only way to stay in their minds and, remember, once you've fallen out of their minds you've lost the sale.

- ## Appeal Personally in a Message

  The very fact that you were expecting these people to purchase indicates that you had some sort of relationship established – a relationship based on a mutual trust and respect. If such a relation-ship exists then it seems inconsistent that the customer would not return your calls. This might be a good time to check in with the customer to see if you've done something that violated the trust you worked so hard to build.

  > *"I haven't heard from you and I wanted to make sure you left on a positive note, and that you have everything you need. I want to help make this as positive an experience for you as possible."*

  Don't purpose to lay a guilt trip on them, but let them know that you thought the time spent together was meaningful, and that you are concerned that you might not have helped them in every way possible.

- ## Create a Sense of Urgency

  I have often taught sales counselors to be aware of the "Closing Triangle", consisting of three elements that must be present in order for a customer to buy. These three factors are:

  1) *"Does the product meet my needs?"*

  2) *"Do I trust the company and the sales representative?"*

  3) *"Do I have an urgency to act on this decision right away?"*

  Have you ever had the prospect who showed you all the right buying signals, who found that the product fit their needs to a tee and who genuinely liked and respected you – but who just wouldn't buy? What caused the indecision? It was a lack of urgency. Without urgency an otherwise strong prospect will sit on the sidelines for ages.

  Make certain that you are instilling a strong sense of urgency during your follow-up calls, even if you are only leaving a message. Without that urgency, the customer will go on believing that it doesn't matter if they buy today or tomorrow – or next month.

- ## Urgency builders:

  ✓ *"We have just two of the Winchester model left, and only one in a location that would meet your needs. You need to come by and look at what we have."*

  ✓ *"It's Thursday and I wanted to let you know that our price increases usually come in on Saturdays. I don't know what will happen this weekend, but it is still possible to lock in your prices today."*

  ✓ *"We've sold six _____ in the last three (hours/days/ weeks). You need to act now to get the best selection."*

Make sure your follow-up calls always have a tone of urgency to them. Don't leave a message unless there is an urgency element to your communication.

- **Make the Final Communication Extremely Positive**

  When you feel it is time to throw in the towel, end the communication on a strong and positive note, preferably in writing. The handwritten note goes a long way towards being memorable. This gives you the best chance of landing the sale when the customer eventually decides to buy.

  (In writing): "I've really enjoyed working with you and I would be honored if you chose us as the company you wish to do business with. I know you would love our product and I promise we'll take very good care of you. Keep us in mind!" "P.S. Stop by sometime just to say hello. I'd love to chat again."

11

Dealing with the Incentive-Driven Prospect

Prospect: *"What are your incentives?"*

Salesperson: *"Well, that depends on what you're looking for. Do you have a particular model in mind?"*

Prospect: *"What are your incentives?"*

Salesperson: *"Heh, heh. You're a smooth one, you are. We've got some great deals right now. Let me show you a model and you can see what you can get."*

Prospect: *"What are your incentives?"*

Salesperson: *"All right, I get it. I'll answer the question, but you have to answer a question for me first. What is the most important aspect of value for you?"*

Prospect: *"What are your incentives?"*

Salesperson: *"Kill me now."*

———————————

It doesn't matter how strong your market is or what the competitors around you are doing. So many shoppers will inevitably ask a question that makes so many sales counselors cringe: "What are your incentives?" The question typically arises in the first couple of minutes of the conversation, and if it is not handled correctly the answer can actually serve to *destroy* the very value that the incentive was intended to create.

Let's start with a question: is buying process primarily an emotional or a logical endeavor? Most would agree that it is an emotional pursuit that is supported by logic. What about incentives – are they emotional or logical? That depends on when they are offered. When we discuss the incentives in the first few moments of the sales conversation, there is no emotional connection yet established in the offering and, therefore, the incentives are logical. Not good. But when we bring up the incentive *after* the shopper is emotionally engaged in the offering then the incentive takes on an emotional appeal.

In short, the earlier you discuss the incentives, the less likely it is you will receive any value from that offering. The longer you wait to bring up the incentives the more likely it is you will receive an emotional return. *Keep in mind that incentives are best used as a closing tool, not as an opening tool.*

Why are customers so taken with this question? For a couple of reasons. The first is that they have been trained by sales counselors to ask this question. Many sales counselors offer incentives as a part of the price description (even when they haven't yet been asked) and so the prospects come to believe this is a normal part of the process.

The other reason the question is so common is that buyers have a perception that incentives (deals, discounts, specials) are a normal part of any big-ticket purchase. They take a cue from advertisements and commercials promoting this month's zero down, zero drive-off extravaganza. Or perhaps they are from a part of the world where negotiation is so common that they expect that a deal will be made *any time* they buy *any product*.

Whether your incentive is $50, $500 or $50,000 you need to protect that valuable sales tool by not playing your cards too quickly. A few ideas...

- **Defer the Conversation Until Emotional Appeal is Secured**

Think back to the last time you bought a car from a dealership. When did you talk about the price, the terms and the final deal? After you took the car for a test drive, correct? Why did the salesperson take you for a test drive before going over the terms? Because she knows that the most important factor in your car buying decision will not be the terms (which are patently logical in nature), but rather the *emotional* appeal of the car. It would be foolish for her to spew out the lowest possible price the moment you walk through the door since there is no emotional value yet established. (Nor would you accept that as the lowest price; this would become your starting point.)

We can learn something from this case study. In fact, we can learn something from just about every big-ticket sales organization on the planet. *Don't talk about terms until an emotional appeal is established.* When you dive too deep into a conversation about "the deal" too early in the process, there is an insufficient emotional appeal established. Tie the customer in emotionally and the value becomes easier to defend.

> *"What are the incentives? Great question, because we've got some great terms. Let's find the car that suits your needs the best and then I'll be happy to share with you the terms on that car."*

> *"I'm glad you asked, because I think you'll like what you hear. Is there a particular model you're interested in? I can tell you the terms once we've established the model you like the best."*

- ## Appeal to the Concept of Fairness for Everyone

  We know that, in many cases, our buyers are dealing with the fear of *not* getting the best available terms. If you can convince the prospect that she is getting the best terms available, and that the next buyer will not get a better deal, you might alleviate some of that fear.

  For most shoppers it is not a case of needing a better deal than everyone else got (though there are certainly some that fit this category). For most it is a question of whether some other customer, even just <u>one</u>, received even *better* terms. Assure them that everyone receives the exact same terms (if this is the case).

  > *"I can appreciate your desire to get the best terms you can get, and that is exactly what is happening. We do not negotiate on our terms, so <u>everyone</u> gets the best deal available."*

- ## Refocus the Value Equation by Redefining "Incentives"

  When shoppers ask about the incentives they are, of course, asking about the financial spiffs available when they purchase. But is this truly the number one incentive for making a purchase decision? No! The number one incentive for making a purchase is…*this is a great product that fulfills my need!* We need to reeducate the prospect as to what the incentive really is.

  > *"What is our incentive? It's the best built home you'll find in this fantastic neighborhood – that's the incentive and that's why people are buying here. Not only that but, if you buy from us, we've got some amazing financial terms as well. We'll get to that later."*

  > *"Our incentives? A great home, a great location, fantastic schools, wonderful neighborhood amenities, 9-foot ceilings…we've got plenty. Let's take a look and I'll show you what I mean."*

- **Talk about Market Factors**

Incentives are a function of pricing and, in reality, pricing is always dictated by the market. You might need to offer a mini-economics lesson to your prospect, explaining that we set our prices according to what the market dictates.

> *"If you were selling your own boat, you wouldn't price it any higher or any lower than the market bears. The fact is that we do not set our prices – the market sets the price. If we set our own prices they would be much higher. If the buyers set the price it would be much lower. The market sets the price, and we price our boats to whatever the market tells us, just like you would if you were selling a boat."*

- **Use the Takeaway Close**

Finally, some prospects just need to know that the deal could not have gotten any better, regardless of their deftness in negotiating. When you get a buyer who is hammering you for more incentives, don't be afraid. Your strength and confidence in your terms might be exactly what that prospect needs to see.

> *"You know, it appears that we are at an impasse because the terms you are asking for are just not consistent with the value of this RV. As much as it pains me to say this, perhaps you need to find an RV where you can feel like you're getting a better deal."*

12
Remembering Customer's Names

Salesperson: *"Hello and welcome to FurnitureMart. My name is Jeff."*

Prospect: *"Hi, I'm Betty."*

Salesperson: *"Nice to meet you, uh…what was your name again?"*

Prospect: *"Betty. You know, like Barney's wife?"*

Salesperson: *"The purple dinosaur is married? I didn't know that."*

Prospect: *"Not that Barney. Barney Rubble… from the Flintstones?"*

Salesperson: *"Oh, yeah. I love that show. So what can I do for you, Wilma?"*

Whether you're a veteran or a newbie in the sales business, remembering the prospect's name seems to be a never-ending challenge. Many are good at getting the name initially, but recalling it even seconds later can be a real problem. This is a critical concern given the importance of using the name as a means of establishing a trust relationship.

I know of what I speak in this regard; remembering names has always been a source of struggle for yours truly. But this is a skill and, like any skill, it can be learned and developed, provided this is truly a priority for you.

We need to start with this reality: retention of any information is more a matter of the will than of technique. We'll talk about technique in just a moment but, if you are not committed to remembering names, all the technique in the world won't do you any good. Those who are extremely strong in this area will tell you that there is both a desire *and* an accompanying action that goes into remembering people's names, but the desire comes first. If this truly is a priority, you'll do what it takes to deal with this issue. So is it truly a priority?

Suppose I said you, "A man in a blue suit is going to walk into your office carrying a briefcase full of cash just for you. All you need to do is introduce yourself, get his name, use it, and remember it five minutes later and the cash is yours." Would you remember the man's name? Of course you would. Why? Because it's important to you! And that's the point. You need to establish in your mind that the person walking in the door of your sales center is equally important, and therefore worthy of you remembering their name.

The first advice I would offer, then, is to incorporate the decision to remember the prospect's name into your "pre-shot routine", that time of mental preparation before the customer walks through the door. In those few moments you can make the commitment to obtain, use and remember the prospect's name. That might sound simplistic, but it works. When you really want to remember something important, *you will*.

A few hints on name recollection…

- **Concentrate**

  99% of remembering someone's name comes through commitment, not through technique. Great salespeople make a commitment to those things that are truly important to the customer... like remembering the name.

  Get in the habit of listening intently for the name as soon as the customer walks through the door. In fact, listen for the name so specifically that it sounds as if they were shouting it at you. Single it out above all else. See the name in your mind. Take a snapshot of the customer's face and see the name written just below the photo.

  You can practice this technique as a part of your normal life – at a store, a restaurant, at church, or a party.

- **Say the Name as Soon as You Hear It**

  When you hear someone say their own name you hear it externally, but when *you* say the name you hear it internally. Our words are loud inside our own head, so say it as soon as possible and you will hear it well.

  > *"Welcome to Peters Brothers. I'm Jeff and you are...Emily. Welcome, Emily and thanks for visiting us today." (The name is actually used twice in this example, further establishing "Emily" in the mind.)*

- **Say the Name Several Times in the First Few Minutes**

  You obviously don't want to get obnoxious about this, but you can use the name as an emphasis provider and thus further cement their name in your brain while showing the prospect that you are personally interested in them.

  > *"Emily, I want to be able to point you in the right direction. Tell me what's most important to you in your new car."*

"I'll tell you what, Emily. You probably want to see a model home. Why don't I get you a brochure…"

- ## Write it Down

  If you're still struggling with remembering names, you might consider taking out a pad of paper and immediately writing down the name (some companies use guest registration cards or CRM software which enable you to capture this information quickly). This might be a tiny bit awkward, but it's a lot better than forgetting the name just seconds after you heard it. Be honest and respectfully explain to the customers that you don't want to forget their names.

  "I'm going to write that down. I meet a lot of people every day and I want to make sure I remember everyone's name – it's important to me."

- ## Associate it with Something

  Memory experts will tell us that associating a person's name with a distinguishing feature (jewelry, clothing, hairline, etc.) will increase your retention. For more on this technique I recommend *The Memory Book* by Jerry Lucas. I read it years ago and found it fascinating and useful…at least the parts of it I remember….

- ## Go out of Your Way to Remember Unusual Names

  It's one thing to remember a name that you are already familiar with. "Emily? Oh, that's my daughter's name!" We can handle the Bill's and the Susan's and the Fred's. But what if the name is something less common to most people – Pushpakar or Hea or Anoop. How do we handle the names that are not necessarily familiar to us?

  Start with the principle that your name can be considered to be one of the most endearing and important aspects of your identity. In many cultures the name is more than what sounds good – it carries deep significance to the family. Don't take this lightly! Go out of your way to slow the conversation down long enough to ensure that you have the name and that you can, if at all possible for you, pronounce it properly.

> *"I'm sorry, I didn't get that and I want to make sure I have it down. Can you repeat your name? An-NOOP. Did I say that correctly? Great. I've not heard that name before. Does it have a special meaning?"*

When we are willing to have this conversation with our customers, we accomplish more than just getting the name set in our own mind. We show the prospect respect and we let them know that we will go out of our way to honor their individuality. Do this because it's the right thing to do, but don't be surprised when you find that your prospect suddenly trusts and respects you right back.

13
He Likes You; She Doesn't (or vice versa)

Salesperson: *"This backyard is perfect for parties. Do you BBQ?"*

Husband: *"Do I BBQ? Dude, I'm the BBQ king! I can cook for 40."*

Wife: *(mumbling) "He can cook hamburgers for 40. I have to prep salad, make the mashed potatoes, bake rolls, cook pies, clean the house, put together seating for 40 and clean up afterwards."*

Salesperson: *"40?! Dude, you rock! You're the BBQ king!"*

Husband: *"Ya' know, I like your style."*

Wife: *(mumbling) "Ya' know, I could clean your clock."*

Salesperson: *"How would you like to call this home your own?"*

Husband: *"How would you like to come over for burgers after we move in?"*

Wife: *(mumbling) "How would you like a fat lip, Slick?"*

It is in the nature of salespeople to want to be liked. That's okay; you don't have to apologize for that. In fact, the desire to please is a cornerstone of effective service. After all, our customers are only pleased when they are well cared for. So when a prospect does *not* like you, it can be painful.

Take a situation where you are working with a couple; she likes you but he doesn't. You end up with a state of affairs that is both painful *and awkward*. Ultimately, a purchase decision is a process that will require cooperation from both parties, so you'd better be able to get your hands around the situation as quickly as possible.

We must start with the question of "Why?" Why doesn't he/she like you? You're a wonderful conversationalist and an incredible human being, right? And wouldn't you say that humility is one of your strong suits? So what's not to like?

Well, for one thing you are a salesperson, and that is quite enough for some prospects to crawl into a defensive posture, even if they have to be discourteous along the way. You and I might hold sales professionals in the highest respect, but your prospect rented "Cadillac Man" last night and has his or her own opinion of the value of the salesperson. Just understand that this is a pre-conceived bias so don't take it personally. Don't get me wrong – the situation still has to be dealt with – but it's not about you!

This bias against salespeople might be based on reputation, or it might be based on past experiences. Regrettably, most of the population can tell you the horror story of dealing with an unscrupulous salesperson and that experience stays with them as they project their fears onto every other sales professional. Again, it's not personal but it is real and it must be dealt with.

There is one other possibility as to why these challenging prospects act as they do and it has nothing to do with the salesperson. It is possible that one person in the relationship just doesn't trust the other, that they are at odds before they walk through the door. The aggravation directed at you might actually be meant for the spouse or significant other. You just happen to be the easy target.

In any event, a customer is a customer and has the right to feel and act as they desire (within the limits of common decency). Sometimes that means they will be less than cordial, just based on the stress levels they are dealing with. I would suggest that this is not the time to pass moral judgments on the prospects, but rather to take them by the hand and show that you can help them through this difficult process.

In my years observing and managing sales representatives I have seen that some sales counselors will handle this situation calmly and strategically, considering it a professional challenge, not unlike 100 other challenges they will face during the course of the day. Others are emotionally affected by this situation, fearing that a lack of approval is a customer's negative reaction to the sales counselor's personality and demeanor.

The difference in response of these two sales representatives is a reflection of their emotional intelligence. One has the maturity and self-confidence to see this as a challenge and an opportunity; the other despairs over the situation and allows it to hamper their own energy and enthusiasm. Success comes when we recognize that everyone is different, everyone is unique, and everyone deserves the benefit of your best efforts, regardless of whether they like you or not.

Some approaches to this situation:

• **Deal with Reality**

   You meet lots of people in your line of work. Many salespeople will talk with more than a thousand prospects each year (and a lot more than that in some fields). But let's be ultra-conservative and suggest that you'll meet with 100 people this year. Is everyone like you? No. Does everyone share your personality style? Of course not. The sales counselor who desires the immediate approval of each and every customer is bound to be disappointed. Getting 100 out of 100 people to love you is, for most, an unattainable goal.

When we recognize that not everyone will like us right off the bat, we further recognize that relationships are a work-in-progress. It is in both the customer's best interest, and in yours as well, to allow time for a process of civilized conversation to develop into a trust relationship based on mutual respect, support and, eventually, likeability.

• Make a Decision in Favor of Unilateral Respect

If we know that not everyone will like us right out of the gate, it leads us to a very important decision: do I need to respect the prospect even if the prospect does not respect me back? The answer is (or should be) "Yes"! Sales counselors with a strong emotional intelligence will make a decision in favor of *unilateral* respect. They provide their best service, their best assistance and even their best attitude to everyone who comes through the door, regardless of the demeanor of the prospect.

Understand that there are all kinds of personality types out there, and the sales approach for one does not necessarily make sense for another. Be patient and respect the boundaries of those who are less comfortable right off the bat.

• "Out-Nice" Difficult People

Suppose you are working with two people but you've only established a trust relationship with one. You must assume that the other will come along in time if you continue to do your best work and provide your strongest service and attentiveness. In the mean time, try to "out-nice" the person.

Suppose he is acting as though he doesn't like you. This might just be a defensive posture that he takes with all new salespeople. He just happens to be more comfortable with strangers. So don't follow his lead! Outlast him with your kindness and respect. Make it your quest to bring him around.

Again, this is a *unilateral* decision. If you need someone to be nice to you in order for you to be nice to them, I'll once again suggest you're in the wrong line of work.

• Don't Play Favorites

The situation we are describing leads to a very serious pitfall for many sales counselors. "I like him, but I don't like her – so I'll be nice to him and tolerate her." Big mistake. When you pay greater attention to your favorite you will only alienate the other partner, thus deepening the problem. That other person will launch into a defensive mindset, fearing that they are outnumbered.

Think 50-50 at all times. Smile equally. When one asks a question, answer both. When one offers an opinion, ask the other if they are in agreement.

• Understand the Uniqueness of Each Prospect

In the case of two people who are shopping together you must understand that couples are often opposite in their personalities. It is therefore likely that you will interact more comfortably with one than the other. Don't panic. This is very, very normal. But you must overcome your tendency towards favoring the person you like the most. This will only alienate you from the person who might be the real decision-maker.

• Find a Victory for the Other Person

Look for even the smallest things to make the grumpy person feel good. Don't overkill this, but see if you can find *something* that makes this person truly feel that you are looking out for their best interests.

Above all else, keep your head on straight. A negative attitude must not be construed as a personal affront, but rather as a signal for attention and assistance. You primary role is to provide positive energy in a situation that is often disquieting to a nervous prospect.

14
Handling Price Objections

Customer: *"The price is too high."*

Salesperson: *"What exactly do you mean by that?"*

Customer: *"I mean it's not too low and it's not just right – it's too high."*

Salesperson: *"And what are you basing that on?"*

Customer: *"On the fact that the price is not where it should be."*

Salesperson: *"All right. Throw me a bone here. I want to help but you need to tell me why you think it's too high."*

Customer: *"I think it's too high because it is overpriced."*

Salesperson: *"That was direct from the Department of Redundancy Department. Can you be more specific?"*

Customer: *"I want a lower price."*

Salesperson: *"Ah. Now we're getting somewhere."*

(Author's admission: This is the longest chapter in the book...and a chapter that could have been much longer. One chapter is hardly enough to provide a solution for every price objection you get, but it will give you some tools to put in your arsenal. Admission number two: I've skipped the hackneyed advice from both trainers and sales managers that says, "Well, buckaroo – you just need to create more value!" I'm figuring you're smart enough to have thought that through already. Let's get to the meaty part!)

I have a factory, and my factory makes designer toothpicks – exclusive and very trendy. I need to sell the toothpicks I produce, so I strive to find that price that will represent appropriate value to my customers. I don't want to overprice my toothpicks because consumers would balk and I would be stuck with too much supply. I don't want to underprice them either; consumers would buy them up and I would have no inventory left to sell. I need to price my toothpicks so that customers will buy them at the exact same pace as I am capable of producing them.

Does this all sound vaguely familiar to you? If so, you might remember this discussion from Econ 101. This is the simplest explanation of the law of supply and demand. One of the most important principles regarding pricing is that I can, at best, *guess* at the appropriate price of my toothpicks. I put my product in front of consumers at the price *I think* they will find attractive, and they respond by either purchasing or passing them over. If they buy my toothpicks at that price, I guessed right. If they buy too many of my toothpicks, I guessed too low. If they don't buy any at all, I guessed too high.

Now let's leave the designer toothpick factory and consider the application to your product. Here is a reality that you must deal with: you are working for a *for-profit organization*. The company you work for wants and needs to make money. Your organization dwells in a capitalistic society and functions in a risk environment. In fact, because of the risky nature of production, your company needs to make as much money as possible whenever it can. When the market shifts downward, your organization is still be on the hook for very real costs: resources, office space, administrative structure, distribution outlets, etc.

All right, so you work for an unashamed, unabashed, financially motivated, capitalistic company. Fine. But here is one other truth I can tell you about your own organization: *your company does not set the price.* You heard that right – the companies that produce goods and services do not set their own prices. Remember that, as true capitalists, we are about maximizing financial opportunity and that means charging the highest price we can. So if your company set the price you would all be selling $200,000 mini-vans or $1,000 sweaters. Guess what - the buyer doesn't set the price either. If that were the case we would all be selling $50,000 beachfront condos or $5,000 Lamborghini's.

It is an inescapable truth of business: ***the market sets the price.*** Always has, always will. The best we can do is attempt to influence market perceptions and then to guess at what the market price is on a given day. Sometimes we guess too low and sell too quickly. Other times we guess too high and get stuck with excess inventory. The market couldn't care less one way or another. The market will determine the appropriate value of the offering and measure that value by a price. This works the same for houses, hip boots, hurricane lamps…and designer toothpicks.

Why the economics lesson? I am trying to do you a favor! *You don't ever have to apologize or even defend the price of your product.* We don't set the price – the market does. If the fundamental sales and marketing disciplines are in order but the product is overpriced, it simply will not sell. Period. Your strongest selling tool might just be your track record.

Try taking the first seven paragraphs of this chapter and condensing it down to a simple explanation of market economics: the market sets the price. The more comfortable you are in explaining this principle to a customer the more likely it is you will overcome the objection.

"Value is an opinion, and so I respect where you're coming from. However, our homes are always priced to market – that is, they are always priced at whatever a homebuyer is willing to pay. It's simple – if our homes are overpriced they won't sell. But we've sold eight homes in the last five weeks. We are actually ahead of our sales pace. The market is confirming that the homes are priced correctly. It appears that the home you are looking at will sell for the price listed; it's only a question of whether you will buy it or if someone else will do it first."

While you do not have to defend the price, you very much need to defend (and enhance) the perceived value of the offering. You cannot affect the purchase price unless you first affect the perceived value. A horrible sales counselor, for example, will turn off the prospect to the product itself, and subsequently the company will have to lower the price to appease the market that has been disturbed by what they see. On the contrary, an outstanding sales counselor will serve to raise the perceived value of the offering, and the company will be rewarded with a higher price.

While you do not need to argue with a customer over whether or not your product is priced to market, you do need to make sure you fully understand the customers' value concern. As with any objection you'll want to question thoroughly to fully understand the basis for the apprehension. When you think about it, "The price is too high" can mean a number of things. Here are some interpretations of that phrase:

- ✓ *"I don't see the value; I don't think it's worth it."*
- ✓ *"I think the deal will get better if I wait."*
- ✓ *"Your competitor charges less than you."*
- ✓ *"I've never spent this much before. It's outside my paradigm."*
- ✓ *"I just need to make sure I'm getting the best deal possible."*
- ✓ *"I can't afford it."*

Note that those are six very, very different interpretations of the same statement. That means that there are six different sales approaches to handle that one initial customer comment. To the extent that you do not understand the true meaning of the phrase, "The price is too high", you will struggle mightily in overcoming this objection.

This is where we turn to perhaps the single-most important word in the vocabulary of a salesperson: "Why?" The "why" question is the quickest path to understanding on a number of levels. The question leads us to a greater insight on the mind of the prospect. It clarifies the last statement the customer made. The "why" question fills in missing information all throughout the sales discussion. You must be certain that before you begin to overcome a price objection you fully understand where that prospect is coming from. Your sales dialogue must get you to a deeper knowledge of the true meaning of the price objection.

"Talk to me. What are you basing that value judgment on?"

"Overpriced? Can you give me an idea as to your comparison point so I can better understand how you come to that conclusion?"

"Value is a matter of opinion, and I definitely respect your opinion. So that I can help you with this issue, can you tell me what you are basing your value judgment on?"

"Can you define 'overpriced' for me? Tell me how you arrive at that."

Take that last example. There is a huge strategic difference in your sales approach when the customer responds, "I've been shopping around and it seems like your prices are higher than your competitor's", versus, "I just can't afford it – it is out of my price range." Those are two entirely different objections initially voiced identically. The "why" question provides the clarity that drives us to the appropriate strategy.

Before we look deeper into those six different categories, I want to clarify one important reality in each of the customer concerns: if they are standing on your sales floor voicing an objection, it means they are on your sales floor voicing an objection. ("Ummmm, Jeff – You just said the same thing twice.") Think this through – the most important observation I can make about the people who are sharing a price objection is that they are still there – they haven't walked out on you. If the price objection was a deal-killer, sayonara. But this is not a deal killer – it is simply a deal-*pauser*. This is the prospect's way of asking for help in justifying the price. You would do the same thing if in their shoes, so don't freak out and don't panic. If anything, you should get excited about the fact that they must be serious *or they would have left by now!*

Now onto the price objections...

- **"I don't see the value; I don't think it's worth it."**

  I love this objection and I'll tell you why. It's all in what you hear the customer say. Many sales professionals interpret the value challenge as, "I want you to lower your price." I hear it as, "I'm very interested, but I'm not there yet. Can you help me?" Remember what we said earlier: if this is a deal-*killer*, they're gone. This is just a deal-*pauser*.

  First words from my mouth: "Thank you. I appreciate you trusting me enough to share that concern. Let's talk it through and maybe I can help. Tell me what you are basing your opinion on." You cannot answer the objection until you fully understand it. I need the prospect to think through the rational basis for their objection. It is important that *they* understand why they feel as they do.

  And "feel" is the right word here. It is up to you to determine whether this value opinion is a feeling or a fact. If it's a fact, your job is to get the customer committed to the emotional reasons why a purchase decision makes sense. If it's a feeling, you can be at the ready with facts that give a more solid and empirical opinion on the valuation. In short, if the prospect's value opinion is based on feelings, counter with facts. If it's based on facts, counter with feelings.

Ultimately, play to the emotional need to improve this aspect of their lives. If they are buying to make their lives better (which is the case), then the sooner they purchase the sooner there lives will be better. Make sense?

- **"I think the deal will get better if I wait."**

I know this doesn't apply to everyone; many of you sell fixed-price, non-negotiable goods or services. If that's the case, take a nap right here (or move on to the next segment).

First question: Is it true? Might the deal get better if they wait? Do you know that? As a salesperson, I don't want to know when the prices and terms are going to change. I want to know what the prices and terms are right now, so that I can get the customer focused on the present value and not on the future price. If it is in your control, plead with your sales manager to keep future pricing discounts, incentives, etc. to her/himself.

Second question: How did the customer arrive at this perception? Do you have a history of sweetening the deal if people wait? Are your competitors "training" your prospects? Are you in a declining price industry? In any event, you need to find the bottom of the market and you to stay firm with the prospect. At some point you might consider this phrasing: "*Congratulations, you have found our last price. The price at which, if you threatened to walk if I don't lower the price by another 1%, I'd let you walk. You now have all the information you need to make a decision, but the price won't change a bit.*" You do your customer a favor when you convince them that they've reached the floor on pricing.

Third question: From your perception, why *should* they buy today? If you cannot answer that question off the top of your head, run (don't walk) straight to your manager and ask for help in nailing down this portion of your presentation. If you are not a true believer in your own value proposition, *why are you there???* You will do your customer (and yourself) no favors by lying through your teeth in convincing them to buy when you don't believe it is in their best interests.

- **"Your competitor charges less than you."**

Is this true? One of the simplest tactics in the buying strategy is to compare apples-to-oranges and then point out a price difference. If this is the case, you need not defend your higher price! In fact, you should boast of your higher price.

Here it is a good idea to relate the prospect to other goods and services where you pay for the stronger value perception. Think of the higher price that goes along with the prestige of owning a quality brand. The fact is that Lexus garners a higher price than Hyundai, even though Hyundai has come to build a fine car. But salespeople at Lexus feel no need to talk about a price adjustment ("It's a Lexus for cryin' out loud!"). Wedgewood crystal should gain a higher price than Macy's brand. Be bold. Be proud. Be everything just short of arrogant about the prestige that your brand carries.

If you don't have the same incredible brand strength but you still have a higher price, you'll need to do a little "symbolic selling". Line up a number of areas where you offer features that your competitor does not, and really hammer those points. You don't need to bash the other guy (bad form!), but by pointing out what you have that they don't you raise the perceived value and you assist in the price justification.

- **"I've never spent this much before. It's outside my paradigm."**

This is actually an issue that is discussed infrequently amongst sales types, but it might be the single-most important obstacle to overcome.

I was in a department store looking at suits not too long ago. I found a really nice black Hugo Boss three-button, nicely tapered, very European. To tell you the truth, I think I looked great in that suit (yeah, I said it!). But the price tag on the suit (not on sale) was way up there. In fact, it was more than I had ever spent on a suit. So not only do I need to deal with the perceived value and the concern over affordability, I also had to deal with the fact that this suit just wasn't consistent with how I see myself. You tell me the greater obstacle – value perception or self-perception????

Since this is an emotion-based issue we must face it on emotional terms first and foremost. You must get the customer to isolate the product, if only for a short time, away from the price: *"Let's pretend that this Rolex was on sale for $100. Why would you want to own it, apart from the great price?"* It is imperative that the *customer* identifies the desire to own the product. They must hear themselves state why they are fond of the offering on an emotional basis, and for a time liberated from the burden of cost.

From that point the customer needs to understand why it makes sense for them to change their paradigm. I'm not a big fan of the "you-owe-it-to-yourself" approach, if only because it sounds so much like you just walked out of a sales training course. But we can paint the picture of how they will enjoy the product down the road, and how much they could resent the compromise of buying the less-desirable offering at the lower price.

This is where you can ask a very powerful value-clarifying question. *"If my product and my competitor's product were both free, and you could only take one, which would you take?"* When my customer admits that if both were free they would take my product, they have also admitted that to take the lower-priced offering would mean compromise. Facing that reality might just build a discomfort they are not ready to accept. They might yet choose to buy from your competitor, but it is your job to make sure they are aware of the potential regrets in purchasing the wrong thing just so that they could save a few bucks, even at the expense of their own contentment.

- **"I just need to make sure I'm getting the best deal possible."**

Oh, yeah – *that* guy! Careful now. Our first thought is to paint this person as one who will not sleep until he knows he is getting significantly better terms than anyone else. But this is not necessarily the case. In many instances this prospect is driven by the desire not to be taken advantage of, and that is a very different motivation.

The question for this prospect is not, "Will I get significantly better terms than anyone else?" but rather, "Will anyone else receive significantly better terms than me?" The fear is that the very next purchaser will receive better terms base on superior negotiation skills.

So we see that there are two very different agendas: 1) Getting a great deal and 2) Not getting a bad deal. Where is your prospect coming from? Get this wrong and you'll end up answering the wrong objection.

Of course, this objection is far simpler if you have a fixed price, non-negotiating policy. The market sets the price and the market further validates that the price is accurate. We have only to stand firm (not that we have a choice) and let the customer know that we will, if necessary, allow the prospect to walk out. Sometimes that is what it takes to convince a prospect that there is not another 2% wiggle room on the price.

Interestingly, this same approach works for those sales professionals who deal with variable or negotiated price and terms. When we continually move on our price we send the message to the prospect that there is more room left to negotiate. At some point the customer needs to know that you are finished, that you have offered him your last price. Be firm about that – you're doing this prospect a favor.

> *"Let me be clear on this – you have found our last price. We don't want to lose your business, but we are not willing to move any further. You now have all the information you need to make a decision on this purchase".*

- **"I can't afford it."**

The key issue here is determining the difference between "I can't afford it", and "I don't think I can afford it." Those are two very different realities. You must begin your defense with that clarification.

> *"Just so I'm clear, are you saying that you don't have the means to purchase or that you are just not comfortable with spending that amount?"*

This is not a question easily asked when there is little trust relationship established, but if you've done your job right and you have assumed a counseling role in the transaction, you should expect your customer to trust you with an accurate answer.

There is a word for prospects who truly cannot afford the product you are selling: "Non-Prospect"! Don't waste your time (or your non-customer's time) trying to sell something that cannot be bought. On the other hand, I've seen prospects do some pretty creative things when they are emotionally attached to a product ("Uncle Louie? It's Bob and Marsha. Say, we're looking at this ski boat, and…")

For the prospect that is just not comfortable with the price, we must understand that people won't make a move unless they perceive that that move will improve their life and that the amount of improvement exceeds the cost. So if a customer has the means but not the comfort level to proceed with the purchase, we can assume that they do not see how owning the product will have an emotional impact strong enough to justify the price. In other words, there is a perception of value issue.

In my experience the first and best option is to clarify the "cost" of doing nothing. If the customer is considering a purchase in the first place it means that there is something about their current situation that needs to be improved. So if they do nothing, they must accept their dissatisfaction. The strong salesperson will point out that the dissatisfaction will grow over time and that the sooner they make a move, the sooner their life will improve.

Then consider telling a third-party story about a similar customer with similar concerns who made the move and today couldn't be happier. Those stories are powerful because the serve as validation from the most credible of all sources – other people.

At the end of the day you cannot force someone to purchase who perceives too great a risk in making the decision. However, you can increase the value perceptions and lower the perceived costs and, in so doing, bring the equation into balance for the prospect.

15

Selling a Heavy Inventory of Your Least Popular Model

Prospect: *"The Winchester Plan suits my needs perfectly. I'll take the Cheyenne."*

Salesperson: *"Huh? I thought you liked the Winchester."*

Prospect: *"We do, but you've got plenty of those and you're sold out of the Cheyenne. Clearly we must be missing out on something."*

Salesperson: *"Missing something like...the best possible product for you?"*

Prospect: *"Yes, and we'd also like the financing plan that isn't available."*

Salesperson: *"And I got out of the restaurant business for this?"*

It's one of the weirdities of the sales business – everyone loves Product A and Product B and we can't give Product C away...until one day for some unknown reason (perhaps tied to the alignment of the planets) everyone simply must have Product C and they passionately hate Product A. I've never been able to figure out this strange shift

119

of the fates of the different offerings, but I have seen some common trends to watch out for.

The most dangerous of those trends is the sales counselor who has fallen out of love with a particular model or product line. He believes what he hears when those around him have suggested it's a lousy product and he has internalized those opinions so strongly that he is no longer capable of selling the line. In his book *Integrity Selling*, author Ron Willingham points out that if a sales counselor does not believe that his product represents a great value for his customer, he can never reach his selling potential. In fact, this "Belief in Product" is so important that a salesperson cannot effectively sell the product without setting aside his own value system.

In my years as a consultant in the home building industry I have frequently come across this situation: a particular floor plan is lagging behind in the sales column. When I query the salesperson as to the situation I'll hear something like this: "Let me tell you why this home won't sell." STOP RIGHT THERE! I don't need to hear any more. I've already discovered the #1 reason why the home won't sell – *because the salesperson is convinced that it won't sell*. In sales this is the ultimate example of a self-fulfilling prophecy.

In the above example, not only did the salesperson have a negative attitude that would prevent him from selling the home, but it is interesting to note that the sales counselor is statistically *dead wrong!* When he says that the home won't sell, that's just not true. Every home sells to someone at some point for some price. This is true for your product as well. Everything sells eventually, but not if you have given up hope.

Great sales counselors ferociously protect their own mindset, staying sharp and positive at all times. They do not allow negative talk to affect how they view their own product, and they possess the emotional intelligence necessary to bounce back when they hear comments that are less than flattering. After all, you are not selling the product to everyone – only to the person who likes it and would like to buy it.

That said, I recognize how frustrating this situation can be. Try these suggestions…

- ## Tie Specific Value to Specific Need

  Every shopper for every product is motivated by the same thing – a perceived need. If the customer has no need, then they are not really a customer in the first place.

  If the customer has a specific need and you have the perfect solution, it hardly matters how many you have as compared to other models. This is the purest form of selling – matching a customer's need with the ideal solution.

  When you find yourself with an abundance of one particular model or line, go first to the deep discovery of the customer's need and see if it doesn't get you both excited about the solution you have in mind.

- ## Convince *Yourself* of the Value

  Get creative and do everything you can think of to make sure you are convinced that this product line represents an awesome value for someone out there. Don't adopt the negative opinion of a few vocal shoppers who for whatever reason didn't appreciate what you had to offer.

  Some specific suggestions:

  - ✓ Talk about the product with a peer, looking for positive attributes as you go along. Sometimes a fresh perspective will lead to value opportunities that you would have missed.

  - ✓ Talk with those people who *have* bought the slow-seller. Ask what attracted them to the product in the first-place and also what they like now that the own it. People have a remarkable way of increasing their appreciation of a product after they have purchased it. As you see that with your own eyes you will gain a greater appreciation of value.

✓ If possible, talk to the producer or manufacturer – someone in authority who had a hand in the creation. No product line is ever drawn as a dud. There was something special that the designer was trying to accomplish. What was it?

✓ Ask yourself the question, "Why will someone purchase this particular product?" Come up with an answer and incorporate that value point into your sales presentation.

- ## Educate the Prospect

  People fear making a mistake, especially on a major decision. Having an abundance of one particular plan might look peculiar to the prospect at first glance, but we in the sales industry know that this scenario is not all that unusual. Assure the prospect that this happens all the time. Some suggested verbiage:

  "I gave up a long time ago trying to figure out why some cars take longer to sell than others. I only know that selecting a car is a personal choice, and that every single car on this lot will soon be sold."

  "It's strange – last month everyone wanted the Plan 2. Now everyone wants the Plan 3. You never know – the Plan 2 could be the huge hit again next month."

  "We only know that it always balances out in the end. We don't expect that everyone will love every boat we build; that's why we offer a variety. I'm not concerned. I know all these boats will sell very soon."

• Learn and Use Third-Party Testimonials

As I have stated previously, no one wants to be alone on a bad decision. For this reason, people seek validation from other buyers. You need to find the one thing about the product that owners really appreciate, and then emphasize that value point when you are describing the line. This works best with actual testimonials from actual buyers. Call a few and find out what they love.

> *"The thing that people have really enjoyed about these shoes is the fact that they can wear them to dress up or wear them with blue jeans, but they're comfortable all the time. People who are on their feet a lot all day really love these."*

> *"My customers tell me that they love how the Accentra feels on the long drives."*

Note that second example one more time. Every product has its plusses and minuses. You want the prospect to look past the potential flaw and forward to the highlight of the product.

16
Dealing with the Relentless Negotiator

Salesperson: *"That's my final price."*

Customer: *"No, it's not."*

Salesperson: *"Yes, it absolutely is. We won't go any lower."*

Customer: *"Yes you will."*

Salesperson: *"Why do you say that? I've talked with my boss and we've offered you our best price."*

Customer: *"Then talk to your boss again, because you want to sell this car and I want the navigation system and the seat heaters."*

Salesperson: *"Look. I don't know how to say it any clearer. The price is the price. The terms are the terms. The deal is the deal. You've already got the best deal and we're simply not going to give you one dime more. I've talked to my sales manager numerous times and she has made it clear she does not want to hear your name until you've signed a contract. We're not giving you the navigation system or the seat heaters. This part of the conversation is now over!"*

(Pause)

Customer: *"Well surely you can at least do the navigation system, and let me tell you why I think it makes sense for you to include the seat heaters as well..."*

———————

Those of us with smaller quantities of hair must be careful at this point not to pull out what little we have left. The relentless negotiator is just that – relentless. He is on a mission and he does not give up easily. For him, the buying process is a sport, a way of life even. He lives to gain stories for his next party or get-together. ("Let me tell you about the watch I bought last week – man did I take those guys to the cleaners!") For others it is not about bragging rights but rather about upbringing. Many people around the world are quite used to negotiating over the price of grapes or eggs. They've got a lot of practice when it comes to cars or jewelry.

Consider this a test. The customer wants to know where the limits are. He wants to know he is getting the best possible deal. He wants to push the envelope whenever he can. But you need to keep something else in mind – your company is doing exactly the same thing. There is no law that mandates sales prices. We are trying to get top dollar for our products at all times. We put a price out there that we believe is not one penny less than market value. We all want the best terms; that's the nature of any sales transaction. Keep in mind that in those times when you think to yourself, "This guy is just being unreasonable with his demands", the prospect is thinking, "This guy is just being unreasonable with his price." Who is right? It all depends on your perspective, does it not?

I believe it is more than okay to acknowledge this to the customer at the beginning of the negotiation.

"Look – you want to buy at the lowest possible price, and that's understandable. We want to sell at the highest possible price, as I'm sure you can appreciate. So our goal is to find a price that is fair to both parties. Agreed?"

This approach is not about winning at the expense of the other party's loss, but rather about a mutually satisfying agreement.

Here are some suggestions for dealing with this oft-frustrating buyer...

- **Understand Their Perspective**

   In the end, this prospect just wants to know that he got the best deal he could get and that there was not one dollar left on the table. The fear of leaving anything behind can be overwhelming. In fact, when the customer believes that he could have gotten more out of the deal he will likely reopen negotiations after the fact to satisfy this disturbing curiosity.

   Does this make the customer wrong? Is he a jerk because he is asking for everything? Not at all. He is the customer and, while he might cause us some frustration through his persistent badgering, we are in no position to offer a moral judgment on his character.

   Before you turn to a hasty and negative reaction, take a moment to try to see things from this customer's perspective. Ask yourself some important questions.

   - ✓ Do I have a strong sense of where this customer is coming from? Have I sought to put myself in his shoes?

   - ✓ Is this customer convinced of the value in the product, or do I have more work to do?

   - ✓ Is there a competitor who is training the customer to ask for more?

   - ✓ Have I done something to indicate that we will, in fact, move on the price?

   - ✓ Am *I* firmly convinced in the value of the offering?

As mentioned previously, negotiation is a way of life in many cultures. This is neither good nor bad – it just *is*. If you are quite accustomed to negotiating over the price of a melon at the market, wouldn't it stand to reason that you would want to negotiate over the price of a ring, or a vacation, or a sofa? I have had customers who were incredulous when I told them we would not negotiate. I remember one man who simply refused to believe me; he even accusing me of lying. Eventually I turned him over to my sales manager, who confirmed that we would not negotiate. By the time he hung up the phone he was furious, and he walked out of my office. My guess is that he bought a different product from someone who was willing to negotiate with him. He bought the best *deal*, but not necessarily the best *value*.

Understand that you might need to offer a (very sensitive) education to the prospect.

> *"You might be used to negotiating the terms of the purchase; in some areas (note that I said "areas", not "cultures" or "countries") it is quite common. Not here. The best price you will ever get is what you've already been quoted. That might not be consistent with your experience, but that's the way we do it at this dealership."*

- ## Understand Their Sense of Emotional Value

In effective negotiations, you must come to an understanding of why the customer needs your particular product more than any other product. If the prospect's needs can be met by any other product and by any other producer, you won't be in a position of strength when it comes to the negotiation. You'll only win by providing the lowest price on the market.

But if there is some emotional attachment to your product – something that provides such a compelling personal value that the prospect simply cannot find elsewhere, your position is strong going into the negotiation. The prospect knows deep down that the choice is clear – buy here or compromise in buying somewhere else. Why do you think car sellers put so much emphasis on the test drive? It is to build exclusive emotional value.

• Find the Win-Win

Whoever said that negotiation has to be about winners and losers? In fact, whoever said that negotiations necessarily need to be battles in the first place?

Too many times we find ourselves on the defensive position, waiting for the customer to finish a talking point so that we can jump in with an explanation of why we are about to say "no". This is the classic symptom of an "I win, you lose" approach. It doesn't have to be that way. You should always be looking for middle ground. Let the prospect know that you desire to help so long as they are willing to understand the company's position as well.

> *"You want the best terms you can get, and I appreciate that. You are aware, I'm sure, that the company has interests that need to be protected as well. So what I want to do is find a solution that works best for both of us. Let's start with a discussion on what is most important to you, and why."*

When you can get your customer talking you will open the lines of communication and obtain a more thorough understanding of their viewpoint and their values. From there you can strategize as to where to take the conversation.

By the way, I highly recommend Leigh Steinberg's excellent book, *Winning with Integrity: Getting what You Want without Selling Your Soul.* This is an outstanding book on negotiating by one of the world's foremost negotiators. The premise focuses on understanding the person you are working with as the key to success in negotiations.

- **Don't Focus on the "Best Price".**

  My long-time mentor, Lisa Kalmbach, taught me that what vigorous shoppers are really looking for is not the best price at all. Labeling something my "best price" is hackneyed and therefore not credible. The response is usually, "Yeah, right."

  Stay away from discussions about the best price; what the customer really wants to know is, "What is your *last* price?" In essence they are saying, "I am looking for the point where you are absolutely done, where if I asked for one dollar more you would turn me down and allow me to walk away." This is the last price, and using this term brings comfort to the customer who needs nothing more than to know there was not one dollar left on the table.

  > *"I appreciate you wanting the best terms you can get, and I respect that. But you need to understand that the price I've given you is not only my* best *price, but it is my* last *price. You need to make a decision as to whether there is enough value here to justify this price."*

- **Threaten the Takeaway**

  Because our customers are often consumed with getting the best possible deal, they often find themselves deep in a logical analysis all the while neglecting the emotional reasons they fell in the love with the product in the first place. When that happens, the positive emotions that caused them to fall in love are diminished. You need to do everything in your power to prevent that from happening. You need to keep them emotionally charged over the purchase of their dream and then threaten to sell it to someone else if you cannot agree on terms.

  Sometimes all a customer needs to know is that you are preparing to sell to someone else. Don't be afraid to be direct with the takeaway.

"Mr. Williams, it does not appear that you love this enough and that you are having a hard time justifying the price. Perhaps you need to be looking at something else. It might be time to throw in the towel on this one."

This is risky (after all, they could walk away) but it does tend to stir people to action if the emotion is strong enough.

17
Handling the Very Needy Customer

Salesperson: *"Hi, Lou Ann."*

Prospect: *"Hello, Jeff."*

Salesperson: *"What can I do for you today, Lou Ann?"*

Prospect: *"I just wanted to see if they had fixed the broken window in the family room?"*

Salesperson: *"You mean the window you told us about yesterday?"*

Prospect: *"Yes. And I wanted to get a loan update as well."*

Salesperson: *"Well, the superintendent has ordered the new window and will install it as soon as the drywall is hung and the siding is installed; that minimizes the risk of breaking the window all over again. As far as the loan goes, it's still approved and waiting for the home to be finished."*

Prospect: *"Oh. Well, I guess I'll go measure a couple of things in the model."*

Salesperson: *(under your breath) "You mean, you don't have the measurements committed to memory by now?"*

Perhaps you've not had the opportunity to work in an office with cubicles all around you. One of the interesting aspects in such a situation is that you are (whether you like it or not) privy to the trials and ordeals of your co-workers. Now imagine that the person in the cubicle next to yours is, shall we say, of the emotional ilk. And let's say that this person tends to take every event in life as if it is a major trauma. And just to complete the picture, let's assume that this person just bought a brand new home. Guess what – you get to hear her talk about the process for the next *six months!*

Buying big-ticket items is a stressful and emotional endeavor, one of the most nerve-racking things we go through in lives. It's like that for anyone, but it is especially trying for those who are detail-oriented and high-strung to start with.

You need to understand how scary this process is to that particular customer. Face it – you see committing to large purchases every day and it might not be that big of a deal to you. The customer goes through this a few times in their entire *life*; it's bound to be a big deal to them. Making a big purchase is scary, and that's a fact. Don't be surprised when some people react to their fear by inundating themselves with information and hounding you for updates. They want nothing to slip through the cracks.

There is one other consideration here: the customer's expectations. As I've pointed out before, many customers simply have a negative expectation about the purchase process. Perhaps they were forced to endure a horrible transaction when they bought their last car. Maybe they have a friend or relative who bought a new home and is insisting that the builder be watched like a hawk. In any event, the customer's expectations about the process, combined with the degree to which they trust you and your company, will determine how diligent they feel they need to watch over the process. Understand the expectations and you will likely understand how to manage those expectations.

How to handle these sometimes-trying customers?

- **Assure Them You're Here to Help**

  One of the curious things about being in sales is that you are there to take care of the *buyer*, but you're getting paid by the *seller*. Whose side are you on, anyway? Well, both. You need to convince your customer that while you are, in fact, being paid by the seller and you do have a responsibility to look after the seller's interests throughout this transaction, you are nevertheless here to make your customer's experience as smooth and as enjoyable as possible. Let them know – specifically – how you will help.

  > *"I will be your eyes and ears on this. I will check on the status regularly and I will track your financing through the approval process. Most importantly, I will call you at least once a week while you're going through this to update you and see if you have any concerns. By the way, I tend to make my update calls on Tuesdays. Does that work for you?"*

- **Stick to Your Promises**

  Now that you've promised your best service you must deliver on what you've pledged to do. Customers will quickly lose confidence when they find that you (or your co-workers) are not living up to your word. When this happens you can expect that they will take it upon themselves to scrutinize everything that happens in the process.

  If you know you cannot come through on a promise, by all means let the customer know about it before the promise is broken. Remember, good news never gets better, but bad news always gets worse.

- ## Beat Them at Their Own Game

Now let's get to the real tough ones, the people who call or come in *almost every day*. While it is possible that some of these buyers are just plain lonely and looking for your companionship, it is more likely that the customer *believes* they need to come in every day in order to ensure that nothing slips through the cracks. The mentality is, "If I want this done right I'm going to have stay on top of these people."

If the real issue is the need to persuade the customer that you are, in fact, on top of things and that you are constantly aware of what's happening with their transaction, you might try beating them at their own game – by calling them incessantly. When someone is calling you literally every day, turn the tables. Make it a point to call them first thing in the morning, *every day for a week*. Start your day by being proactive in calling your customer.

> *"Good morning, it's Jeff. I talked to Steve about the wall in the family room and he says he had already seen the bow, that he has already talked to the framer, and that it should be fixed by the end of the day. I'll check that before I leave today and call you tomorrow morning to let you know that it got taken care of. If you need anything before that, just call."*

The trick is not to do this once, but *every day* for several days. Then notice whether the customer's calls diminish. You are trying to teach your customer that you are already looking at the things they are concerned about, and that it is not necessary to call or come in every day because we are already here and we are looking after the home and the process.

- ## E-mail Early in the Day

If you have access to e-mail you could consider sending them a brief daily update first thing each morning. Even if you have nothing new to report you are still being proactive, and the 30 seconds it takes to send an e-mail to this person might save you 15 minutes in phone calls or office visits. It doesn't have to be detailed; it only has to be frequent and consistent.

"Checked in on your ring setting this morning. Looks great – right on schedule. I'll get you an update tomorrow. Jeff"

- ## Remind Them that You have Other Customers

In the worst-case scenario it might be necessary to politely inform people that you have a great many customers to serve and you need to be able to do that. Be sensitive, apologetic, and contrite.

"I enjoy spending time with you and I really appreciate your diligence in staying on top of the progress. I do need to let you know that we are currently working with twenty different customers and I need to spend time with each one of them. You're welcome to come by every day, but please understand and forgive me when I cannot spend a great deal of time with you on every visit."

One more thing on this subject - a personal lesson that I learned the hard way. When I was selling new homes, I once had a homebuyer (we'll call her Susan) who came into my sales office *every day*. I mean that – every day! It got to the point where I shuddered when she pulled in because I knew she was about to eat up more of my time.

After Susan closed she got a survey from our company. One of the questions on the survey asked, "Did the salesperson keep you informed?" Susan marked "Not at all". I was furious. Sometime later Susan came back into my sales office, looking sheepish.

Susan said, "Jeff, I got this survey and I…"

I interrupted. "And you said I didn't keep you informed. I know – I saw the survey! Susan, how could you say that? I talked to you *every single day!*"

Susan replied, "No, Jeff. I talked to *you* every single day. You never called me one time in the entire six months the home was being built."

Now, you might be thinking to yourself that this was totally unfair and that I got a bum deal (and I'd be thinking that I agree with you). But the lesson was invaluable. The buyer calling us for updates *doesn't count*. The only thing that counts is when we *proactively* call the buyer (and in my opinion each and every week during an extended sales process). If you've promised to call the buyer every Tuesday, call them every Tuesday – even if the buyer had been in your office on Monday. The proactivity is what counts.

18
Dealing with Market-Based Objections

Prospect: *"This is a terrible market – a really bad time to buy."*

Salesperson: *"May I ask how you arrive at that conclusion."*

Prospect: *"Well, no one else is buying right now."*

Salesperson: *"Wouldn't that make it a good time to buy?"*

Prospect: *"Hey now – don't go trying that logic stuff on me. I'm perfectly happy in my paranoiac misery, thank you."*

Salesperson: *"Don't know what came over me. I'll be careful."*

Prospect: *"Thanks. By the way, we're all going to die very, very soon."*

Salesperson: *("We didn't go over this in sales training.")*

As I've discussed in other chapters, fear is a real and healthy emotion for all prospects – especially when it comes to large ticket purchases. In fact, it's so pervasive that there is actually an acronym to

139

describe it: FUD...Fear, Uncertainty and Doubt. Just watch the news or read the daily headlines and, trust me, you'll get an earful of FUD.

The world today constantly bombards us with a real-time stream of information, news and data and, let's face it, these outside sources greatly influence our perceptions. This sound-bite driven culture is fueled by, but certainly not limited to:

- Media

- Co-workers

- Family members

- Facebook and Twitter posts

- Overheard conversations

- Other salespeople

This unending stream of opinions can wear a prospect down. And who can blame them? It's hard not to listen!

Here's the key: the prospect has heard all those things *and is interested anyway.* They're on your sales floor, right? What does that tell us? Something is seriously wrong with their current situation and they're looking for a solution. Stay focused on the problem and let the product provide the solution

MARKET OBJECTIONS ARE "NORMAL"

Let's agree that market-based objections are simply *normal behavior* for customers and should, frankly, be expected from the get go. I might go so far as to suggest that it would be AB-normal to work with a customer who doesn't have a care in the world (and also may call into question what world they are actually living in!).

Market concerns can be based on things real or imagined and, quite honestly, it is sometimes hard for prospects to even know which is which. Here's where your role as a sales *counselor* kicks in. It's your responsibility to get them fact-based about their current situation and to offer some much-needed perspective about their future.

When confronted with a market-based objection, start to dig deeper by asking simply, "What are you basing that upon?" Listen carefully to their response while keeping in mind this very important fact: fear-based perceptions are stronger than reality. Whatever the customer is telling you doesn't have to be *true* in order to sway their emotions. The economy could be growing by 25% a quarter, but if they *perceive* tough times then they will filter the world through that lens and all your facts and figures to the contrary aren't going to shift this.

Now that you've listened carefully to their concerns, what question should be pounding your brain? "Well then, if financial Armageddon is just 12 months away, why are you here?" Answer: there must be something wrong, there must be some real dissatisfaction in their life, that brings them to you in the first place *despite* what is happening in the market. Your job right now is to figure out what that current dissatisfaction is in order to offer them a future promise that will overcome their fears.

Here is a simple formula to put this in perspective:

Current Dissatisfaction x Future Promise > Fear + Cost™

The stronger your understanding of their pain (current dissatisfaction), the more pop you will get from your solution (future promise) in order to overcome their fears and close the sale. Get them thinking about how their life will be so much better with that new RV and how much more family time that gives them or how many new locales they'll be able to enjoy or whatever the dominant motivation is for this customer. Build emotional attachment to the solution you are offering because those feelings are market-proof!

So here's the funny thing about dealing with market-based objections – your job is *not* to overcome the objection directly. No need to go out and stock up on copies of the Wall Street Journal and The Economist in order to dazzle customers with your keen insight into today's macro-, micro- and nano-economics. Instead, your job is to discover what got them thinking about this purchase in the first place and then get them emotionally engaged in a solution that will change their world.

So let's talk about what these market-based objections sound like...

- **"I think this will go on sale if I wait."**

  Start this one by gaining their perspective – why do they feel this way? Have they been conditioned by past experience? Are they just *hoping* this to be true? Again, you're not going to argue with them about things that may or may not happen in the future but you do want to show respect for their feelings and understand their perspective.

  Next, either determine or re-visit *why* they are interested in the first place. You want to narrow this down to a current need – for example, a new baby being born into a family with a car that's just too small. Reinforce with the customer that the need is *now* and so is the solution.

  "Matt and Shauna, I understand your hesitation and your hope that you might find a better deal on this car down the road, I really do. I also know that none of us can predict or control the future. What we do know is that your current car just doesn't meet your needs anymore. And we know that you love this model because of the extra storage space, the great safety record and the beautiful color. With your new baby just a few weeks away, I'd hate to see you remain stuck in car that's going to continue frustrating you

every time you drive it. Let's put in you in place to really enjoy the coming weeks and months instead of living in frustration."

Remember, sell to their emotions and get them thinking about how that pain will still be there if they walk away today.

- **"Not many people are buying right now, so the choices will still be there if I wait."**

In the last example, we focused on the customer's current dissatisfaction. For this one, let's zoom in on the future promise that our solution offers. Let's face it, people buy to improve their lives. And the sooner they buy, the sooner their lives improve, right? One of the true blessings of being a sales professional is that we get to help our customers enjoy life more, so play to that strength and get your customer on board to improve their life!

First, get the customer talking about the solution emotionally. Remember, they're here today for a reason – tap into that dominant motivation and bring it back to the surface. For example, if you're working with someone considering the purchase of a new home so that they're commuting less and spending more time with their family, you might say,

> *"Bill, you're right in some respects – you will always have choices no matter how long you wait. At the same time, I know how much you're looking forward to spending more time with your daughter. As we think about the right choice for you, tell me some more about what you want to do with that extra time together?"*

Next, confirm with them that this choice, today, actually provides the right solution in their life. And, if so, ask the question, "What's wrong with making the *right* choice *today*?" Remember, none of us can control the future – we can only deal in today.

Now, I've got no doubt that you've worked with customers who decided to wait. And, more than that, I'm sure you've seen customers who have lost out on their best choice because they waited too long. That perfect home on the perfect cul-de-sac. That perfect car in just the right color. That perfect ring in the perfect setting. Be honest and straightforward about these realities with your customer and help them make a good choice today:

> *"Bill, I get it – there are a lot of choices out there. You may choose to wait and see what else you find down the road. But let me tell you about one of the worst parts of my job, and I mean really the worst. It's working with someone like you who has found the perfect solution and chose to wait, only to come back in a couple of weeks to find that someone else just bought your perfect home. This home is going to change your world, Bill – let's make it yours <u>today</u>, okay?"*

- **"The economy is bad."**

"The economy is bad" sounds like "your price is too high" – you've got nothing to work with here and it's next to impossible to effectively handle vague objections like this. Seek clarification by asking, "Tell me what you mean by that."

Listen carefully, then go deeper into a personal application of this concern, "How does this affect you personally?" Remember that if a customer is seriously concerned about losing their job, they wouldn't be out shopping for a new car, or expensive jewelry or whatever non-essential item you are selling,

I think Warren Buffet's famous saying holds true here, "Be fearful when others are greedy. Be greedy when others are fearful." So take that contrarian thinking and turn it around for your customer.

> *"That's right, Kim, it is tough out there! But have you considered that tough conditions are really the best time to buy? Demand is off, prices are down and financing is available at historic lows.*

What happens down the road when things improve and prices start going up? In so many ways, this is the smart move and you enjoy the benefits today."

- **"I can buy this cheaper if I buy it used."**

With the explosion of services like Craigslist and eBay, consumers truly do have a wide range of choices for buying things second hand. Tack that onto the existing huge markets for used cars and re-sale homes and this can become a legitimate objection for a buyer. So, let's agree that, yes, possibly they could buy something similar for less money. But, again, here's the key question: why are they here today?

Go ahead and ask them how they're looking at the pros and cons of new versus used. Bring out a sheet of paper and use the Ben Franklin approach that we discussed earlier – draw a t-chart down the middle of the page and ask your customer to write out the positives and negatives. This approach will narrow down the real objections into tangible issues that you can address clearly and succinctly.

It's also worth asking the customer very directly, "What has prevented you from buying used so far?" Chances are, this will provide an opportunity for your prospect to begin overcoming their own objection. It will certainly give you concrete topics to discuss in lieu of the very generalized "I can buy it used" objection.

In many cases, you'll find that the decision really comes down to value, so don't shy away from engaging in that conversation. Sure, a used car may be less expensive but the warranty isn't nearly as long or comprehensive. Absolutely, the resale home may cost less but what about the energy and maintenance costs? "Less expensive" can quickly become a relative point when you consider the cost and time associated with the used alternative. Knowing your customer's mission and dominant motivations will go a long way toward building a value equation that tilts in your favor when faced with this particular objection.

19

Getting "Up" When You're Feeling Down

Salesperson: *(Deep sigh)*

Salesperson's Wife: *"What's the matter, dear?"*

Salesperson: *"Nothing."* *(Deeper sigh)*

Wife: *"Will you just tell me what's going on?"*

Salesperson: *(Sigh)* *"I'm down. Down, down, down."*

Wife: *"Now dear, it's going to be all right. You just need to think positive, that's all."*

Salesperson: *"That's easy for you to say. You don't have to go to work and pretend you like people."*

Wife: *"Have you considered not pretending, and actually trying to like people?"*

Salesperson: *(sigh)* *"Now you're just talking crazy!"*

Wife: *(sigh)*

Consider this important question: What is the single-most important thing you bring to your customers? Is there a more important question to grapple with? I think not. So what is it that you bring that offers more value than anything else? Is it knowledge, a deep understanding of your product or your marketplace? Perhaps it is guidance, the ability to connect and walk the prospect through a sometimes-difficult and scary process. How about compassion, and your purpose in empathetically connecting with your customer on a deep level?

All are important, of course, and I believe sales professionals must have all of the above in some measure. But can any of them be called the "most important"? I believe that the single-most important element we bring to a prospect is *positive energy*.

To a prospect who is weary from the process and laden with fear, who considers the buying process from a victim's perspective even before the conversation begins, positive energy is like a warm fire on a cold day. In fact, it is the foundation for the entire sales process, and every element in that process is enhanced with the presence of positive energy. Get the prospect in a positive frame of mind and the transaction becomes more enjoyable and ultimately more successful for both parties.

Put this in real-life perspective for a moment. A customer is approaching a mattress store. We can presume without much of a stretch that there is a need – people don't window shop for mattresses! A couple pulls up to the store and as they are getting out of the car they are saying things like, "Now let's get this straight – we're just looking and we have several other stops, right? We're not giving in to the first salesperson." Or worse, "That last guy was a creep. Let's just tell this guy to back off and we'll look around on our own." Will your product knowledge save you in this situation? Will your well-rehearsed product demonstration save the day here? In reality, even your very deep compassion will be meaningless if you cannot break down the pre-determined defenses.

Top professionals make a concerted effort in favor of positive energy, *regardless of the demeanor or personality of the customer*. Poor performers are really nice with really nice people, but what good is that? The niche for working only with nice people is already filled!

So positive energy is critical, right? Now here's the rub: you can only give out that which you have inside. And if you are charged with giving out positive energy all day long, you'd better be eating positive energy for breakfast! And you had better be snacking on it all day long. In short, protecting your own positive energy is critical to your success.

In the course of our day we take in so much negative energy. It comes in the form of negative customers, irritating executives, tough market conditions and a media that is in love with bad news. It's only a matter of time before the negativity becomes infectious. And when we are infected we infect those around us. This is why slumps are so debilitating. When unchecked we become carriers of a negative virus, and an already-negative customer adopts that same demeanor.

It all starts with the mindset. I can give you a bunch of techniques and tips (which I will), but you need to start with your mindset each and every day. The primary advice here is not how to throw some sort of magical (and mythical) positive energy switch whenever a new customer comes through the door. Rather, it is to live positive energy at all times. In the next chapter we'll talk about staying positive on the fly, but here we'll talk about positive energy as a lifestyle. Let's consider a few simple ideas for feeding yourself positive energy consistently:

- **Don't start your day negative.** Controlling what we allow into our minds is always important, but let me suggest that it is *critically* important when it comes to starting your day. Consider what you hear on the average cable news network in the morning – rabid reactions to the latest economic indicators, pundits lambasting the latest partisan political ploy and the latest dire predictions on the environment. Now, I consider myself a well-read and well-informed individual and I intend to stay that way. At the same time, that kind of noise does nothing to improve my disposition as I prepare for a day where I need to be "on". Kinda like mom used to say, "If you can't find something nice to say (or listen to), then don't say (or listen to) anything at all!"

- **Exercise early.** Boy, let me tell you that this really sets the tone for the day. Personally, I can always tell a difference on the mornings I exercise. There's a feeling of achievement, clarity and energy that just can't be duplicated by an extra cup of coffee (not that there's anything wrong with that, either!). And it's a great alternative to those negative inputs we talked about above when starting your day!

- **Use your drive time wisely.** Audio books, podcasts, training seminars and so much more can help you maintain a positive mindset during your daily drive. Not that every moment of your life needs to be filled with some form of stimulation, mind you. The point here is to *consciously choose* the best way to spend this time. Perhaps pumping yourself up with music gets your energy flowing – great! On the other hand, you might use a quiet drive to decompress from home life and transition into being "on"…or vice versa. Again, there are no right answers; I simply encourage you to *reflectively consider* how to best use this time for your own benefit.

- **Look for mental snacks all throughout the day.** Find time and ways to recharge yourself during your long day. Do you subscribe to an email newsletter? Take a few minutes to digest it. Working long stretches alone? Call up a colleague to find out what's hot in their world. Text your son or daughter with an encouraging word or to find out what's going on. Yes, we're in a world driven by our customers and our employers, but *you're* responsible for keeping yourself operating at peak performance all day long and *you* know best what it takes. Be smart, be thoughtful and create opportunities to "sharpen the saw" (thank you, Mr. Stephen Covey!).

- **5-minute reading bursts.** Perhaps not the best way to work your way through Tolstoy's "War and Peace", but it's another really effective way to boost your energy levels in small bites. Reading through a book like the one you're reading right now is a great example – read one chapter a day for five or ten minutes and then work on immediately applying what you've learned during the rest of your workday. Blogs, web sites and newsletters also offer wonderful inspiration and practical application to improving your selling skills every single day.

- **Deep breaths and stretching.** Okay, I admit it – I'm not really much of a yoga guy. But I've tried it and I know that the principles work. Now, I'm not suggesting that you bust out a Downward Facing Tree Pose on the sales floor. But, at an appropriate place and time, stretching allows more blood to flow to our muscles, improving circulation, while deep breaths bring more oxygen to our brains. Face it, our bodies are dynamic organisms that require intentional care and maintenance to operate at their best. And, on that note, remember to eat throughout your day, too – your brain and your metabolism will thank you!

- **Establish a "default" positive energy activity.** File this under "what gets me centered". For you, this may be exercise, prayer, meditation, music…again, whatever gets you consistently centered within yourself. This is your "go to" activity when you feel that positive energy waning in your world. Yes, work to create energy-building activities throughout your day. And, know for yourself, when all else fails, that you have a tried and true mechanism for regaining focus and positive energy to get you back on track.

Beyond all of these strategies and activities, however, it's worth noting that maintaining a positive attitude in life is really a choice. It is *your* choice. Life may throw you a curveball or you might find yourself in a rut, but that choice always comes back to you. Let me illustrate this monumental truth by sharing two powerful lessons that I've learned over the years...

A LESSON IN A TRAGEDY

Getting very serious for a moment, let me share with you a personal story. Several years ago, on a Sunday afternoon, my dog was shot. I can assure you this was not something I ever could have, or would have, predicted that I would experience on a sleepy Sunday afternoon at home. Responding as quickly as our shocked hearts and minds allowed, we rushed her to the vet but she did not make it out of surgery.

Needless to say, I was devastated. This dog was part of our family and truly held a special place in the hearts of my wife, our three children and me. I knew in an instant that this would affect my spirit for some time – this is not something one just bounces back from overnight.

Well, that was going to be a huge problem because at 8:30 am on Monday morning I was slated to stand in front of a sales team for a daylong training session. Let's be real – how much do you think I wanted to do that?

At this point I had to make a decision. I had to decide how I would choose to handle this. And it was *my* decision.

Victor Frankl, in his excellent book *Man's Search for Meaning*, writes, "Everything else can be taken from a man except for the last of the human freedoms, the ability to choose one's attitude in any given set of circumstances."

Yes, I concluded – my response was up to me. And so, that Monday morning I made a conscious decision. I decided to absolutely pour my heart and soul into the people I was to train. I decided to become so engaged in their welfare that I wouldn't have time to think about my own situation. I concentrated on that sales team with all I had and gave them the very best I had to offer. And it worked.

Not only did I feel good because I gave this team what I had promised, what they expected and what they deserved, but I received, in return, positive energy back from them. And that's just what I needed that day and that week in order to work through this loss with my family.

A LESSON FROM YUL BRENNER

Years ago, I watched an interview with the late Yul Brenner – you remember him, right? The deeply tanned bald guy with the deeply sonorous voice. Brenner was most famous for his role in Rodgers and Hammerstein's "The King and I". Now, aside from his memorable performance in the movie of the same name, he performed that role over 5,000 times on stage!

As I marveled at that fact, I asked myself, "How do you do it?" How do you stay "up" for 5,000 shows? Wouldn't you just want to mail it in at some point?

In fact, the interviewer asked that very question and Brenner replied, "Row G, Seat 6." He went on to clarify, stating that it didn't matter how many times he had done the show – for the guy in Row G, Seat 6, it was opening night.

The real question was this: "Who is the performance about?" If the show is about Yul Brenner, he might mail it in because, hey, this is just show number 3,757. But if the show is about the guy who is there for the first time, it is opening night and he deserves the very best performance possible.

And so I wonder if a mindset shift is in order. Who is your sales presentation about – you or your customer? I'm not asking you to get over yourself – I'm suggesting you get outside yourself! Keep your positive energy charged up, make a conscious choice to change your customer's world and, who knows, you might be surprised at just how many more sales you make and how good you feel in the process!

20

Bouncing Back from a Difficult Conversation

Receptionist: *"John, your 2:00 appointment is here."*

Salesperson: *"What?! What 2:00 appointment?"*

Receptionist: *"The Stuarts. They are waiting in the customer lounge."*

Salesperson: *"Oh man – I totally forgot about that. Tell them I'm not here today."*

Receptionist: *"I already told them you are here. Are you still smarting from your meeting with the boss?"*

Salesperson: *"How did you know I got chewed out? Does everyone know?!"*

Receptionist: *"I never said anything about being chewed out. But for the record, we could hear the yelling from down the hall. Yeah, everyone knows."*

Salesperson: *"Oh, great. That's just great. Tell the Stuarts that my grandma just died."*

Receptionist: *"Sorry, John. I'm not going to lie for you."*

Salesperson: *"Tell them I just had a cerebral hemorrhage."*

Receptionist: *"I'm going to tell them you'll be right up. And John, the head of finance has some questions for you about your commission request."*

Salesperson: *"Tell him I'm meeting with the Stuarts...and I'll be a while."*

It is the nature of sales that we will, from time to time, find ourselves in less-than-comfortable conversations with prospects, clients, suppliers, and, yes, even our own boss. This is not a question of "if", but "when". You've already armed yourself with strategies to create positive energy and stay "up"; now it's time to get tactical in your thinking so that you're equipped to handle that unplanned and emotionally challenging encounter on the job.

So, let's assume that you're already employing the positive energy strategies discussed in the previous chapter. You woke up early, exercised, ate a balanced breakfast and listened to your favorite seminar speaker (a pretty cool guy by the name of Jeff Shore) on CD during your drive to work. Strategically positive? Check! With energy to spare!

All right, pop quiz: First phone call of the day arrives and it's your boss. And she's not happy. It seems that your famously high-maintenance customer is now calling *her* for further maintenance. And apparently he is, shall we say, ticked off. What in the world? You talk to this guy almost every single day! Not to mention the emails...and the text messages! And now he's calling your manager with a problem he hasn't even told you about? Who does this guy think he is? And to top it off, now your sales manager is questioning you about your customer service skills. Oh, and she wants this taken care of *right away* when, of course, you're scheduled to meet with another customer five minutes from now. And she'll call you after lunch for an update. Click.

As Keanu Reeves famously quoted in the movie *Speed*: "What do you do? What. Do. You. Do?"

The time to decide is not in the heat of battle. Emotion is too strong a pull and will cloud your logic. Yes, you've come to the battle strategically armed with positive energy but this customer and your boss have just exploded a mortar shell in your emotional nerve center. Right now, it's time to think tactically to ensure a clear-headed response and generate positive forward momentum so as not to derail your entire day.

Think of a soldier – why do they drill the same tactics over and over again? First objective: learn the skill. Second objective: master the skill. Third objective: commit the skill to your subconscious – make it instinctive so that when you're on the battlefield, you just do what you prepared for.

This same principle holds true for difficult conversations. You need to have the mechanism in place to switch into performance mode, deal with it and move forward positively. Otherwise you will carry the negative energy from one conversation into a discussion with a new prospect.

Bouncing back is a critical sales discipline and the true professionals seem to have this down pat. Conversely, I've seen a lot of mediocre salespeople lose their focus for hours on end or even an entire day (even more at times!) as a result of a difficult exchange. And that's a real shame because, in that case, they have completely taken the power to control themselves and given it to another person. No thanks!

Want to maintain control of your own world and improve your abilities in this arena? Here are some basic tactics for bouncing back and moving forward in a positive direction:

- **Take a deep breath.** Okay, sounds too simple, right? But it works. And let's avoid the dramatic sigh, here. This is a measured, deep breath to clear your head and slow down.

- **"Throw it away"** (or some other physical action). This is your trigger, a practiced and deliberate motion that allows you to capture this emotion and put it in its place. Much like a batter's deliberate and practiced pre-pitch ritual or a basketball player's pre-shot dribbles at the free throw line, create your own physical "switch" to stay focused on the next goal facing you. Or simply say to yourself, "Next play."

- **Commit to 100% engagement outside of yourself.** Trust me, if you're doing your job and maintaining a consistently professional demeanor then, chances are, this whole exchange was way more about the other person than about you. So view it that way! In other words, focus on the customer's (or co-worker's) experience, understand where they are coming from (reasonable or not!), clarify what needs to be done and make that the issue to be dealt with – not your bruised ego or wounded sensibilities.

- **Give yourself permission to get emotional in the future.** The previous step notwithstanding, it's okay to get hacked over the conversation, just not right now. Remind yourself that you will have plenty of time to offload the encounter to a colleague or a friend later on and express your (legitimate) frustration. Now is not the time to replay the exchange over and over again inside your head and identify all the ways in which you were wronged. Right now, you need to deal with it and move on. You can feel free to talk your way through it later as needed.

- **Get a corrective thought engrained in your brain.** Remember the Victor Frankl quote I shared in the last chapter? Would it shock you to know that I've memorized it almost verbatim? And even if I'm off by a word or two, it serves me well when confronted by someone or something that is making my life particularly difficult. I encourage you to use this approach, too – whether it's the Frankl quote itself or some other phrase, passage or lyric that can put your mental train of thought back on track.

- **Take action.** If there is some action or next step required on your part coming out of this difficult encounter, now is the time to either do it or to make a clear plan to do it. Time permitting, deal with the issue *now* so that you can completely move beyond it. If you've got other customers or meetings to attend to, then write it down in your calendar or your task list this very moment so that you've closed out the issue mentally for the time being.

- **Smile before your next customer greeting or phone call.** Smile in advance. Let the customer see it, hear it and feel it. Next play.

21
Doing the Uncomfortable Stuff

Salesperson: *(Talking to self)* *"Okay...Monday morning. Here we go. Let's see...wow, alrighty then, 103 unread emails in my inbox...how did that happen? Another email from Bob? I told you I'd get back to you when I got an answer – chill out, man. Okay, sales meeting in two hours – got to give an update on my top prospects. No problemo, I'm smokin' the competition this month! Okay, dang, didn't get that paperwork done yet that I promised to send over to finance...what a pain and I need those final numbers from Adam to do it, so I'll make a note to call him later. And I still owe the Jenkins' a call to talk about the delay on their delivery date. Right...better do that later – I don't want to ruin a perfectly good Monday morning for them. Man, I really thought I could knock all this out first thing today before the sales meeting. Good times at happy hour Friday afternoon, though – glad I decided to go! Oh well, time to get moving on all of this...right...after...I check the box score from last night's game...what a blowout..."*

Let's get our hands around a common problem in all humans (some more than others). We all have a desire for comfort that many times dictates our actions. There is, it seems, always an easier way. Key word being "seems".

Because you're in sales you might have less of an issue when it comes to, as an example, talking to new people. I've known others who would rather be duct taped to the scorching black vinyl seats of a '77 T-top Camaro during the middle of summer while wearing shorts and a tank top than strike up a conversation with someone they don't know. But we salespeople find our challenges in plenty of other areas…paperwork, organization, reports or having the tough talk with a customer or boss. Boy…just shoot me now! But the fact is, our desire for, and pursuit of, comfort can be debilitating to our success.

One area where this manifests itself most consistently is in our tendency towards procrastination. Notice that we do not procrastinate on things we find comfortable. I mean there's always time for the latest episode of our favorite TV show, a round of golf, a quick shopping excursion or a lingering meal with friends. When it's fun and pleasurable, why put it off, right? Exactly. Procrastination is all about how we deal with the *un*comfortable things in life.

My business coach, Marty Nemko, calls procrastination a pandemic in today's world. It afflicts literally tens of millions of people every single day in America, costing salespeople and corporations billions of dollars in lost sales and productivity annually. And, in the most acute cases, this issue literally costs people their careers.

Let's clear up one misconception on this matter. It's been said that top performers do the things that others find uncomfortable. That is only partially true. The fact is that top performers do the things that *they themselves* find uncomfortable…but they do them anyway. After all, what is uncomfortable to one person is perfectly simple to another. Doing only those things we find most comfortable is a recipe for a short and unproductive career.

With that in mind, we can rightly say that procrastination is a choice. And if that is true, than swift action on uncomfortable tasks is also a choice. That might sound obvious, but it is important to understand. Procrastination is an active choice, a firm decision to be less then fully productive. We tend to think of procrastination as a non-action. That is not the case; it is an active decision. Don't kid yourself.

If you believe you struggle with putting off uncomfortable things, I want to share four resources and suggestions that will help:

- *Eat That Frog* **by Brian Tracy.** This is an excellent book that takes a very simple look at productively handling uncomfortable tasks early in the day. You'll find this book to be very inspirational. You'll also find that the act of reading the book is a positive step that leads to other positive steps. Just see if you don't immediately get some things done that have been on the uncomfortable list for a while.

- **Fight for the moment.** I learned from prominent career coach Marty Nemko this valuable tip: Be honest in the "Moment of Truth". I refer here to the moment at which you are tempted to defer on a task that you can and should do right in the moment. Many people have grown numb to the nagging feeling that says, "You should do this right now". You'll know the moment when you either get pricked by your own conscience or you find yourself making up a rationalization for why you are deferring (a very natural occurrence when ignoring an unpleasant task!).

- *Never Check E-mail in the Morning* **By Julie Morgenstern.** This is an excellent book with some great tips for increasing productivity at work, especially early in the day. The book is an excellent companion for *Eat That Frog* (see above).

- **Find someone really productive to interview.** I don't know about you, but I am inspired by people who get so much done in so little time. Remember that we all share one trait. You, me, Donald

Trump, Mark Zuckerberg – we all have the exact same 24 hours in each day. It's not about how much time we have; that is invariable. It is only about how we use those hours. Talk to people around you who maximize their days.

In the spirit of immediate application, here are also a couple of quick tips that have worked extraordinarily well for me personally:

- **Use a daily disciplines checklist.** Make up a list of things that you know you should do every single day, and check them off the list as you go along. You'll find that self-accountability goes a long way towards increased productivity.

- **Start early in the day.** For many, the answer might come in getting up 30 minutes earlier in the morning. The start of the day can be an incredibly productive time. Once the day is in full swing we tend to be at the mercy of those around us. Get up early and get something done right out of the gate. See if that doesn't make you more productive throughout the day.

- **Clump tasks together in small blocks of time.** Designate several small blocks of time to handle a number of minor tasks. Find 15 minutes and a list of two-bit tasks – then just pound away. No new e-mails, no phone calls. Just put your head down and knock 'em out.

- **Reward yourself for getting things done.** Find a specific reward when you finish difficult tasks. Got a 90-minute project that you really need to move forward on? Tell yourself that a walk to Starbucks is in order when you're done. Or that you will take 10 minutes to goof off once the task is complete.

The power to choose your attitude and to chart a positive, productive course each day starts and ends with you. And dealing with the uncomfortable stuff *first* enables you to focus on the things the energize you and create more capability within yourself. So… what's your choice today? Are you ready to "Deal With It!"?

About the Author

Few sales leaders possess more extensive experience — and irresistible enthusiasm — than Jeff Shore. A voracious student of life and self-proclaimed sales "junkie," Jeff believes that sales is a noble profession and that salespeople who act in the best interest of their customers provide a valuable service to society.

After several years selling resale homes, Jeff began his homebuilding career in 1987 as a sales counselor in Northern California. Thriving in a tough market, Jeff honed his craft during the California real estate downturn of the 1990's and moved quickly through a series of progressive sales management and executive positions for billion-dollar Fortune 500 homebuilder, KB Home. He later he served in a corporate role as their National Sales Director creating training programs, coaching managers, and directing sales strategy nationwide.

Today, Jeff provides sales strategy and training for sales organizations across the country, working with both executive and sales teams alike. Continually pressing for new levels of personal and professional performance, he delivers hard-hitting experiences that electrify teams with quick-witted humor, personal challenges and relentless positivity.

A member of the National Speaker's Association and a regularly featured speaker at the International Builders Show, the Pacific Coast Builder's Conference, and SMC's across the country, Jeff's coast-to-coast seminars garner ecstatic reviews from sales counselors and managers who describe them as "authentic," "entertaining," "inspiring," and "compelling." Drawing thousands upon thousands of attendees from across the United States, his Tough Market New Home Sales Seminar remains one of the most popular seminars in the industry.

When he's not on an airplane or working with sales teams, Jeff resides in Auburn, California with his wife Karen and a neurotic Jack Russell "Terrorist." Jeff and Karen find deep happiness spending time with their three grown children and enjoying friends, community and church activities and the overall small town life of their rural Northern California surroundings.

Visit www.jeffshore.com or send an e-mail to jeff@jeffshore.com.

Booking Information for Keynotes and Seminars

Jeff Shore keeps his audience thinking, laughing and, most importantly, changing the way they do business. Seamlessly incorporating over two decades of sales success and executive experience, Jeff provides proven strategies for professionals who want to "Deal With It!" by facing challenges head-on, leading real change and creating thriving sales organizations.

Offering real-world tools and solutions for selling in a tough market, Jeff's reputation for clarity, humor, authority, and sincerity makes him one of the most requested speakers among businesses and sales and marketing organizations across the United States. Watch Jeff's blend of savvy, substance and style in action and connect with him online at jeffshore.com.

For more information about booking Jeff, please contact Cassandra Grauer at (530) 558-9109 or email cassandra@jeffshore.com.

ORDER DISCOUNTED MULTIPLE COPIES FOR YOUR SALES TEAM

We have heard from countless sales managers over the past several years who use Deal With It! to enhance their sales meetings by asking the team to read a chapter each week, with reports of engaging and highly applicable group discussions.

If you would like to order multiple copies for your sales team, we happily offer bulk discounts. Please contact Cassandra Grauer at (530) 558-9109 or email cassandra@jeffshore.com.

CPSIA information can be obtained at www.ICGtesting.com
Printed in the USA
BVOW011428041112

304446BV00003B/3/P